Virtual Research Environments

Virtual Research Environments

From portals to science gateways

ROBERT ALLAN

Chandos Publishing
Oxford • Cambridge • New Delhi

Chandos Publishing
TBAC Business Centre
Avenue 4
Station Lane
Witney
Oxford OX28 4BN
UK
Tel: +44 (0) 1993 848726
Email: info@chandospublishing.com
www.chandospublishing.com

Chandos Publishing is an imprint of Woodhead Publishing Limited

Woodhead Publishing Limited
Abington Hall
Granta Park
Great Abington
Cambridge CB21 6AH
UK
www.woodheadpublishing.com

First published in 2009

ISBN:
978 1 84334 562 6

© STFC 2009

Neither the STFC nor its collaborators accept any responsibility for loss or damage arising from the use of information contained in any of their reports or in any communication about their tests or investigations.

British Library Cataloguing-in-Publication Data.
A catalogue record for this book is available from the British Library.

All rights reserved. No part of this publication may be reproduced, stored in or introduced into a retrieval system, or transmitted, in any form, or by any means (electronic, mechanical, photocopying, recording or otherwise) without the prior written permission of the Publishers. This publication may not be lent, resold, hired out or otherwise disposed of by way of trade in any form of binding or cover other than that in which it is published without the prior consent of the Publishers. Any person who does any unauthorised act in relation to this publication may be liable to criminal prosecution and civil claims for damages.

The Publishers make no representation, express or implied, with regard to the accuracy of the information contained in this publication and cannot accept any legal responsibility or liability for any errors or omissions.

The material contained in this publication constitutes general guidelines only and does not represent to be advice on any particular matter. No reader or purchaser should act on the basis of material contained in this publication without first taking professional advice appropriate to their particular circumstances. All screenshots in this publication are the copyright of the website owner(s), unless indicated otherwise.

Typeset by Domex e-Data Pvt. Ltd.
Printed in the UK and USA.

Contents

List of figures and tables	ix
About the author	xi
Acknowledgments	xiii
Preface	xv

1 Introduction — 1
- What is e-research? — 3
- What is a VRE? — 11
- Portals and science gateways for e-research — 14
- A service-oriented architecture approach — 16
- Development methodology — 18
- Note — 19

2 Motivation and requirements — 21
- Research lifecycle: data, information and knowledge — 21
- Generic usage scenario and requirements — 23
- What functionality does an e-researcher need? — 26
- What components need to be integrated for e-research? — 27
- Illustrative examples — 31

3 Creating and using research data — 39
- Characteristics of data — 39
- High-performance computing in e-research — 42
- Managing research data — 47

4 Managing and using digital information — 55
- Information sources used by researchers — 55
- E-research and the wider information environment — 73

5	**Collaboration, trust and security**	**79**
	Virtual organisations and their implementation	81
	Collaborative working	85
	Collaboration tools	86
	Security in a VRE: authentication and authorisation	95
6	**Domain differences and usability**	**99**
	E-research, e-learning and digital information	99
	Differences between research domains	101
	Usability	104
7	**VRE architecture: the technology**	**107**
	Don't reinvent the wheel	108
	N-tier architecture	110
	Web services and service-oriented architecture	111
	Security frameworks	115
	VRE service definitions	122
	What e-infrastructure is available?	129
8	**E-infrastructure and grid resources**	**133**
	What is grid computing?	133
	Grid applications	137
	Middleware	139
	E-infrastructure, SOA and services	143
9	**Desktop environments and the web**	**145**
	Lightweight grid computing	145
	Desktop e-research tools	148
	E-research portals	152
10	**The Sakai collaborative learning and research framework**	**161**
	Working with Sakai	165
	Portal prototype – the Sakai VRE Demonstrator	167
	Portal organisation and use cases	169
11	**Example 1: E-infrastructure for social science research**	**173**
	A scenario from social science research	174

	Social science research data	178
	High-performance modelling and software development	182
	Training and outreach	184
	E-infrastructure for social science research	185
	Experiences with the NCeSS VRE	190
12	**Example 2: E-infrastructure for experimental facilities**	**193**
	Requirements and prerequisites	194
	Mapping requirements to data flow, data models and analysis	200
	Project management and other issues	204
13	**Conclusions: lessons learned and limitations**	**209**
	Top ten e-research requirements	209
	Impact of e-research	210
	Future	211

Appendix A	**213**
Appendix B	**227**
Appendix C	**235**
Appendix D	**239**
Bibliography	**249**
Index	**263**

List of figures and tables

Figures

1.1	Service-oriented architecture	17
2.1	The e-research data and information lifecycle	22
2.2	Go-geo! in the JISC landscape	33
5.1	Areas of expertise within the eMinerals VO	81
5.2	Screenshot of PAG in a GridSphere portal	90
5.3	Screenshot of Agora in a Sakai portal	92
6.1	Commonality of e-research domains	100
7.1	E-research service classification	123
9.1	Yahoo! map mashup in Sakai	158
10.1	Context, role and account relationships in Sakai	166
10.2	File transfer portlet accessed from Sakai using WSRP	168
11.1	Extended information environment architecture	176
11.2	Grid hosted data gateway	180
12.1	Diamond user office processes	195
12.2	MX beamline processes	197
12.3	Diamond Light Source e-infrastructure	199
12.4	DLS data and information flow	200

Tables

1.1	Some e-research and VRE activities worldwide	9–10
3.1	CCPs and their funding source	45
7.1	Some e-research projects and prerequisites	109
A.1	US TeraGrid Science Gateways	213–15
A.2	UK information portals	216–17
A.3	UK JISC VRE-1 Projects	217–18
A.4	UK JISC VRE-2 Projects	219
A.5	UK JISC VRE-3 and related projects	219–20
A.6	UK research portals	221
A.7	European research portals	222–3
A.8	Portals and science gateways in Australia and New Zealand	223
C.1	Generic commercial portal engines	235–6
C.2	Generic public domain portal engines	237

About the author

Rob Allan is leader of the HPC and Grid Technology Group in the Computational Science and Engineering Department at STFC's Daresbury Laboratory. Staff of the department collaborate with many research groups throughout the UK and worldwide, principally through the Collaborative Computational Projects, and support them through the application of computational simulation and modelling and advanced ICT.

Following a BSc in physics at the University of London, a PhD in atomic physics at the University of Newcastle upon Tyne, and three years of work in France and Germany, Rob started his career as a research physicist at Daresbury Laboratory in January 1985. In 1987 he moved into the Advanced Research Computing Group, developing new tools to enable heritage applications to run on high-performance parallel computers.

He became responsible for a group of around ten people, working in high-performance computer modelling and simulation and the design of novel numerical algorithms and methodology. This included an interest in distributed computing, including the computational grid.

In 2000 he was asked to help set up the CCLRC e-Science Centre and UK Grid Support Centre, which meant moving on and establishing another group of ten developers. Following an evaluation of grid middleware commissioned by the Department of Trade and Industry, they focused on the delivery of grid resources and services to end users via web-based portals and lightweight desktop interfaces – what are now known as virtual research environments (VREs). In addition to leading software development for projects such as e-HTPX and eMinerals, the e-Infrastructure for Social Science, and the GROWL VRE and Sakai VRE Demonstrator, the group has been involved in developing and deploying the e-infrastructure for STFC's large-scale experimental facilities, including the Diamond Light Source.

Rob chaired the UK Grid Engineering Task Force for two years and helped to set up the National Grid Service, for which he produced the original technical roadmap. He also chaired the Service Delivery Board of the National Centre for e-Social Science and currently chairs the Operations Board of the North West Grid, arguably the largest regional UK grid project, involving staff and resources at Daresbury and the universities of Lancaster, Central Lancashire, Liverpool and Manchester.

Rob is a member of the Institute of Physics and the European Physical Society and is a Chartered Physicist.

The author may be contacted at:

Computational Science and Engineering Department
STFC Daresbury Laboratory
Daresbury
Warrington WA4 4AD
UK
E-mail: *robert.allan@stfc.ac.uk*

Acknowledgments

I thank the following organisations for funding the research upon which this book is based: BBSRC, DTI, EPSRC, ESRC, JISC, NERC, NWDA and STFC (formerly CCLRC). They supported my research group from 2000 to 2008. This was a significant period in the evolution of e-research technologies and I am grateful to have been able to play a small part.

Most of the text is based on personal experiences involving research and software development in this domain. However, I thank the following collaborators and contributors who have provided valued input and advice: Cliff Addison, Asif Akram, Ties van Ark, Alun Ashton, Malcolm Atkinson, Chris Awre, Mark Baker, Richard Blake, Ann Borda, Ian Boston, David Boyd, Adam Braimah, John Brooke, Dharmesh Chohan, Keith Cole, Phil Couch, Rob Crouchley, Mike Daw, Mihaela Dediu, Greg Diakun, Maia Dimitrova, Ian Dolphin, Martin Dove, Glen Drinkwater, Paul Durham, Jim Farmer, June Finch, Adrian Fish, Michael Gleaves, Miguel Gonzalez Losa, Dan Grose, Martyn Guest, Tony Hey, Caroline Ingram, Catherine Jones, John Kewley, Kerstin Kleese van Dam, Gregor von Laszewski, Adam Marshall, David Meredith, Colin Nave, Kevin O'Neill, John Norman, Jason Novotny, Stephen Pickles, Andrew Richards, Jamie Rintelman, Mike Russell, Derek Sergeant, Charles Severance, Shoaib Sufi, Steve Swinsburg, Jens Thomas, Mary Thomas, Frederique van Till, Andy Turner, Rik Tyer, Xiao Dong Wang, Paul Watry, Graeme Winter and Xiaobo Yang.

Thanks also to all those too numerous to mention who have helped in one way or another to guide me in the right direction both in carrying out the work and in writing this book.

Preface

This is a book about making information and communication technologies (ICT) usable by researchers working to solve 'grand challenge' problems in many research domains, from social science to particle physics. It is driven by the work my research group and I have carried out to evaluate researchers' requirements in using information services and grid services via web portals and in adapting collaborative learning and information management tools to meet their more diverse needs, particularly in multidisciplinary scientific studies.

This is the motivation for what we have helped to develop into the UK's virtual research environment (VRE) programme. The book illustrates generic aspects of this with specific instances of studies comparing portal and grid technologies and evaluating usability. This work, and further development of collaboration and web-based research tools has been carried out with international colleagues, in particular using the Sakai framework and other recent Java language based portal programming frameworks and associated standards.

Two principal case studies form the basis for discussions in this book: first, a virtual research environment for social scientists engaged in many research areas including statistical modelling on high-performance computers; second, a virtual research environment for scientists using a large-scale experimental facility. These case studies are built from our practical experiences of developing e-research infrastructures and virtual research environments in related areas.

Administrative 'back-office' processes, while equally important to researchers embedded in institutional and funding agency processes, will be covered in less depth. They are however mentioned in the chapter on the e-infrastructure for the Diamond Synchrotron and were a feature of work carried out at the University of Leeds in the EVIE project. Integrating administrative procedures across institutions is a complex task and new initiatives such as the UK Research Councils Shared Services Centre mean that many of the processes are currently in flux and the desktop and web-based tools are changing. Perhaps it will be easier in future as a spin-off from the kind of e-business technology that shared services will employ.

I focus mainly on web-based access to research services in an approach which has developed from the concept of a 'portal' to what is often now termed a 'virtual research environment' or 'science gateway'. In principle at least, the technologies involved are easily extensible to cover administrative procedures and in fact should include a web-based interface to research support services within the host institutions, as is the case in many university institutional portals. I illustrate the approach taken and practical deployment using the Sakai Java-based collaborative framework, but also describe extensions which include Web 2.0 technologies and methodologies.

Most of the examples and background work cited are from four sources. First, the UK e-Science Programme (see *http://www.rcuk.ac.uk/escience* and *http://www.nesc.ac.uk*); second, the UK Joint Infrastructure Systems Committee (JISC) VRE Programme (see *http://www.jisc.ac.uk/whatwedo/programmes/vre2.aspx*); third, the US TeraGrid Programme (see *http://www.teragrid.org*); and finally VeRSI, the Victorian E-Research Strategic Initiative in Australia which is associated with the Victorian Partnership for Advanced Computing (see *http://www.versi.edu.au*). There are of course similar initiatives in other parts of the world.

In any discussion on e-research, there is plenty of jargon, particularly relating to the technology. I provide an extensive glossary with web links and references to specialist introductions to the more relevant topics. Any references I have omitted can usually be found using Google or Wikipedia – both of which illustrate valuable broad search information tools which will be discussed later. To help with understanding the overall motivation and goals of e-research, two short publicity films were produced by the JISC at the end of its VRE-1 Programme (2003–2006). These address both technologies (see *http://www.jisc.ac.uk/media/avfiles/programmes/vre/technicalsolutions.wmv*) and applications (see *http://www.jisc.ac.uk/media/avfiles/programmes/vre/researchneeds.wmv*). A video is also available introducing e-research in Australasia (see *http://espace.library.uq.edu.au/view/UQ:155728*).

In writing this book I wavered between several messages and questions including who is the audience and what am I trying to say? In the end I settled on a description of the motivations of e-researchers, the benefits to be gained and some of the examples with which I have been personally involved. A full technical discussion of how to deploy a VRE would require a separate in-depth publication and is in any case a moving target. I have mentioned a few software products, mostly open source as they tend to be used by the academic research community. One should however bear in mind that there are many commercial products suitable for building a VRE and which are widely used in e-business; the appendices list those found at the time of writing.

1

Introduction

In certain respects, people in large (distributed) project teams trying to solve research problems are in much the same position as blind men trying to describe an elephant.[1] They all view the problem from a different perspective or have a different set of information, all of which needs to be brought together in a true collaboration to solve the problem. ICT support can play a significant role in achieving this goal. For many people, however, their understanding of the e-research technology space is informed by their initial experience of using a certain type of ICT to solve a previous problem. Many e-research applications could make use of a wider spectrum of technologies, such as the following:

- A multi-site computational grid system (Foster and Kesselman, 1998) implemented using middleware such as Globus (*http://www.globus.org*) provides mechanisms to harness distributed resources (mainly computational but also data movement) using global identity credentials that work across a multi-institution grid.
- A data grid system implemented using software such as the Storage Resource Broker (SRB) (*http://www.sdsc.edu/srb/index.php*) or Fedora, the Flexible Extensible Digital Object and Repository Architecture (*http://www.fedora-commons.org*) allows for long-term storage and retrieval of data and metadata. Such a system can be used both for basic storage, retrieval and archiving of data, and also to support the publication or e-publication activities of the team.
- A collaborative system such as Sakai (*http://www.sakaiproject.org/portal*) allows people to interact and work together as a distributed team. Groups can dynamically form to work on projects or subprojects or for purposes requiring specific tools and authorisation. Data in Sakai is maintained in a database and can be archived to associate the collaborative activity with computed or experimental data associated with a particular research effort.

- Portal systems such as GridSphere (*http://www.gridsphere.org*) and uPortal (*http://www.uportal.org*) are widely used. Portals that support standards such as JSR 168 (*http://jcp.org/en/jsr/detail?id=168*) or WSRP (*http://www.oasis-open.org/committees/download.php/3343/oasis-200304-wsrp-specification-1.0.pdf*) provide an excellent mechanism to collate the tools from disparate resources into a single gateway or portal, making them easy for the team to use.
- Knowledge-building tools and software such as Data2Knowledge (*http://www.data2knowledge.de/d2k/index.php*) and Kepler (*http://kepler-project.org*) allow scientific workflows to be produced and can be used to orchestrate scientific procedures and software services.
- Large and valuable data sets need to be conserved, such as those from the National Virtual Observatory (NVO) (*http://www.astrogrid.org*, see Berman et al., 2003). Important data sources, such as astronomical telescopes, utilise very specialised pieces of equipment that need to be managed with appropriate security to gather data using advanced observation and analysis techniques. Once gathered, the data is made available to the e-research efforts through some form of repository to include in more complex models of the cosmos.

Many e-research projects still have relatively small staff complements and short lifetimes that lead the team to ignore the larger potential scope of their domain or even new multi-domain opportunities. In terms of ICT, projects usually adopt an ad hoc approach to provisioning themselves with core e-collaboration tools and services; as a result, each component (e.g. wiki, intranet, e-mail list and forum) usually requires a separate logon. Once a particular way of working or tool has been adopted, the co-workers become reluctant to replace these tools with something that would integrate with their other domain-specific tools and services due to the additional work that this would entail – for example, a database would need converting to another format, an interface would need to be re-branded or the team would have to learn about a new tool. The lack of standards for describing the underlying information structures exacerbates this situation. However, were these projects to start by recognising the bigger picture of open standards (which allows for integration and interoperability), then any new project would be able to pick up on earlier developments made on core tools and services. This would also enable them to reuse the data and allow staff to concentrate more of their effort on the actual scientific challenges to be solved. The collaborators should then be able to work more efficiently, for example, by cross-searching the various information and data sources and using them together.

Although this book concentrates on web technology for virtual research environments (VREs), the above argument can just as easily be applied to any of the scenarios discussed. Desktop office software suites provide some of this kind of capability, but need to be linked into scientific applications and repositories of publications and data. By using the appropriate exchange standards, we can create a common e-research infrastructure that enables us to hide much of the underlying complexity. A strong theme for VREs is reusability – this can be achieved by using open standards, packaging tools as services and exposing them through a variety of interfaces. We refer to this either as a service-oriented architecture (SOA) or as a pluggable framework.

Research resources in this architecture comprise of software, grid-enabled data sets and the infrastructure on which these will reside. They also comprise of people, i.e. the researchers, students and consumers of the research outputs. We stress the importance of enabling people to access the software, data and computer systems, and enabling them to collaborate and interact in a rich variety of ways.

There are a number of important cross-cutting aspects such as global identity and global access control that are also an important part of any cross-application, multi-site and multidisciplinary integration. The Globus Grid middleware toolkit is commonly used to provide this cross-application identity and cross-institution security in an e-research grid. Architectural issues including security will be considered further in Chapter 7.

What is e-research?

Some of the following notes are adapted from an Australian government website (*http://www.dest.gov.au/sectors/research_sector/policies_issues_ reviews/key_issues/e_research_consult*).

The research sector worldwide is experiencing enormous change driven by advances in ICT. Research is increasingly characterised by national and international multidisciplinary collaboration and most countries participating in the international Organisation for Economic Cooperation and Development (OECD) are investing heavily in those capabilities and the associated coordinating mechanisms.

Do not confuse the virtual research environment with virtualisation in the sense of 'cloud computing'. Do not confuse e-research with educational research. For our purposes, the term 'e-research' encapsulates research activities that use a spectrum of advanced ICT capabilities and which embrace new research methodologies emerging from increasing access to:

- broadband communications networks, research instruments and facilities, sensor networks and data repositories;
- software and infrastructure services that enable secure connectivity and interoperability;
- applications that encompass domain-specific tools and information and data management and collaboration tools.

E-research capabilities serve to advance and augment, rather than replace traditional research methodologies, but there is a growing dependence on e-research capabilities. Improved access to data, information and knowledge will enable researchers to perform their research more creatively, efficiently and collaboratively across long distances and disseminate their research outcomes with greater effect. Using ICT methodologies, researchers can work seamlessly from desk-to-desk within and between organisations. A very simple example is that web-based search engines such as Google and Yahoo! have become an essential part of library services and Wikipedia is often the first place to look for definitions of terms and concepts. This is causing a change in business model for people previously occupied with traditional information services. Such sources are however driven by popular demand and emphasise the more popular topics, possibly to the detriment of less popular topics or those conceived to be 'harder', which of course encompass most of today's research challenges.

As research is about pushing the boundaries of human knowledge, there is a requirement for access to 'deep search' in addition to 'broad search' across information services. Entirely new domains of research, hitherto unavailable, are also emerging, using new techniques for data mining and analysis, advanced computational algorithms and resource sharing networks plus social research based on analysis of the use of the internet itself.

At the start of the twenty-first century, e-science was a new paradigm of research, often said to be characterised by a 'deluge' of data analysed by massive distributed computing power, i.e. the grid. E-science research collaborations are frequently large, distributed and multidisciplinary, involving many institutions across the globe. Grid technology, rising to respond to these challenges, promised to enable exciting possibilities for better research, even creating new disciplines such as astro-informatics.

In this context, a wide range of national and international initiatives started, such as the UK's E-Science Programme and National Grid Service, EGEE in Europe, the TeraGrid in the USA, China's CROWN Grid and similar projects in other Asian and Pacific countries.

The concept of e-science is now broadening and generally evolving into e-research, to encompass the social sciences and the arts and humanities, which also have a need to collaborate and share data. At the same time, it must be recognised that different communities are at very different stages as regards their awareness of the new uses of ICT. As such, the current needs of a large international scientific collaboration are likely to be much more complex than those of the lone humanities researcher, wishing to collaborate more effectively with a handful of colleagues worldwide in the same domain of interest. In our thinking, we try to keep the whole range of requirements in view.

At the high end, the new developments appear to be making the process of conducting research more complex and demanding. The aim of a VRE is to help researchers manage this complexity by providing an infrastructure, framework and user interfaces specifically designed to support all the activities carried out within their research teams, on both small and large scales. VREs aim to add value to the research process across all domains by complementing and interworking with existing resources and by being flexible and adaptable to changing requirements.

The ICT challenge is to create and sustain a robust shared infrastructure, ideally usable on a routine basis by researchers from all domains to enhance their productivity and effectiveness. Meeting this challenge is a task for those building the infrastructure, its potential user communities, the institutions to which users belong, the organisations that fund research, and other stakeholders in the research process. These developments cannot happen in isolation but need to work with other components of the infrastructure being provided by funding organisations and research institutions themselves, such as learning environments, digital libraries and national large-scale research facilities.

Atkins et al. (2003) suggest 'cyberinfrastructure' to be the basis for building 'new types of scientific and engineering knowledge environments and organizations and ... [pursuing] research in new ways and with new efficiency'. In the EU, distributed e-research services use the GEANT network and in the UK they use JANET, both of which are high bandwidth (multi Gb/s) and free at the point of delivery for academic use.

The above discussion has focused on research in the academic sector, but many of the issues and factors are similar for commercial research, albeit typically within the bounds of a single large organisation. This is especially so in organisations that work across multiple sites worldwide. Such organisations might also be engaged in e-business processes with suppliers or customers. Indeed e-research is sometimes thought of as an extension of e-business and the concept of workflow, introduced to manage manufacturing processes in the early part of the twentieth century and into software in the 1980s, is now being considered for automation of research processes which have to be managed, recorded or repeated.

It has been unclear, a priori, what type of framework a VRE should adopt, on which technologies it could be based, how it can be developed sustainably and how usability and take-up can be ensured. The target user community includes all those engaged in research, from developers to end users, and we now have experience of several attempts to investigate these questions.

Domains, and communities within domains (especially in non-science subject areas), have to identify for themselves the potential in the technology. They may have to overcome cultural obstacles to collaboration and may need training to develop relevant skills. Associated legal issues need to be understood and clarified, while formal and informal codes of practice must be updated to recognise novel forms of collaboration involving data and information sharing. The barriers to the uptake of e-research technologies outside of well-organised commercial environments are significant, particularly as a goal is to span multiple organisations with diverse cultures and practices.

Locally, institutions need to understand the business case for supporting research collaborations and how they can be reconciled with continuing competition for funding. Wider impacts will be felt through changes in scholarly communication and in the complexities of managing and sustaining long-term open access to data and information for reuse. New business models in publishing are emerging, for instance through open access (Jones, 2007).

Paul Bonnington, former Director of E-Research at the University of Auckland, New Zealand and Director of BeSTGrid describes e-research as follows:

> research enhanced by advanced information technology, particularly data capture and storage, computational processing and simulation, and advanced collaborative tools (such as, multi-point video conferencing and web portals). This is how many international science and engineering researchers are working

now – on large-scale collaborative projects based on global e-research collaboratories. We have also seen a simultaneous movement in Europe and North America towards funding of collaboratories. We have to participate in and be members of this international community. (Hyphen, 2007)

For more information on e-research, the following sources are useful. E-research in Australia is supported by the Department of Education, Employment and Workplace Relations (DEEWR). Formerly the Department for Education, Science and Training, DEEWR supports a strategic accessibility framework for research outputs (*http://www.deewr.gov.au*). The New Zealand government has a digital strategy and is supporting a number of open access repository and e-research programmes (see *http://www.digitalstrategy.govt.nz* and *http://www.morst.govt.nz/current-work/science-infrastructure/eresearch*). Development of an open access repository at the University of Otago is described by Jones (2007). In the UK, open access repositories and e-research are supported by the Joint Infrastructure Systems Committee (*http://www.jisc.ac.uk/whatwedo/themes/eresearch.aspx*). The UK Research Councils support the use of ICT in research in a wider sense, for instance through the E-Science Programme (*http://www.rcuk.ac.uk/e-science*). In the USA, TeraGrid is an important example of deploying and making accessible distributed resources for research (*http://www.teragrid.org*).

Cox (2004) reports on collaborative e-research environments and provides additional background material and a rationale for the UK's efforts to create VREs. The report summarises the proceedings and breakout group discussions from two awareness-raising workshops held in 2004 at the universities of Edinburgh and Warwick. This led to the development of a roadmap and programme of funded work on VRE prototypes (Allan et al., 2004a), largely based on experiences with virtual learning environments (VLEs) and the management of digital information. The projects which were subsequently funded in the first two phases of the VRE programme are listed in Appendix A.

Background material from the UK E-Science Grid, compiled by the Grid Architecture Task Force, is contained in the report by Atkinson et al. (2002). This vision was tested through the work of the UK's Grid Engineering Task Force and in 2005 was introduced into the National Grid Service (*http://www.ngs.ac.uk*). This provided a shared computational infrastructure, which is now being supplemented with other services required for research.

In the UK's Joint Information Systems Committee (JISC), there is substantial activity to maintain a critical mass of digital information resources to support researchers, learners, teachers and administrators in their work and study. The production of information is on the increase and ways to deal with this effectively are required. There remains a need to ensure that 'quality' information is not lost among the masses of digital data created every day. If we can continue to improve the management, discovery and serving of quality information, there is huge potential to enhance knowledge creation across the learning and research communities. Knowledge management is now recognised as being as important in academic institutions, both for teaching and research, as it is in commercial enterprises. Almost all research funding now also comes with a requirement to carry out knowledge exchange.

JISC's mission is to provide world-class leadership in the innovative use of ICT to support education and research. JISC funds a portfolio of national services and a range of development programmes.

The aim of the JISC Information Environment (IE) (*http://www.jisc.ac.uk/whatwedo/themes/information_environment.aspx*) is to help provide convenient access to information resources for research and learning through the use of discovery and management tools and the development of better services and practices. The IE aims to allow discovery, access and use of resources for research and learning irrespective of their location. Work on developing a distributed architecture for the IE is described by Powell and Lyon (2001) and Wilson et al. (2003). In the UK, common services such as those in the IE and the National Grid Service should be reused to underpin VRE developments.

In Australia, the VeRSI Programme is informing debate on major issues such as:

- How can the benefits of e-research be measured?
- How does one manage the paradox of collaboration and the competitive nature of research?
- There is a growing acceptance of the availability of advanced tools and technologies in 'everyday' research, but is this change fast enough?
- Expertise is a key issue, so how do we attract and reward ICT people to support research?

In their analysis of work in New Zealand, Lawson and Butson (2007) describe e-research as a vague concept, but point out that it covers the entire general area of ICT aiding researchers in their activities. In their report, they review the contemporary status of e-research in the USA, UK, Australia and New Zealand, co-incidentally some of the partners in the JISC e-Framework for Education and Research (*http://www.e-framework.org*). Further examples of work in Australia are given by O'Brien (2005). While the USA and the UK are today leading research in the e-research domain, Australia, New Zealand and also China are catching up. In summary, Lawson and Butson list six points where e-research can add value to today's research activities:

- new domains of study;
- increased quality of research;
- savings in cost and time;
- multidisciplinary and inter-institutional research;
- increased impact of research output;
- comparative benefits.

Table 1.1 lists further e-research and VRE activities worldwide.

Table 1.1 Some e-research and VRE activities worldwide

Country	Initiative	Project and goals
UK	RCUK	National E-Science Programme
UK	Edinburgh University	National E-Science Centre and support for the RCUK E-Science Programme
UK	JISC	Services including repositories, JANET, Shibboleth and the National Grid Service
UK	JISC	VRE, repositories and middleware development programmes.
UK	Oxford University	Interdisciplinary E-Research Centre
UK	STFC	E-infrastructure for large-scale facilities
UK	NW-GRID	North West England Regional Grid
EU	DEISA	European high-performance computing Grid
EU	EGEE	Enabling Grids for E-Science in Europe, infrastructure and middleware
EU	LHC Grid	Hierarchical grid for analysis of CERN LHC data

Table 1.1 Some e-research and VRE activities worldwide (Cont'd)

Country	Initiative	Project and goals
EU	NorduGrid	Nordic testbed for wide area computing, data management and middleware development
EU	D-Grid	Funded by the German Ministry of Education and Research (BMBF) and industrial partners
Australia	NCRIS	Platforms for collaboration: national computation, collaboration and data services
Australia	Melbourne, Monash and La Trope University	VeRSI: Victorian E-Research Stimulation Initiative
New Zealand	Otago University	Using the KAREN network for collaborative research
New Zealand	Auckland University	Bioinformatics, including CellML and the Physiome project
New Zealand	Auckland, Canterbury and Massey University	BeSTGrid: Broadband enabled Science and Technology Grid
USA	NSF TeraGrid	Supercomputing grid based on computers and data stores on a high-performance network
USA	NSF OCI Program	Advanced cyberinfrastructure
USA	NSF NMI	National Middleware Initiative, including the Open Grid Computing Environment (OGCE) portal
USA	NSF Open Science Grid	Computing grid for data-intensive research
China	CROWN	China Research and Development environment Over Wide area network, Grid testbed, middleware and portal development
Japan	Riken ITBL	Information Technology Based Laboratories, an R&D and collaboration platform involving computers, data and experimental facilities
Japan	NAREGI	National Research Grid for Japan
Korea	KISTI	Korean Institute of Science and Technology Information

What is a VRE?

The nature of a VRE means that it is more realistic to describe it in terms of its intended capabilities rather than its component parts as the latter are likely to (and indeed should) evolve over time, depending on contemporary standards and requirements.

In our view therefore, a VRE should do the following:

- Support the processes of conducting research, including marshalling of resources, scholarly discourse and publication, and the creation and maintenance of collaborations across domains, institutions and countries, including support for meetings and organisational processes.
- Be designed to meet user requirements and address usability and accessibility, with appropriate evaluation mechanisms and benchmarks for new service and tool development.
- Include modes of access which (almost) any user can download and install on their laptop/desktop/PDA/mobile phone/home computer, with 'servers' that can be easily installed by system administrators without specialist knowledge and national-level servers as appropriate, so that tools work 'out of the box'.
- Be secure and trustworthy – the VRE components should interoperate with federated cross-institutional authentication and authorisation mechanisms.
- Be accountable, by providing adequate logging and probity including supporting queries about provenance.
- Be compatible with other widely used and deployed systems, including at least: web, e-mail, instant messaging, SMS, wikis and video-conferencing tools from lightweight desktop applications through to high-end video conferencing via Access Grid.
- Support the creation, sharing and curation of digital content, through ease of authoring, publishing, discovery and access. This implies adoption of appropriate metadata schemas and support for automatic generation of metadata. Resources to be described will include data, publications, computation, experimental or observational facilities and human researchers.
- Be based, as far as possible, on loosely coupled, distributed, interoperable services and tools, rather than monolithic applications.
- Be extensible with enhanced or new tools (possibly domain-specific) from any developer, through the use of published standards and

software development kits, software libraries, etc. It should be as easy as possible to make existing software and services (e.g. e-print repositories, portals and proprietary software) interoperate with the VRE.

- Be open source and standards-compliant wherever possible. The licensing of the software should encourage and support improvements to the tools and development of new tools by the community. Intellectual property rights (IPR) issues need to be investigated and understood.
- Support tailoring of the environment by individuals or groups to reflect their domain interests and personal preferences.
- Support the delegation of routine tasks to intelligent personal agents where the means to realise these exists, e.g. by incorporation into workflow processes.

To achieve all this is a tall order. We will revisit these items in the rest of this book and see how they have evolved since the original vision.

Based on the background and examples given, a VRE can be considered as a set of applications, services and resources integrated by a standards-based, service-oriented framework which will be populated by the research and ICT communities working in partnership. The scope of the components needed to build this framework is discussed further with examples in the following chapters.

Multiple domain-specific or community-specific gateways to the VRE will exist in parallel, serving the needs of different communities but achieving maximum synergy and cost-effectiveness by being based on a common infrastructure which enables reuse of generic open source or open access components, referred to as services. The use of portals is just one example; lightweight programming libraries is another, permitting integration with 'heritage' applications.

It is not currently possible to produce a single complete VRE and indeed it may never happen. Rather, work is contributing to the definition of and helping to develop a common framework and associated standards and to encourage others to work within this framework to develop and populate overlapping VREs with applications, services and resources appropriate to their needs. The intention is to maximise the value and benefit of future investment in this area by a variety of funding bodies to secure community contributions and to promote sustainability.

VREs must cater for a wide range of scale and complexity of research activities, from small research collaborations with a few partners to large teams with many partners in many institutions. A balance must be achieved between meeting the needs of specific domains and developing capabilities of widespread utility. The wide variety of research activities means that in each case a judgment must be made as regards the appropriateness of including specific capabilities for the application in question.

In the long term, VREs will have to become self-sustaining within their user communities and service providers. They will therefore have to be seen to provide sufficient additional benefit to motivate this effort. While VREs, gateways and resources will 'belong' to their user communities and will respond to and track their communities' evolving requirements, it is expected that there would be mutual benefit in coordinating these separate activities through a common framework with reusable services and associated standards. This is one of the aims of the international E-Framework for Education and Research.

It is important for any VRE development activity to have strong links with other related activities such as virtual and managed learning (Weller, 2007) and digital information management. In this respect, we make particular reference to the Sakai project in the USA. It has many components and services in common with all of these. Indeed, turning full circle, VREs can also be used for education, possibly simulating access to computers and instruments for training purposes in addition to accessing course material and other information.

Fraser (2005) gives an overview of a typical VRE and three JISC-funded VRE-1 projects: Integrative Biology VRE (IBVRE); Building a VRE for the Humanities (BVREH); and Sakai VRE Demonstrator, all with end users at the University of Oxford. Although focusing on different domains, these projects all keep user requirements and technical open standards in mind (see Appendix A). Fraser defines a VRE as 'a framework into which tools, services and resources can be plugged' – a philosophy which we endorse.

While people may give various definitions of VRE, we argue that the core of VRE is about collaboration. VRE can be treated as an implementation of an e-infrastructure for research. Through a VRE, researchers should be able to work collaboratively, share data and other artefacts, and use many of the tools specific to their research domain. Consequently, such a system should provide services for communication and resource integration. For example, NEESit (*http://it.nees.org*) tries to link earthquake engineers across the USA by providing them with software and services so that they can easily organise and share data, participate in remote experiments and perform hybrid simulations. NEESit is one of the TeraGrid Science Gateways and NEES has used both the CHEF and Sakai frameworks for its evolving VRE.

Portals and science gateways for e-research

The idea of a web portal has been around for a number of years. An early significant example illustrating the capabilities, architecture and goals was the Extensible Computational Chemistry Environment (ECCE), which formed part of the Molecular Science Software Suite developed at Batelle Pacific Northwest National Laboratory in the USA (Schuchardt et al., 2002). At the time, this was referred to as a problem-solving environment, but it had all the attributes of an e-research portal and used grid and semantic technologies. Another example – SCIRun – comes from the University of Utah and is based on a powerful workflow (dataflow) driven rich-visualisation client (Johnson et al., 2002; *http://software.sci.utah.edu/scirun.html*).

Portals have been used for institutional e-learning and administration systems and for access to the information environment (Dolphin et al., 2002; P. Miller, 2003). We organised the Portals and Portlets 2003 workshop (Allan et al., 2004b) at the time when two significant pieces of technology, the JSR 168 portlet standard from the Java Community Process and the Web Services for Remote Portlets standard (WSRP 1.0) from OASIS were being agreed (see *http://jcp.org/en/jsr/detail?id=168* and *http://www.oasis-open.org/committees/download.php/3343/oasis-200304-wsrp-specification-1.0.pdf* respectively). Since then, a number of open source and commercial portal projects have been launched to support research. One example from the UK is the portal for the National Grid Service (*http://www.ngs.ac.uk*). This evolved from HPCPortal, which was initially a Perl and C programming language environment for launching and monitoring grid jobs similar to the GridPort and HotPage portals from the San Diego Supercomputer Center (M. Thomas et al. 2002; Berman et al., 2003). Other work in the USA focused on the Java language (Novotny, 2002; Berman et al., 2003) and eventually led to the development of GridSphere (Novotny et al., 2004; *http://www.gridsphere.org*). After briefly using PHP technology, we have now evolved to using Java with JSR 168 portlets (Yang et al., 2005) first in the GridSphere and StringBeans (*http://www.nabh.com/projects/sbportal*) frameworks and more recently in uPortal (*http://www.uportal.org*).

In the Sakai VRE Demonstrator (Allan et al. 2007; Crouchley et al., 2007; Severance et al., 2007) we were thus able to benefit from a huge experience of portal development and integrate many tools funded through other projects. The aim was to bring all these tools together in one place, i.e. to create a portal-based VRE. However, we have separately

Introduction

argued that Sakai is not in fact a portal, but rather a collection of tightly-coupled hosted services which enable user participation in a manner similar to hosted Web 2.0 services (Allan and Severance, 2006). Sakai now also includes loosely-coupled and remote services through the adoption of JSR 168 and WSRP.

A VRE is more than just a portal. While the NGS portal has a number of tools to encourage people to share artefacts, such as descriptions of computational tasks or workflows, it has very little built-in community support. It is important to address this if e-research technologies and the grid are going to be taken up more widely. In the USA this is done through the concept of 'science gateways'. The TeraGrid website lists a number of such gateways. Many of these are home-grown web applications rather than fully-functional portals. However, a few such as DOE Fusion, QuakeSim, NEESit, nanoHub, NVO, LEAD, BIRN, caBIG and SCEC go much further, and some are based on portal components from the Open Grid Computing Environment (OGCE) (Alameda et al., 2007; *http://www.collab-ogce.org/nmi/portal*), which has many of the characteristics of a VRE. The TeraGrid User Portal is a generic interface built on OGCE with GridSphere. See also Appendix A.

According to Dennis Gannon (2009), TeraGrid science gateways take three common forms:

- a gateway that is packaged as a web portal with users as clients accessing TeraGrid services;
- grid bridging gateways for communities who host their own grid resources devoted to their areas of science – in these cases the science gateway is a mechanism to extend the reach of the community grid so it may use the resources of the TeraGrid;
- a gateway that involves rich application programs running on users' machines (i.e. workstations and desktops) and accesses services on TeraGrid (and elsewhere).

Science gateways can have varying goals and implementations. Some expose specific sets of community codes so that anonymous scientists can run them. Others may serve as a 'meta-portal' – a portal that brings a broad range of new services and applications to a particular community. A common trait of all three types is their interaction with the grid through the various interfaces to hosted services. Although the gateways may be instantiated on managed grid resources, it is expected that many will be instantiated on community resources and be administered by the community.

We envisage a portal-based VRE to be capable of doing many of the things described above, such as submitting jobs to remote resources on a national grid service or clusters in collaborators' institutions or managing diverse resources on a 'campus grid' within the user's own institution. We furthermore consider that a VRE should be able to support all kinds of research by containing a comprehensive suite of data and information management and community-building tools in addition to those for grid computing.

A significant TeraGrid example is caBIG (caGrid Project, 2008), the US Cancer Biomedical Informatics Grid, which hosts a comprehensive portal using the LifeRay framework (*http://www.liferay.com*). This has portlets for discovery, service metadata exploration, data service query (using its own XML-based caGrid query language which can be shared), grid status, news (RSS) and events, calendar (iCal), map-based services and analytics. Additional community portlets can be deployed from a shared repository.

A service-oriented architecture approach

A service-oriented architecture (SOA) is an approach to joining up independent services to provide integrated capabilities. Although a relatively new approach, it has rapidly gained in popularity because of the lower costs of integration coupled with flexibility and simplified configuration. SOA is becoming best practice for commercial distributed software development and there are now quite a few books and references, only a few of which are noted here (Atkinson et al., 2002; Erl, 2004, 2007; Hashimi, 2003; Ruh, 2003; Stevens, 2003; Tabor, 2006; *http://www.service-architecture.com*).

An SOA of the form we will describe further in Chapter 7 builds upon the use of web services, the present industry standard for building and integrating distributed systems (Allan et al. 2003; Graham et al., 2004; see also *http://roadmap.cbdiforum.com/reports/protocols/summary.php* and *http://www.service-architecture.com*). Previously, it was the norm to use software systems such as CORBA (*http://www.omg.org*).

A rationale for using an SOA in the context of managed learning and virtual learning environments is given by Powell and Lyon (2001). Other relevant projects worldwide are deploying similar approaches and architectures. In the world of computational grids, the same approach is used and has been formalised through activities of the Open Grid Forum (*http://www.ogf.org*) which has established the Web Services Resource Framework standard (*http://www.oasis-open.org/committees/wsrf*).

Introduction

Figure 1.1 Service-oriented architecture

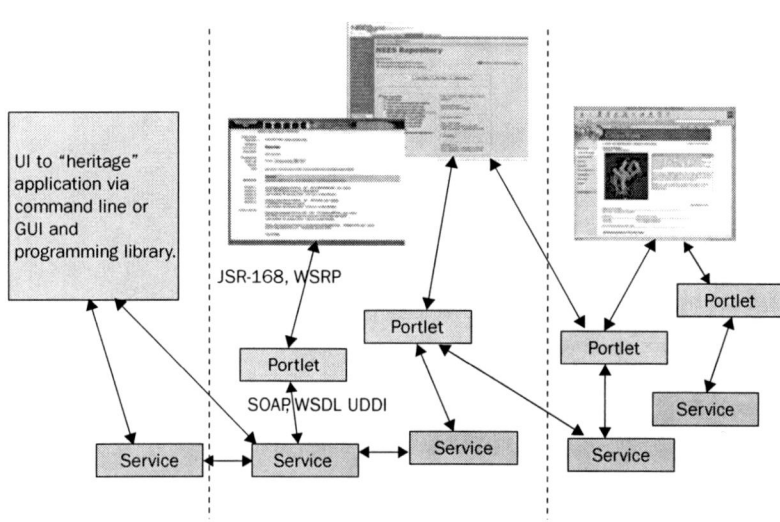

Figure 1.1 highlights some aspects of an SOA relevant to deploying a VRE with appropriate user interfaces such as portals, online commands, drag-and-drop desktops and programming libraries. A key aspect of the architecture is to maximise the reuse of common services and middleware, including portlets. There are web service interfaces for all these components.

An SOA clearly does not preclude the concurrent use of cloud computing or data warehouses and is in fact agnostic with respect to how the rest of the enterprise is configured, which is why it makes a good approach for a framework. Services are autonomously configured, maintained, published and upgraded but one must make available a well-defined application programming interface via the web service software stack so that they can be used and reused. In addition, because integration occurs in this fashion, it becomes a simple task to update the systems that provide services within the architecture or to look up new ones via a service registry. Because service consumers are configured to access a service without any knowledge of the system that provides the service, we can replace the underlying service components without affecting the systems using it.

These generic services are an abstraction of actual services, some of which might be made available in the VRE. Broadly speaking these might cover:

- authentication, authorisation and access control;
- grid services, data and information services, semantic services, resource discovery, etc.;
- collaboration services;
- support and management services.

More details will be provided in Chapter 7.

Development methodology

DEEWR in Australia and JISC in the UK, together with other international partners including SURF in the Netherlands and the New Zealand Ministry for Education (and previously Canada) are working to define a common language for describing an e-framework (*http://www.e-framework.org*). We contributed to the early stages of this work and use the e-framework vocabulary in this book. It describes all stages in the process of designing and creating software and virtual environments for education and research.

A number of key issues emerged from early discussions about VREs, as listed below:

- positive incentives;
- barriers;
- institutions;
- disciplinary communities;
- user needs;
- a virtual e-research framework;
- usability;
- awareness;
- threats;
- IPR and legal issues;
- the rhetoric of 'collaboration';
- scholarly publishing and open data.

More detailed accounts and conclusions of the discussion groups can be found in the summary of awareness-raising workshops (Cox, 2004).

It was expected that VRE development would address these issues in a technical sense. Nevertheless, non-technical aspects continue to be a source of debate at meetings. We will only address them superficially in this book through the use cases and examples.

The e-framework has really evolved from the idea of service classification and reuse as depicted in Figure 7.1 and is now being expanded to encompass:

- *Service genre*: A collection of related behaviours that describe an abstract capability. This allows people to see how adopting a service-oriented view with smaller, reusable services is more efficient and ultimately can be more economical than supporting a monolithic system. It helps to avoid funding development of similar applications again and again. The documented service genres show that common components are readily reusable.

- *Service usage model*: The relationships among technical components (services) used for software applications. This allows people to look at examples of how different functional services can work together to provide a new application without starting from scratch every time.

- *Service expression*: A specific way to realise a service genre with particular interfaces and standards. This allows people to see the published e-framework service components and those currently under development. Insight can be gained for building specific applications.

We will see later how a number of research scenarios can be expressed using this terminology.

Note

1. The story of the blind men and the elephant is thought to have originated in India. It is best known in the West through the work of nineteenth-century American poet John Godfrey Saxe.

2

Motivation and requirements

This chapter draws upon discussions with developers and users in the UK Research Councils (RCUK) E-Science Programme, JISC VRE Programme and the user requirements studies they have conducted. We have ourselves carried out such surveys and have participated in several workshops on usability and requirements. Results of this work have been provided in a number of reports to JISC (Allan et al., 2006a, 2006b, 2006c, 2006d, 2006e, 2006f, 2006g).

Research lifecycle: data, information and knowledge

We consider the activities involved in conducting research to be ultimately driven by knowledge creation. In October 2004, we made the following definitions:

- *data*: bits and bytes arising from an observation (non-repeatable), an experiment (repeatable) or a computer simulation (calculated);
- *information*: relationship between items of data of the form 'A is always associated with B in some way';
- *knowledge*: understanding of causality in relationships, e.g. 'B happens after A because of X' – this knowledge is shared globally.

The research activity could be described at the highest level as creating knowledge from data. In sharing or reusing data, information and knowledge in collaborative research, we meet the problem of metadata and representation. Bits and bytes, no matter how well curated, are of no use unless they can be interpreted.

Virtual Research Environments

Figure 2.1 shows our own version of the steps in the research lifecycle which we believe to be appropriate in e-research activities.

For simplicity, we have omitted from this the all-important administrative activities involved with grant proposals and funding, project management, collaboration forming, actual collaboration and computing. While it is at least in theory possible and desirable to link VREs to institutional and organisational processes, this is currently very challenging.

This book does not discuss knowledge management, but has a lot to say about data and information, the latter typically in the form of published research outcomes such as journal papers and technical reports.

In discussions of data and information management, the term 'metadata' is frequently encountered. Metadata is often defined as *data about data*. Classical metadata will have information such as description, provenance and location referring to a data set or collection. Each of these can be a complex set of information; for instance, location could refer to one or more copies of the data with different access rights, the sort of information required for a link resolver such as OpenURL. Metadata is typically accessed in the form of a catalogue and is extremely useful for search purposes. A particularly important aspect of e-research is the capability to automatically generate and maintain accurate metadata as it has been found that many users do not like entering metadata or are prone to making mistakes.

Figure 2.1 The e-research data and information lifecycle

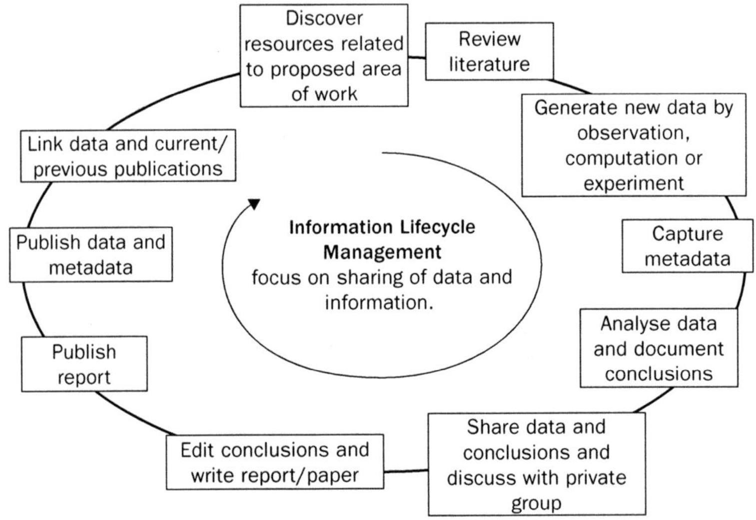

XML, the eXtended Markup Language which is a generalisation of HTML for web pages, is now popular (W3C, 2007). It is only really applicable to data and information in the form of text and of no use for binary data such as images, except for representing their metadata. XML requires a 'schema' to be defined so that the meaning and relationship of its 'tags' can be published. For HTML this is not a problem as the underlying standard is well known and fixed. Another problem with XML is that it can only represent a tree-like organisational structure. As such, it is useful for catalogues, but not so useful for representing complex procedures that may include cyclic behaviour, such as a laboratory workflow.

Other XML-based computer languages must be used to convey the relationships required to represent and form deductions from data, i.e. knowledge. These include the Resource Description Framework (RDF) and the Web Ontology Language (OWL). Both these will be met in discussions of the Semantic Web. RDF and OWL are also important for data interoperability, as they permit terms (XML tags) to be given meaning (e.g. via a dictionary). UK e-science projects have used a family of XML-based technologies, most notably RDF, to provide a mechanism for representing resource metadata. Ontologies capture the meaning of metadata terms and their interrelationships. OWL provides a vocabulary for describing classes of RDF resources and their properties (including relations between classes, cardinality, etc.).

In addition to its use for information and metadata, XML forms the basis of web services that use the SOAP protocol, because it can be ingested and consumed by software written in other computer languages. Web services are a bit like e-mail, with a header and data packet. Binary data can be transported as attachments. Security assertions can be provided via the Security Assertion Markup Language (SAML), which again is XML-based. We will refer to web services again when discussing a service-oriented architecture (SOA) for e-research systems.

Generic usage scenario and requirements

We have found that the key areas that need to be addressed are those of integrating information (in the form of publications, notes, etc.) and data; long-term archival and persistent access with appropriate access control; seamless search and discovery from a (portal) interface alongside other research tools; publication of data following peer review from personal and group information management systems; and collaborative working in discovering, interpreting and using data and information. These areas, with subject-specific differences in detail and usage pattern, are constituents in the generic research lifecycle and some aspects overlap with e-learning and digital information management. We refer to the infrastructure required for a VRE to support these areas as the 'wider information environment'.

In fact, it turns out that while the lifecycle is similar, the activities of creating research data are extremely varied from one domain to another and there is little opportunity to share services at this level. Within an individual domain, such as bioinformatics, certain procedures can however be encapsulated and reused as workflows, e.g. with the Taverna tool in the myGrid and myExperiment projects. Each domain is therefore likely to have specialist tools built into a VRE customised for its specific research community.

We therefore focus on a simple all-embracing generic use case for 'discovery to delivery' in research which might be as follows:

> A researcher wants to carry out a subject-specific search via one or more portal interfaces and to be able to find relevant publications and data associated with their studies and to be able to find other papers which cite them. They may also want to find associated grant references and appropriate funding opportunities for related work.
>
> The researcher then wants to access and download some of the data sets and carry out a similar piece of work using a new model, new insight or adding new data to the previous study. In an experimental study, they might be repeating a recommended procedure on one or more new samples or applying an improved procedure to a benchmark sample. This might involve downloading and using an existing workflow description.
>
> The researcher will afterwards discuss and share results with a peer group, using appropriate personal and group information management software, and will eventually create reports and publish the results together with data and information related to their model or hypothesis.

Klyne (2005) describes some more specific requirements for VREs that affect the provision of repository services and personal information systems from the Sakai VRE project. These include:

- access to best practice documentation, and support for best practices, within the VRE;
- capture and storing of collaborative discussions;

- support in training new researchers;
- searchable list of conferences, lectures and other events;
- ability to locate other researchers;
- selective delivery of information;
- supporting grant applications;
- forums and 'spaces' for internal communication and recruitment;
- access to searchable databases of digital (or digitised) artefacts;
- data repositories.

Sergeant et al. (2006) describe another set of stated requirements, this time from the EVIE VRE project:

- find and acquire published information such as articles, conference proceedings, literature;
- find out about funding opportunities, apply for funding, manage funded projects;
- collaboration with partners in the university or at other institutions;
- share or archive research results such as preprints, postprints, technical reports, software or data sets;
- other activities, not just related to research.

Peer review and citation

What has been described above mostly concerns teams of people engaged in research activities. We also have to consider the before and after – the competitive process by which researchers get funding and the process of judging the effectiveness or importance of their work. Both these are essentially carried out on merit by peer review. There are of course policy issues, which determine what areas of research are favoured at any particular time, e.g. environmental studies, energy conservation or poverty; these are outside the scope of this book.

Research-led institutions such as universities are judged by the amount and quality of research carried out by their staff. In the UK, this is done through the Research Assessment Exercise (RAE; *http://www.rae.ac.uk*) which is conducted by the Higher Education Funding Council for England (HEFCE) and its equivalents in Scotland, Wales and Northern Ireland. The four bodies use the RAE quality profiles to determine their research grants to the institutions they fund over the following two years.

An important factor in devising a rating is the number of citations of research publications. Citation is considered to reflect the importance of the work reported.

Citation indexes list citations between publications, allowing a user to determine which publications have been cited by later ones. These were originally provided as printed compilations for the sciences, social sciences and arts and humanities, and were available in most research libraries. Citation index services are now available online, the principal ones being published by Thomson Scientific (Web of Science and Web of Knowledge) and Elsevier (Scopus). CiteSeer, RePec and Google Scholar can be used to get similar information.

What functionality does an e-researcher need?

The abovementioned EVIE report also identified priorities in terms of portal functionality and usability. We assume that this functionality will be delivered via a web portal, perhaps through tools in a science gateway or institutional portal. Current portals only address some, but not all aspects of the use cases. We here identify the broad requirements for resource discovery and portals within the e-research community. It is also important to bear in mind that web-based solutions might not always be the best. Many desktop tools used by the research community could be extended or repurposed to form a VRE. A simple example is Microsoft Outlook, which is widely used as an institutional tool.

A typical portal-based VRE might involve effort from staff across the university or collaboratory and could provide seamless access to the following:

- MyResearch profile;
- data warehouses that deliver business intelligence on research applications, awards and income;
- costing and project management tools;
- research publication databases and research expertise systems;
- peer-review tools;
- library catalogues, bibliographic research resources and digital repositories;

Motivation and requirements

- access to shared facilities on the grid and to primary research data and metadata associated with relevant projects;
- service portals provided by research councils, government departments, etc.;
- asynchronous communications – e-mail and discussion fora;
- synchronous communications – chat and shared whiteboard;
- desktop video conferencing;
- calendaring and meeting management;
- news – blog and RSS feeds;
- collaborative writing – wiki;
- in the UK, the RAE tool and the RCUK Je-S online application process.

All these can be realised through a web-based portal accessing distributed services in an SOA. As a further illustration, the functionality of Google and other major internet search engines can be cited. Google is now providing a range of services that can be used for research purposes, some particularly aimed at scholarly activities.

In this context, we note again that web browsers are only one client for research services and that others, such as web services which are aimed at machine-to-machine communication and can be linked into 'heritage' applications, graphical user interfaces (GUIs) etc., are likely to be of increasing future importance. Andy Powell (2005) also notes the potential of using RSS, iPod or Firefox (browser) plugins. We have shown that this is possible using pattern-based Java technologies such as J2EE (Yang et al., 2007a).

End users are likely to require a variety of client tools for both machine and human-oriented access including ones which can be used for management of their personal data and information which is growing in size and complexity. It is arguable that this is where e-research technology can make the biggest impact and provide functionality through active links to a wide range of resources *not* simply accessible from a web browser.

What components need to be integrated for e-research?

Components come in the form of: (1) software service interfaces which can be combined into designs for actual applications, including portals;

(2) fusion layer services, including security; and (3) infrastructure such as data servers and computers which host the services. We envisage the use of an SOA paradigm consistent with the JISC E-Framework for Education and Research.

In a separate document (Allan et al., 2006e), we have discussed the service usage models and implied components additional to the JISC Information Environment (IE) Architecture originally proposed by Powell and Lyon (2001). This is taken as an example of an information infrastructure to underpin e-research.

From scenarios, use cases and reference models

The following conclusions arose from an analysis of a number of previously documented use cases and scenarios from relevant projects (Powell and Lyon, 2001):

- researchers want access to data and information (e.g. scholarly publications) for a variety of reasons, and they want to access all sources in a seamless way and to have a uniform style of presentation;
- they want to use the results of such discovery for a variety of purposes, fusing data and information from multiple sources;
- they want to use previously stored data and also create new data and information from computational or experimental procedures;
- they want to publish new data and information, potentially from personal repositories into public repositories;
- service usage models (SUMs) can be developed based on research processes outlined in the scenarios and use cases;
- these SUMs represent parts of the generic research lifecycle;
- SUMs can be realised as designs using generic service components (this hypothesis is yet to be fully tested);
- the IE architecture can be extended with additional components to accommodate an implementation of these designs in service expressions;
- multiple context-based user interfaces are required to access components in the extended IE architecture;
- use of the components and services can be facilitated by workflows supporting the research process;

- many activities worldwide are beginning to implement parts of this overall architecture and we need to integrate with them;
- however, toolkits to support the implementation of most are not yet available.

From interviews and questionnaires

These conclusions arose from an analysis of a number of previous surveys and questionnaires supplemented with interviews with key stakeholders (Allan et al., 2006a).

Linking research practice, resource discovery and information retrieval needs an environment within which they are all integrated. We found that previous surveys have taken too narrow a view of this, as they have mostly been domain-specific or have focused on one aspect of this activity. The joint requirements still need further investigation, i.e. computing and collaboration, or personal information management and admin functions.

However, with regard to research, some key conclusions can be drawn from previous studies, including the following:

- researchers need access to data storage and computational resources, as well as software and services;
- provenance is key to establishing the quality, reliability and value of data in the discovery process (this has also been noted by the DCC);
- any interface needs to present the views of multiple grid services in a way that is easy for users and administrators to access and customise;
- there is a need for a more comprehensive understanding of the domain differences in user requirements (this is considered further by Allan et al., 2006e) – the research issues raised in previous studies are related to data format diversity as well as metadata, mapping and vocabulary;
- existing services and methodologies could be shared and web-based presentation layers customised for delivery to users, e.g. in portals;
- a range of toolkits (thin clients, portals, scripting languages, GUIs etc.) should be developed to extend and simplify access to grid resources and information systems, leading to the eventual emergence of one or more interfaces to a virtual research and information environment.

With the development of (multidisciplinary) e-research groups, new needs appear to have emerged. It is likely that the needs that will be important for a given institution will vary according to the areas of research strength, extent of infrastructural development and the strength of collaborative networks.

A portal for e-research is likely to require the following (though we note that this would need further testing with users, a process now underway):

- a mechanism to set up virtual organisation members and resources in collaborative sessions – to include shared access to data repositories for searching, replication and updating;
- generic tools such as text chat, white boards, etc. with shared updates to text message streams;
- audio-video conferencing and collaboration tools – to share events specifying changes in compressed streams;
- applications such as web pages, presentations – all of which share key clicks to control a master document;
- visualisation – to share events corresponding to changes in pixels of a frame buffer, maybe using scalable vector graphics;
- shared maps, instruments (e.g. medical) – controlled as above and possibly with added mashups;
- access to full-text resources as well as tools to cross-search both free and subscription-based services – the results pages should identify subscription-based resources and whether the user can gain access to them;
- alert services, promotion and training opportunities on how to use services accessed from the portal – how to contact information specialists;
- access to departmental and local resources and repositories as well as external resources from a single interface.

Any online provision also needs to be supported by assistance with organising and managing research data sets, information and knowledge, as well as a training programme.

It is worth remembering that 'a portal is not a repository, and a repository is not a portal' (P. Burnhill, personal communication). Even though all repository facilities are likely to have websites, these are not all portals and therefore the interfaces to their services are hard to reuse and preclude machine-to-machine access. The complementarity of portals and repositories has also been noted (Allan et al., 2006b). Additionally, what is functionally useful in a repository is not necessarily important for portal functionality; in other words, a portal could do without a repository if users are depositing in institutional and other digital repositories. In terms of e-research, the value of a portal could be enhanced if it were also an interface to create and support a community of users, a space that people use for their collaborative research. However, the portal must point to some repository or other, or it loses much of its usefulness for information and data management.

It is clear from the surveys of user requirements that researchers need access to scientific and other data as well as publications. While it is probably not within the remit of a single e-research system to host all such data, it may consider hosting corresponding metadata or providing search facilities and mechanisms to link data to publications and vice versa. As noted above, this functionality may be provided by separate services.

Overall, researchers appear to need more support for learning, adapting and writing software specific to their research problems than is currently available. In addition, researchers who are generating and using large data sets need help managing their data. This need will become more pressing as data enters long-lived archives and therefore the public arena through preservation rather than simple publication of links.

We suggest that a VRE might usefully link into a wide range of data services by accessing a number of reusable components within the surrounding architecture. These include private and commercial as well as open services.

Illustrative examples

We have chosen five short examples to illustrate how ICT can add value to existing research programmes and processes.

Geo-spatial data and information

This example illustrates work that could be composed from services already being developed or put into production in a number of JISC funded projects: GRADE, geoCrossWalk, HEIRPORT, Go-geo!, DCC, and projects delivering things such as OpenURL resolvers and aggregators. Work on geo-spatial data is already relatively advanced as several projects at EDINA and elsewhere have addressed this area. There are also a number of projects funded by the Research Councils. See also the DCC briefing paper 'Curating geo-spatial data' (McGarva, 2006).

The Go-Geo! portal is a science gateway that simplifies the discovery of geo-spatial data and related resources. An extension to the original project has developed portlets deployable into subject, media-specific, data centre and institutional portals operating within a JSR 168 framework. Go-Geo! has been proposed as a grid portal for the UK academic geographic information science community. The project is also investigating metadata creation in the community. There is a related broker service, which gives access to the academic catalogues forming a geo-data grid. Figure 2.2 shows how Go-geo! links into the JISC landscape.

Further integration might enhance existing e-research components to include geo-spatial data plus census data and associated publications. Some e-research projects are already investigating this. For example, Grid Enabling MIMAS Services (GEMS) aims to make such data available via data management services hosted on the NGS, while the Historic Environment Resources Network (HEIRNET) is using geo-spatial data to enhance research into historical monuments and finds. Other projects, such as those in the domain of archaeology, might usefully contribute or benefit from this kind of approach.

Work on linking geo-spatial data to other relevant data and publications still needs to be increased in other disciplines where studies are made of historical and current activities, particularly in social science.

In the case of map-based data, there is a need in the UK to embrace the activities of the Ordnance Survey. While not completely free to use, Ordnance Survey map information is widely used, and often forms the basis of valuable 'derived data', some of which may be related to a particular time or event. Sharing such data can maximise research (increasingly multidisciplinary) and/or business benefits (Smith, 2005).

To facilitate multidisciplinary work and cross-searching, appropriate metadata should be used – not simply metadata specific to geo-spatial data. Standards must also be applied, for instance to place names which may have changed over long periods of time, making correlation between historical research and geography difficult. Gazetteers are important in this respect. The international Open Geo-spatial Consortium is involved in a wide range of other relevant standards.

Some required services include:

- user registration;
- authentication;
- metadata creation and editing;
- packaging;

Figure 2.2 Go-geo! in the JISC landscape

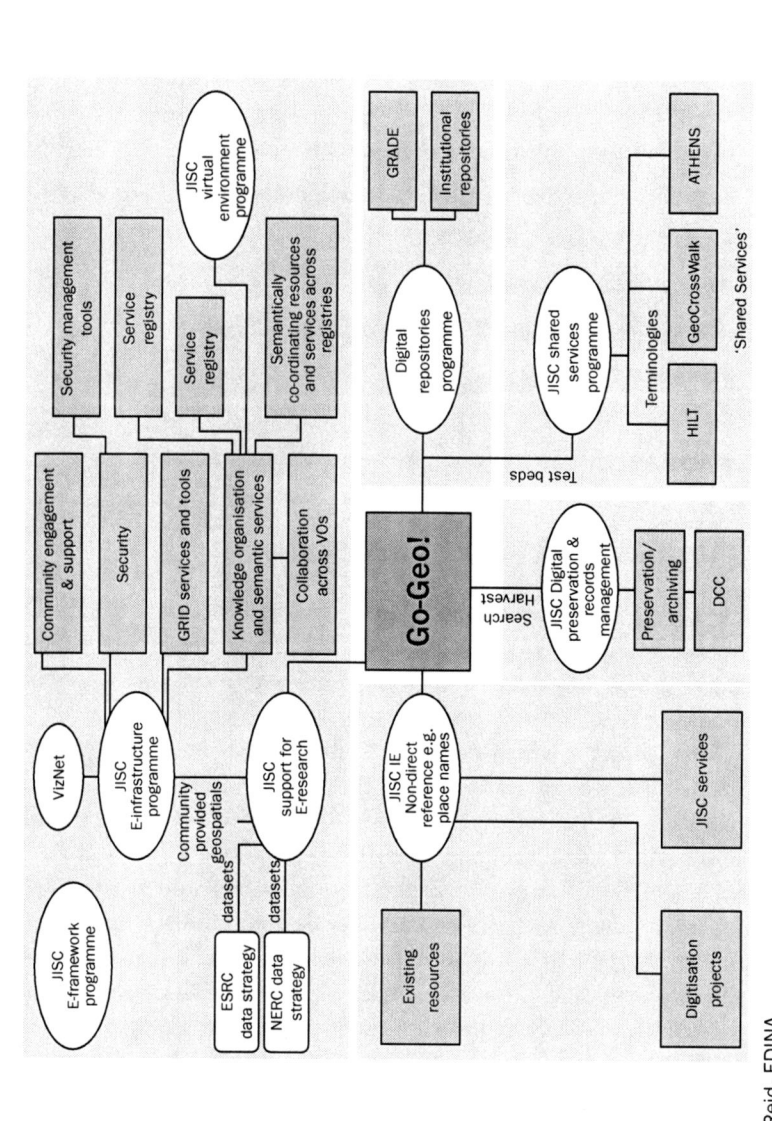

Source: James Reid, EDINA

- data and information upload;
- validation;
- notification;
- rights information creation and editing;
- authorisation;
- recording and editing provenance;
- representation information repository;
- search and discovery (possibly in collaboration);
- location (based on rights);
- aggregation and overlay;
- visualisation or analysis (possibly in collaboration);
- access and download;
- adding links – proposals, data, publications and citations;
- resolving and interpreting terms (metadata and 'names').

Chemical data and information

This example is based on the eBank, ePrints, PSIGate, ALPSP, eCrystals, SMART-Tea and R4L projects. Other projects such as e-CCP have related goals. One can use Google to find information about these projects.

Other projects which might usefully contribute or benefit from this include Integrative Biology VRE and e-HTPX. Computationally-generated data produced by the UK Collaborative Computational Projects (CCP) Programme might also be included – for instance, CCP1, CCP4 and CCP5 are now generating metadata and storing results as enabled in the NERC-funded eMinerals and BBSRC funded e-HTPX projects. Protein structure data produced by e-HTPX and its associated metadata is uploaded for archival in the Protein Data Bank (PDB) at the European Biomolecular Institute in Hinxton, near Cambridge.

It is necessary to capture data and metadata as they are generated in the laboratory, often in 'one-shot' or high-throughput experiments. Once such data is captured in a laboratory information management system or electronic lab notebook, it can be managed and used in other parts of the research lifecycle, for instance, the automatic generation of laboratory reports.

Motivation and requirements

There is a similar set of services required to those in the first example. However in this case we are handling chemical and bio-chemical data rather than geographical data. Place names and map references are replaced by chemical names, compounds and identifiers such as InChI, LSID and terms from schema such as Chemical Markup Language (CML). Semantic services are necessary to work with such identifiers and terms. There is a further similarity to the place names, in that chemical and bio-chemical names and identifiers are not unique and have changed with time.

In the e-CCP project, application-specific vocabularies have been collected and semantic tools based on ontologies are used to map data between applications. Thus, output from one application can be interpreted with tools designed for a different one. So far this has addressed the computational chemistry domain and is based on work on the XML-based CML. Extensions of the generic e-CCP methodology (now known as AgentX) are however applicable to other areas and there is a requirement to store the vocabularies and ontologies in a registry such as IEMSR for reuse.

Social science data and information

ESRC has recently established a project to deliver a prototype e-infrastructure for social scientists. This project makes use of collaboration tools and middleware being developed in JISC VRE projects such as GROWL and the Sakai Demonstrator to access NGS resources and data sources such as UKDA and MIMAS. It plans to link to census data via OGSA-DAI middleware and services being deployed in the GEMS project by extending the GROWL toolkit. Geo-spatial data is also involved, for instance in defining land boundaries for policy makers. The outcomes of the project, which will also deliver a range of semantic tools and possibly use AgentX, could be incorporated into existing e-research services from the information environment, such as the IESR or IEMSR.

This project does not however have any provision for using other IE services, such as other means of data and information discovery or publication of results – these are areas which could usefully be explored. A simple first step would be to include the SPP portlets in the Sakai portal to be deployed at NCeSS hub and nodes, thus enabling interaction with SOSIG and other Resource Discovery Network (RDN) repositories. Portlet interfaces to MIMAS and UKDA and other services useful to social scientists should be explored, as should the licensing of widely used commercial software to run on the NGS and the linking of remote data sets into such software. The services could then offer an interface that researchers could 'plug in' to the relevant project for their work.

For social scientists investigating worldwide policy and trends, other sources of data and information outside the UK will also be required.

Another worked example scenario of a social science researcher has been described by Allan et al. (2006e).

Our experiences of developing a virtual research environment for the social sciences are described in Chapter 11.

E-mail, data and shared services

This example is based on JISCmail which, as well as providing a list server and management tools, has a searchable archive (see *http://www.jiscmail.ac.uk*). JISCmail is an example of a tool which already supports thousands of 'virtual communities', each via its own mailing list. Communities have overlapping membership lists, but JISCmail maintains separate content.

Pennock (2006) notes that e-mail is now a significant tool in decision making for both administrative and research purposes. Records of how such decisions are made are no longer documented separately, and curating e-mails and attachments may be the only way to provide an audit trail in the event of problems or for future reference. E-mail is just one component of what is sometimes referred to as 'grey literature'. For such archives to be widely useful, search and discovery mechanisms need to be provided alongside the tools to mark up e-mail in a useful way (e.g. separating out the 'to' and 'from' headers as XML elements). This is a challenging area as many e-mails typically contain abbreviations, colloquialisms and material which is simply not directly relevant. There is often no reference to formal 'threads' of conversation and the 'subject' headers may be wildly misleading. This area requires as much a culture change as software services and could be a fruitful area for longer-term work.

Portal interfaces for the search and discovery of e-mail archives, with appropriate rights-based mechanisms for access may become increasingly useful, but only if supported by semantic and text-mining tools. Access rights may usefully be more fine-grained than at the list level, but there is no mechanism for capturing this granularity or other metadata not already in the mail headers. Sakai is a portal which also supports virtual organisations through its 'worksite' structure. Each worksite could therefore be easily linked to a different JISCmail list. Additional worksite services would then be immediately available to JISCmail users.

The utility of such services is already indicated by the fact the Google searches often turn up e-mail contributions to thread-based discussion fora and blogs, particularly for resolving problems with computer software. However, such results also confirm the potential problems outlined above. In addition, Google cannot access e-mail archives which are stored in a database. These should be linked into an e-research system in other ways to enable cross-searching.

JISCmail is considering additional services related to collaboration, for instance a calendaring service to support setting up meetings. This is already available in Sakai, but would require further integration. We believe that additional integration is also necessary with institutional services, such that JISCmail and calendaring can be accessible, closely coupled with MS Exchange via suitable interchange standards.

The use of list servers, such as LISTSERV which underpins JISCmail, is further discussed in Chapter 5.

Large-scale experimental facilities

The new Diamond Light Source experimental facility built on the Harwell Science and Innovation Campus in Oxfordshire is the largest single investment in science in the UK for 40 years (*http://www.diamond.ac.uk*). Our use case and experiences of developing an e-infrastructure for Diamond are recorded in Chapter 12.

During an exercise to document requirements and develop a workplan for the rollout of e-science technology to support staff and users of the Diamond Light Source in 2005, we identified the key needs to preserve experimental data and associated metadata and link it to both grant proposals made to the Research Councils and publications arising from the work (Gleaves and Ashtun, 2006). Considerable experience was gained from previous work on high-throughput protein crystallography experiments in the e-HTPX project and other work on the Synchrotron Radiation Facility at Daresbury (Allan et al. 2005; Wang et al., 2006; Akram et al., 2007).

A number of early users were consulted in eliciting requirements, including ones from e-HTPX and the National Crystallography Service who are also using eCrystal, eBank, R4L and PDB. However, there remains a considerable amount of work to be done to deploy all the required services and link them into other services, such as those provided by NGS, DCC, CCPs and ePubs. A VRE integrating interfaces from the various administrative and research services from the views of users, user office staff and station scientists still needs to be specified and developed.

3

Creating and using research data

The activities of research are concerned with creating or accessing data and interpreting its meaning. In order of historical importance, the creation of data might be from observations, experimentation or (nowadays) simulation and modelling using computers. We have excluded here original thought, philosophy and mathematics which of course underpin all aspects of research.

The nature of scholarly communication is changing, with researchers wanting access to primary research data, often in digital form. Such data may have been expensive to produce and has an intrinsic value for further research. Scholarly communication now requires more than journal publications as were previously managed, made accessible and preserved in libraries. Indeed, it is speculated that libraries may risk fading from existence if they do not respond effectively to the changing research environment and business model. In e-research, it is becoming more common for primary research data to be managed, made accessible, curated and linked to other research outcomes. As reported by Goldenberg-Hart (2004), Clifford Lynch of CNI argues that the role of libraries will shift from primarily acquiring published scholarship to managing scholarship in collaboration with researchers who develop and use this data. Librarians are becoming 'information specialists', able to respond to a wide range of requirements to make use of digital information and data.

Characteristics of data

Below we consider some differences between observational, experimental and simulation data and how they are used. The current trend is to keep (curate) all such data for either research purposes or legal reasons. However, our ability to generate data is also growing exponentially and in the future we will have to give careful consideration to how much and which data is to be kept and for how long. For now, e-research is concerned with keeping the data and creating metadata for it so that it can be searched, accessed and potentially reused.

Observation

Observational data is important in many domains of research, particularly in studies of living organisms (both functional and behavioural), our planet, climate and the universe at large. Medical data is mostly from observations. Such data is associated with processes which cannot be repeated and are therefore not appropriate for experimentation.

A characteristic of observational data is that cause and effect is very hard to recognise. Such data may be subjected to statistical techniques, such as longitudinal modelling (if observations have been repeated at many intervals on a given population) or data mining. Genetics has used such techniques to associate the changes in particular genes, chromosomes or proteins with certain medical conditions.

Another characteristic is that such data may be confidential (in studies of human populations) or only of use to the person who collected it. Its intrinsic value varies greatly between research domains.

Experimentation

In experimentation, any study is performed under closely controlled conditions and the outcome recorded. The experiment may be repeated many times to get 'error bounds' on the data, allowing interpretation based on a hypothetical model to help establish cause and effect. Similar experiments may be repeated under slightly changed conditions to establish trends.

Some experimental data may require complex analysis based on an underlying physical or chemical or other model. This differs from analysis of observational data which is likely to be statistical in nature. We cite our work on the e-HTPX project, further described in Chapter 12, in which X-ray crystallographic spectra are analysed by a variety of computational techniques to identify three-dimensional protein structures. The computer software to do this is maintained by the Collaborative Computational Project for Protein Crystallography (CCP4) – see below. In this case, the primary data may need to be stored in case improved computational techniques are developed and the data can be re-analysed (such analysis does not always give unique answers). The data can also be analysed for trends, e.g. the likely effectiveness of a particular drug in combating a disease in which a family of proteins are involved or in determining the function of such proteins. It is however likely that secondary rather than primary data will be used for this purpose.

Simulation and modelling

Simulation and modelling is now recognised as the third main methodology of research. High-performance computers are enabling mathematical models of reality, based on our hypotheses, to be translated back into numerical results. These results can in turn be compared with experimental or observational data. The importance of simulation is that it allows parameters to be changed in the models to understand cause and effect at a level which is not possible in other ways. It also permits phenomena to be studied which might be too expensive or dangerous for conventional experimental methods. Another reason for comparison is to validate the theoretical and mathematical model and to indicate how it might be enhanced if results do not match.

The report from the US President's Information Technology Advisory Committee in 2005 recognised the importance of computational science:

> Computational science provides a unique window through which researchers can investigate problems that are otherwise impractical or impossible to address, ranging from scientific investigations of the biochemical processes of the human brain and the fundamental forces of physics shaping the universe, to analysis of the spread of infectious disease or airborne toxic agents in a terrorist attack, to supporting advanced industrial methods with significant economic benefits, such as rapidly designing more efficient airplane wings computationally rather than through expensive and time consuming wind tunnel experiments. (PITAC, 2005)

There is a great deal of literature about high-performance computing and computational grids, which we will not repeat here. Most academic and commercial research organisations have access to high-performance computing (HPC). National and regional grids are discussed in Chapter 8. The use of HPC to generate data will be described in the next section.

There are a number of different types of data grid worldwide. The largest in the UK is GridPP, which is part of the European EGEE project and is designed as a hierarchical network of servers relaying data on demand from CERN, to national Tier-1 centres and then to regional Tier-2 clouds such as NorthGrid or to individual research groups. The data is cached at each level and will allow outcomes of the large hadron collider (LHC) experiments to be analysed in the race to win a Nobel Prize. The Natural Environment Research Council (NERC) data grid is under development and currently supports discovery with access to thousands of data sets from the British Atmospheric Data Centre (BADC) and other NERC data centres; a gateway with database and vocabulary servers; and an underpinning XML data model.

Combined methodologies

It is now possible to combine the above methodologies for generating data. Using sophisticated computer models together with observational data forms the basis of the weather forecasting that affects our daily lives. Simulations may be compared with trends in climate change in an attempt to establish the causes of change; this clearly requires data to be accessible. High-throughput experimentation can be combined with computer analysis and modelling as the basis of screening for new effective (targeted) or personalised pharmaceuticals.

High-performance computing in e-research

It may currently be a step too far to include control of experimental or observational facilities in a VRE, but it is certainly possible to include running applications on high-performance computers as available on the grid (see Chapter 8).

Over the past 30 years, HPC has been used to model and predict accurately a wide range of physical properties and phenomena. More recently, large-scale simulations of our environment are being used for urban policy making, and statistical and financial models are being used to understand social trends. Commercial organisations are using realistic simulations to avoid destructive testing of prototypes. The results of such simulations can even be sufficient to gain safety accreditation, e.g. for vehicles or jet engines. Many of these applications have had an important impact in contributing to wealth creation and improving quality of life through developing new products and processes with greater efficacy, efficiency or reduced harmful side effects and in contributing to our ability to understand and describe the world around us.

The pressure on computational science and engineering now is to study more complex and larger systems and to increase the realism and detail of the modelling. In their 1992 report, a scientific working group chaired by Professor Catlow of the Royal Institution of Great Britain presented a scientific case for future supercomputing requirements across many of the most exciting and urgent areas of relevance to the missions of the UK Research Councils (Catlow, 1992). The report highlighted a number of domains at the forefront of science in which computational work would play a central role. It was noted that to make progress in these most computationally demanding and challenging problems, increases of two to three orders of magnitude in computing resources such as processing power, memory and storage rates and capacity would be required. The report led ultimately to the procurement of a Cray Research Inc T3D system, which went into operation at the University of Edinburgh in the summer of 1994. The High Performance Computing Initiative (HPCI) was set up in November 1994 to support the efficient and effective exploitation of the Cray T3D and future generations of systems by consortia working in the 'frontier' areas of computational research.

The enhancement of the Cray T3D in 1997 to 512 processors gave a very significant increase in computing power compared with previous national facilities, allowing simulations to move forward on a number of fronts including the following:

- improved resolution and accuracy – this is particularly important in mesh-based applications where numerical artefacts can distort physical effects and, for example, make computational fluid dynamics simulations more diffusive than the physics dictates;
- moving from two spatial dimensions, which can typically be accommodated on a workstation, to three spatial dimensions;
- moving from static, steady-state or time-averaged simulations to dynamic simulations – for example, the study of non-equilibrium properties and the calculation of extremal instantaneous behaviour;
- larger systems – for example in materials simulations moving away from periodic simple three-dimensional systems to more chemically and physically interesting surface and defect systems, modelling systems of sufficient scale to eliminate finite size computational effects;
- long timescale studies enabling the determination of the low-frequency dynamic response of systems;
- increasingly complex or strongly interacting systems – for example nonlinear interactions or materials properties, moving beyond mean

field or averaged interactions, to systems under extreme conditions, multi-phase and multi-physics simulations;
- optimisation studies within large parameter spaces, model parameterisations, trends and sensitivity analyses.

Subsequent national computer facilities, the CSAR Service (Manchester, November 1998 to June 2006), HPCx (Daresbury Laboratory, December 2002 to early 2010) and HECToR (University of Edinburgh, April 2007 to 2013) have enabled more and greater challenges to be tackled. Projects wishing to use facilities such as these typically need to apply for a Research Council grant or equivalent. These Tier-1 facilities are complemented by Tier-2 facilities on grids. Access to grid resources is currently easier, but the business model is changing.

We next describe how development of large-scale computer applications in science and engineering is managed in the UK and how efficient exploitation of national supercomputer facilities is assured. Other countries have different ways of doing this; for instance, many large computing projects in the USA receive funding from the National Science Foundation or the Department of Energy (DoE). One example is the DoE's Scientific Discovery through Advanced Computing programme (see *http://www.scidac.gov*).

The UK Collaborative Computational Projects

Many researchers in the physical sciences in the UK will know all about, and possibly participate in, the Collaborative Computational Projects (CCPs). The CCPs bring together leading UK expertise in key domains of computational research to tackle large-scale scientific software development, maintenance and distribution projects. Each project represents many years of intellectual and financial investment. The aim is to capitalise on this investment by encouraging widespread and long-term use of the software they develop, and by fostering initiatives such as new research consortia.

The CCPs currently cover a range of research areas as shown in Table 3.1.

The collaborative research carried out by participants in the CCPs enriches UK computational science and engineering research in various ways. The CCPs provide a software infrastructure on which important individual research projects can be built. They support both the R&D and exploitation phases of computational research projects. They ensure the development of software that makes optimum use of the whole range

Table 3.1 CCPs and their funding source

CCP	Title	Funding source
CCP1	The Electronic Structure of Molecules	EPSRC
CCP2	Continuum States of Atoms and Molecules	EPSRC
CCP3	Computational Studies of Surfaces	EPSRC
CCP4	Protein Crystallography	BBSRC
CCP5	Computer Simulation of Condensed Phases	EPSRC
CCP6	Heavy Particle Dynamics	EPSRC
CCP7	Analysis of Astronomical Spectra	no longer active
CCP8	Nuclear Structure	no longer active
CCP9	Electronic Structure of Solids	EPSRC
CCP10	Plasma Physics	no longer active
CCP11	Biosequence and Structure Analysis	no longer active
CCP12	High Performance Computational Engineering	EPSRC
CCP13	Fibre Diffraction	no longer active
CCP14	Powder and Single Crystal Diffraction	EPSRC
CCPN	NMR Analysis	BBSRC
CCPB	Biomolecular Simulation	BBSRC
CCPP	Computational Plasma Physics	EPSRC

of computer hardware available to the scientific community, from the desktop to the most powerful national supercomputing facilities. The training activities of CCPs have been outstandingly successful, benefiting several hundred students and postdoctorates each year. In Europe, the Centre Européen de Calcul Atomique et Moléculaire (CECAM) fulfils a similar but more centralised role.

The main activities of the CCPs are as follows:

- carry out flagship code development projects;
- maintain and distribute code libraries;
- organise training in the use of applications, sometimes in the form of annual schools;
- hold meetings and workshops;
- invite overseas researchers for lecture tours and collaborative visits;
- issue regular newsletters.

Flagship projects represent innovative software developments at the leading edge of a CCP's area of science or engineering. They normally last for three years and may support a postdoctoral researcher associated with the project. At the end of a flagship project, the resulting software usually becomes part of the code library. CCPs maintain, distribute and develop the new code according to demand from member and user research programmes.

This flagship model suits most CCPs. It provides a mechanism for responding to advances in its subject area and maintains the interest of participating staff in cutting-edge research. Other CCPs, especially those involved closely with experimental research (CCP4, CCP14, CCPN), focus more on the collation, standardisation and development of data analysis codes. Here it is vital to keep pace with rapid developments in instrumentation and there may be particular relevance to commercial users.

The collaborative approach makes the community almost uniquely able to adapt and respond to developments in computer science, information technology and hardware. One of the strengths of the scheme is that the focus of each CCP has evolved to maintain international scientific topicality and leadership within its community. The CCPs are increasingly represented in science and engineering as advances in computational techniques and hardware make it feasible to tackle problems of real practical significance.

Each CCP has a chair and a working group, which sets the scientific agenda, decides the work programme and monitors progress. Currently, more than 300 groups participate in the CCPs, including several outside the UK and in industrial research. There are probably more than 1,000 individual researchers and research students in the UK supported by CCPs. The CCP programmes produce more than 500 papers per year. About 12 per cent of these are in the 'hot news' category, publishing in journals such as *Nature*, *Science* and *Physical Review Letters*.

CCPs have a high profile overseas. Many have links with European networks or programmes. The CCP steering panel includes international scientists. CCPs also provide opportunities for links with foreign institutions and scientists. CCPs maintain high visibility to industrial researchers by publicising their software, meetings, training and other activities, and by including industrial members on working groups and on the steering panel. The CCPs are funded competitively through regular Research Council grants. Since 1978, they have also benefited from support by staff at STFC's Daresbury Laboratory, funded via an agreement with the Research Councils. These staff provide expert technical and administrative support, perform many of the functions outlined above, and are frequently involved in large-scale application development projects.

The whole CCP programme is overseen by a steering panel which, with the addition of its chairman, comprises the chairs of all CCPs and a few international advisers, the director of STFC's Computational Science and Engineering Department and the director of CECAM. The steering panel looks actively at areas for co-working between CCPs; joint meetings, workshops and training events are common. All CCPs have a strong interest in e-research and grid computing and are developing common approaches to using ICT.

Managing research data

Data will typically be stored in some form of repository (see Chapter 4). This may be alongside information such as reports and other published research outcomes and the information may be cross-referenced. It is becoming widely expected that publications should cite the source of the data they use and that the data should be accessible for future investigations or reappraisal of its conclusions.

Such publications are themselves a valuable form of metadata. In fact, techniques of indexing and text mining can extract keywords from which metadata records could be constructed. In this respect we refer to work of the UK's National Centre for Text Mining (NACTeM; *http://www.nactem.ac.uk*). Some people have suggested that such techniques and others involving natural language processing might be used to enhance the Semantic Web in a 'bottom-up' approach that would be a significant feature of Web 3.0. This automates the idea of 'social tagging' used in Web 2.0 and complements 'top-down' metadata created by the original author or classification by an information scientist with knowledge of the research domain. Significantly, these different ways of creating metadata can result in different terminologies, which may cause problems in an e-research context if the usage of terms changes in the future. It also makes discovery and reuse hard where a standard thesaurus or ontology is not adhered to, but generally any such data model is a consensus and not fixed for all time.

For now, however, we shall ignore this problem and return to the classical form of metadata as described in Chapter 2. This typically is provided as database or other records complying with a predefined XML schema known as a data model. The existence of a metadata database makes scientific data reusable. Typically, it will be used in a discovery service involving a catalogue browser or domain-specific keyword search.

In discussing research data and metadata, the issue of granularity must be considered. There are often related data sets or collections which could be described by a single metadata entry. This could however be suboptimal at the point when the data has to be accessed. Alternatively, describing data sets at a very fine level leads to a growth in the volume of metadata and can slow or confuse the discovery process.

The report from the US President's Information Technology Advisory Committee in 2005 recognised the importance of data management alongside access to high-performance computers in realising computational science as a significant branch of ICT-based research. The committee noted:

> These enormous repositories of digital information require a new generation of more powerful analysis tools. What was appropriate for a modest volume of manually collected data is wholly inadequate for a multiple petabyte archive. Large-scale data sets cannot be analyzed and understood in a reasonable time without computational models, data and text mining, visualizations, and other knowledge discovery tools. Moreover, extraction of knowledge across heterogeneous or federated sources requires contextual knowledge, typically provided through metadata. For example, knowledge to be derived from data captured through an instrument requires some knowledge of the instrument's characteristics, the conditions in which it was used and the calibration record of the instrument. Metadata is necessary to determine the accuracy and provenance (heredity) of the individual data sets as well as the validity of combining data across sets.
>
> Computational science researchers often gather multi-channel, multi-modal and sensor data from real-time collection instruments, access large distributed databases and rely on sophisticated simulation and visualization systems for exploring large-scale, complex, multidimensional systems. Managing such large-scale computations requires powerful, sometimes distributed, computing resources and efficient, scalable and transparent software that frees the user to engage the complexity of the problem rather than of the tools themselves. Such computational application software does not currently exist.

Data-intensive computational science, based on the emergence of ubiquitous sensors and high-resolution detectors, is a new opportunity to couple observation driven computation and analysis, particularly in response to transient phenomena (e.g. earthquakes or unexpected stellar events). Moreover, the explosive growth in the resolution of sensors and scientific instruments – a consequence of increased computing capability – is creating unprecedented volumes of experimental data. Such devices will soon routinely produce petabytes of data. (PITAC, 2005)

Digital curation

We here refer to curation of digital data, which means more than just archiving. Curation of digital data is the process of establishing and developing long-term repositories of digital assets for current and future reference by researchers, scientists, historians and scholars generally (Abbott, 2006).

The Digital Curation Centre

The Digital Curation Centre was established by the UK E-Science Programme and JISC to provide a national focus for research and development into curation issues and to promote expertise and good practice, both national and international, for the management of all research outputs in digital format (see *http://www.dcc.ac.uk*).

The DCC has its own conceptual lifecycle for digital information, similar to Figure 2.1 (see *http://www.dcc.ac.uk/docs/publications/ DCCLifecycle.pdf*). They have additional actions, important for curation, appraisal and migration. Part of the appraisal action may include a decision about whether to continue to curate a piece of data or to dispose of it. Such decisions are critical, as the volume of relevant data is growing faster than our ability to store it. In 2007, data centres already consumed some 2 per cent of the world's electricity supply (EPA, 2007), although many are storing transactional, financial and internet web pages rather than pure research data. The DCC will provide advice on how such decisions should be taken and implemented.

The CASPAR project

CASPAR stands for Cultural, Artistic and Scientific Knowledge for Preservation, Access and Retrieval. This is a digital preservation project funded in part by the European Union and running from 2006 to 2009. CASPAR brings together a consortium covering important digital holdings, with appropriate scientific, cultural and creative expertise, commercial partners, and leaders in the domain of information preservation.

CASPAR has its own conceptual lifecycle, which includes parts for creating, curating and consuming data. It has activities related to finding, packaging and storing data and includes consideration of repository information via a registry and knowledge creation through discovery.

An important part of the work of CASPAR is to implement, extend and validate the ISO 14721 Open Archival Information System reference model (OAIS; *http://www.oais.org*). An OAIS must be usable to enable the following:

- negotiate for and accept appropriate information from producers;
- obtain sufficient control of the information provided to ensure long-term preservation;
- determine which communities should become the designated community and therefore, should be able to understand the information provided;
- ensure that the information to be preserved is independently understandable to the designated community – in other words, the community should be able to understand the information without needing the assistance of the experts who produced the information;
- follow documented policies and procedures which ensure that the information is preserved against all reasonable contingencies and which enable the information to be disseminated as authenticated copies of the original, or traceable to the original;
- make the preserved information available to the designated community.

In response to these requirements, the OAIS reference model will provide a framework for the following:

- the understanding and increased awareness of archival concepts needed for long-term digital information preservation and access;
- concepts needed by non-archival organisations to be effective participants in the preservation process;
- terminology and concepts for describing and comparing architectures and operations of existing and future archives;

Creating and using research data

- describing and comparing different long-term preservation strategies and techniques;
- comparing the data models of digital information preserved by archives and for discussing how data models and the underlying information may change over time;
- potential expansion by other efforts to cover long-term preservation of information that is not in digital form (e.g. physical media and physical samples);
- expanding consensus on the elements and processes for long-term digital information preservation and access, and promoting a larger market that vendors can support;
- guiding the identification and production of OAIS-related standards.

Data discovery

To illustrate how data discovery and reuse is facilitated by metadata, we give an example of iCAT.

iCAT: the STFC Information Catalogue

The Information Catalogue, iCAT, was developed in STFC's e-Science Centre to add value to scientific data collected from the large-scale facilities managed by STFC. The name 'iCAT' is somewhat confusing, as it is also used for the iRODS Catalogue developed at the San Diego Supercomputing Center. iRODS is data grid software based on the previous Storage Resource Broker. Data referenced by STFC's iCAT is also typically accessed using the SRB.

iCAT software comprises a metadata schema and a suite of tools which provides access to specific information within large distributed data collections, large both in terms of complexity and size (into the petabyte range). iCAT consists of three main components: the metadata model used to describe the data location and content; the iCAT application programming interface (API) – a programmable interface to the catalogue dealing with access, selection and security; and the DataPortal, which uses the API to provide secure web access to the iCAT catalogue and underlying data in an e-research context. Other tools, such as command line search and metadata management, can be provided using the same web service API.

51

The iCAT catalogue uses its metadata schema to describe core components of the data such as the following:

- *topic indexing*: catalogue of keywords describing and categorising the data;
- *provenance*: where the data came from, when and why it was produced, and by whom;
- *data holding*: information about the organisation, location and key content of the data;
- *related material*: any existing information that has been correlated with the data or has resulted from correlating the data with other information;
- *access conditions*: who is allowed or is specifically denied access to this data.

The iCAT XML schema enables discovery and access to information and data in a wide variety of formats from different and distributed sources. Parameter fields allow for customisation of the schema for other research domains. The latter has been successfully proven through a number of implementations and deployments for domains such as environmental science, chemistry, physics, materials and nanotechnology.

To enable efficient access to the content of iCAT, an API was developed which fulfils requirements for interactions with the catalogue. The API shields the developer from specific database and storage layers and insulates applications from any changes to the underlying structures and contents. Its functionality not only includes retrieval and submission of information from the catalogue, but physical data access also requires appropriate control. The iCAT API uses web services as recommended by the Web Services Interoperability Consortium (WS-I). The web services API allows, for example, access from web applications, customisations to pre-existing GUIs, command line tools and plugins to access the same underlying calls, allowing for flexible integration into new and existing applications. Additionally, it decreases the maintenance burden in deployed environments by being firewall friendly.

The use of WS-I allows the ICAT API to be consumed by a wide range of languages as well as being platform-independent. The API has over 90 different methods to create, read, update and delete information pertaining to different entities held in the iCAT schema.

The DataPortal is a web-based interface for users to directly interact with information in the iCAT and the underlying data. The DataPortal uses the functionality of the iCAT API to interact with the metadata held in the iCAT. The DataPortal provides secure access to all the functionality enabled by the catalogue. It also offers the option to link multiple iCAT schemas together, making these distributed resources cross-searchable through one interface. In this way, information can be collated across different data holdings.

The DataPortal has been through extensive evaluation on projects in which it has been deployed. For more information see Chapter 12.

The iCAT metadata schema focuses on the concept of a study comprised of a number of investigations. Each one is of a particular type and uses a particular instrument on an experimental facility and is carried out in a particular access cycle. Associated with each investigation is a title and grant reference number and there can be a number of the following: investigator, keyword, topic list, topic, sample, data set and publication. Samples have associated data sets and sample parameters. Data sets have data-set parameters and data files which have format information. There is also information about access permissions built into the schema and associated with individual investigations and data sets.

This schema was devised in consultation with users and staff of major experimental facilities managed by STFC, including Diamond and ISIS and the Central Laser Facility. It has also been discussed with staff at the Oak Ridge National Laboratory Spallation Neutron Source (USA), Australian Synchrotron and Neutron facilities and the Canadian Light Source.

Data access

Access to data has two strands: access control and physical access. Following data discovery via systems as described above, which may also be subject to access control, the data sets or collections need to be downloaded, moved or modified in some way.

Access control

Access control is related to security and identity management, which will be discussed in Chapter 5.

Access control based on authorisation is the ability to permit or deny the use of a particular resource by a particular entity (person, service, etc.). Access control mechanisms can be used in managing physical resources, logical resources or digital resources. They could be identity or token-based. For digital data and information, this is mostly for reasons of confidentiality, but can also be extended for logging access, particularly if the resources are modified by users.

While there are a number of access control techniques in use for digital resources, we will restrict our discussion to role-based access control (RBAC). This is slightly different for computational resources on the grid, which effectively use access control lists by mapping a user's digital identity onto underlying resources. An example of how RBAC is implemented in a portal is given in Chapter 10.

Physical access

Once access has been granted, data can be downloaded or moved, possibly to another grid resource for analysis. Research data sets can be large, so high-performance data transfer protocols or physical media are preferred. Large means the order of several gigabytes in size. Transferring a 1 GB file can take around 15 minutes over a 10 Mb/s broadband link. For comparison, a typical data CD holds up to 680 MB and a DVD holds 8.5 GB. For small data sets and documents, http or https web-style access may be sufficient. This might still be possible for larger data sets that can be compressed, such as textual or spreadsheet data. Compression followed by uu-encoding is a useful technique to allow data sets to be sent via e-mail or via web services.

High-performance transfer, particularly of binary data, requires protocols such as SCP, FTP and GridFTP. Distributed or logically distributed file systems such as SRB will employ the same underlying protocols to achieve good performance, for instance, SRB can use GridFTP. Distributed file systems add an abstraction layer whereby the user can see data sets simultaneously from several sources, and perhaps drag and drop between them (see Abbas, 2004). It is not easy to transfer data between systems using different protocols, but the Apache Virtual File System (VFS) attempts to do this and has now been built into the NGS Portal.

Physical data transfer can be on CD or DVD, tape or even firewire disc containing up to 1 TB per disc pack. This represents the highest bandwidth for transmission but rather poor latency, e.g. the time taken to load and drive a vehicle from source to destination.

4

Managing and using digital information

Linking people to resources, researchers to scholarly materials, has been the role of the librarian for centuries. Libraries have traditionally been central to the research endeavour, managing and preserving scholarly resources, increasingly in digital form, and making these resources accessible to the researcher, often in collaboration and partnership with other libraries. Access to information from libraries tells a researcher what is already known about his subject and will suggest new lines of investigation. Librarians have know-how not only in managing, making accessible, and preserving scholarly resources but also in forming federations and collaborations to share published scholarly work. A VRE needs to incorporate such information services and provide access to them as part of the research lifecycle.

Information sources used by researchers

The online resources already accessible in some way via the JISC programmes are noted in their Collections Catalogue (*http://www.jisc-collections.ac.uk*). These are classified primarily by subject and then separated into those which are free of charge and those which are subscription-based. Many of them are referenced below where we list some existing information services which are of interest to researchers. These are only examples rather than a complete list.

Common standards are needed to search the service catalogues and access information content. The Open Access Initiative (OAI) community (Jones, 2007) has made good progress in developing tools for the OAI harvesting standard. Links are needed between commercial and institutional repositories in order to get them to work together and make information access seamless.

Virtual Research Environments

As an example, the user requirements report from the EVIE VRE project (Sergeant et al., 2006) listed some of the key resources that the respondents used across a broad range of disciplines: Web of Science (39); Google (29); Medline (14); PubMed (6); Cinahl (4); Embase (4); Cochrane Library (3); Google Scholar (3); SOSIG (3); AMED (2); arXiv (2); Biosis (2); JStor (2); Psychinfo (2); Psychlit (2); Science Direct (2).

National services in the UK

In the UK, JISC maintains the Information Environment (*http://www.jisc.ac.uk/whatwedo/themes/information_environment.aspx*) as a focus for providers and consumers of digital information. This initially targeted images, geo-spatial data, moving pictures and sound, e-learning, journals, e-prints and scholarly communication.

There are two major aspects to the tools and mechanisms that an information environment enables researchers to use. The first relates to users of the services. Being able to cross-search and use customised services with added value can considerably simplify users' interactions with online resources. This should encourage take-up and lead to improved access to resources. This means that information would disseminate throughout the research community more quickly. Institutions would also be able to incorporate a range of these services within their own online environments for learning and research, presenting local content alongside national and international resources. Portals are an important aspect of this as many institutions have their own portals, e.g. for administration or teaching. Facilities can be provided for institutions and individuals to create and share content and in many cases to adapt it to local use.

The second aspect relates to making the information environment actually work. This requires the implementation of a range of services using widely agreed technical standards and protocols. This is not easy, as it involves influencing national resource providers and service providers, commercial suppliers and vendors as well as content creators, and requires considerable ongoing investment. In the UK, JISC is responsible for this important activity. A few of the available services are listed below:

- *The UK Arts and Humanities Data Service (AHDS)*: AHDS is a national service aiding the discovery, creation and preservation of digital resources in and for research, teaching and learning in the arts and humanities. It currently covers five subject areas: archaeology; history; visual arts; literature; languages and linguistics; and performing arts. It is organised via an executive at King's College London and five AHDS centres in these domains, hosted by various higher education institutions (see *http://ahds.ac.uk*).

- *Archives Hub*: The Archives Hub is a national gateway to currently 19,723 descriptions of archives in 145 UK universities and colleges. These are primarily at collection level, although complete catalogue descriptions are provided where they are available. The Archives Hub forms one part of the UK's National Archives Network, alongside a number of related networking projects. The hub also has a blog and provides training and advice on issues relating to the electronic cataloguing of archives (see *http://www.archiveshub.ac.uk*).

- *Combined University Catalogue (COPAC)*: COPAC is a union catalogue. It provides free access to the merged online catalogues of 24 major university research libraries in the UK and Ireland plus the British Library, the National Library of Scotland and the National Library of Wales/Llyfrgell Gened-laethol Cymru (see *http://copac.ac.uk*). COPAC is a MIMAS service funded by JISC with records supplied by the Consortium of University Research Libraries (CURL).

- *EDINA*: Based in Edinburgh, EDINA provides a range of online services to support geo-spatial research, some listed below (see *http://edina.ac.uk*).

- *Information Environment Service Registry (IESR)*: IESR is a machine-readable registry of electronic resources. It is designed to make it easier for other applications to discover and use materials that will help with their learning, teaching and research. The IESR currently holds this information for a selected set of electronic resources within the JISC information environment, provided by AHDS, EDINA, MIMAS, the Resource Discovery Network, the UK Data Archive and the UK Mirror Service (now JISC National Mirror Service). The project partners are MIMAS, UKOLN and the University of Liverpool (see *http://ies. ac.uk/about*).

- *JISCmail*: This mail list management service has archiving facilities. Archived e-mails can be quoted as references in publications. JISCmail can also host discussions and surveys and is looking into providing a wiki service (see *http://www.jiscmail.ac.uk*).

- *JORUM*: JORUM is a free online repository service for teaching and support staff in UK further and higher education institutions, helping to build a community for the sharing, reuse and repurposing of learning and teaching materials (see *http://www.jorum.ac.uk*).

Virtual Research Environments

- *LandMap*: LandMap is a MIMAS service for satellite image data (see *http://landmap.mimas.ac.uk*).
- *MIMAS*: Based in Manchester, MIMAS provides a range of online services, some listed below (see *http://www.mimas.ac.uk*).
- *Resource Discovery Network (RDN)*: The RDN is a free service dedicated to providing effective access to high-quality internet resources for learning, teaching and research. The collection includes: Artefact (arts and humanities); EEVL (engineering, mathematics and computing); Geosource (geography and environment); Biome (health, medicine and life sciences); ALTIS (hospitality, leisure, sports and tourism); HUMBUL (humanities); PSIGate (physical sciences); and SOSIG (social science, business and law). The RDN selects, catalogues and delivers high-quality web resources for further and higher education. The Subject Portals Project (SPP) provides common interfaces to RDN resources. RDN is now known as Intute (see *http://www.intute.ac.uk*).
- *JISC Regional Support Centres (RSCs)*: Based around the UK, the RSCs advise learning providers on deploying ICT to achieve their organisational mission.
- *The UK Data Archive (UKDA)*: The UKDA is a national resource centre that acquires, disseminates, preserves and promotes the largest collection of digital data in the social sciences and humanities in the UK, including census data (see *http://www.data-archive.ac.uk*).
- *Z39.50 Table Of Contents (ZETOC)*: ZETOC provides access to the British Library's electronic table of contents of around 20,000 current journals and around 16,000 conference proceedings published each year. The database covers from 1993 to date, and is updated on a daily basis. It includes an e-mail alerting service, to enable one to keep up-to-date with relevant new articles and papers. ZETOC is free to use for members of JISC-sponsored UK higher and further education institutions. It is also available to English National Health Service (NHS) regions, NHS Scotland and Northern Ireland. A small number of other institutions are eligible to subscribe. Research Council institutions are currently not eligible so have to use the British Library Citation Service instead. It is run from MIMAS on behalf of the British Library and JISC. ZETOC also provides an RSS news-feed service (see *http://zetoc.mimas.ac.uk/zetoc*).

Institutional services

There are many institutional services; the list below just shows some examples:

Managing and using digital information

- *AIM25*: This project aims to provide electronic access to collection-level descriptions of the archives of over 50 higher education institutions and learned societies within the greater London area (inside the M25 motorway, hence the name). It is coordinated at King's College London (see *http://www.aim25.ac.uk*).
- *Centres for Excellence in Teaching and Learning (CETLs)*: HEFCE has been funding 74 CETLs since 2005. This has been its largest initiative, with CETLs covering most subject domains and many institutions.
- *The Consortium of University Research Libraries (CURL)*: CURL provides a variety of institutional services and acts as a discussion forum (see *http://www.curl.ac.uk*). Its mission is to increase the ability of research libraries to share resources for the benefit of the local, national and international research community.
- *ePubs*: ePubs is STFC's system for research publications relating to staff and facility users (Jones, 2007; see *http://epubs.stfc.ac.uk*).
- *Royal Society Library*: The Royal Society is the UK's national academy of science. It provides comprehensive library services including a digital archive dating back to 1665 (see *http://royalsociety.org/page.asp?id=1646*).
- *Regional libraries*: These include, for example, Manchester City Library online services (see *http://www.manchester.gov.uk/libraries/online*).
- *Society of College, National and University Libraries (SCONUL)*: All universities in the UK and Ireland are SCONUL members; so too are many of the UK's colleges of higher education. Other members are the major national libraries both sides of the Irish Sea. Most of its activities are carried out by the heads of library services, often through SCONUL's range of expert groups or their executive board (see *http://www.sconul.ac.uk*).

Subject-specific services

There are also many subject-specific services – here is a small selection:

- British Atmospheric Data Centre *(BADC)*: The BADC is one of the seven NERC Data Services (see *http://badc.nerc.ac.uk*)
- *The British Medical Association.*
- *BUBL*: A large collection of links arranged by subject. Produced for the Higher Education community with free access (see *http://www.bubl.ac.uk*).

Virtual Research Environments

- *Daresbury Chemical Database Service (CDS)*: The Daresbury CDS is an online broker for a variety of chemical database services. UK academics can register free of charge for this service (see *http://cds.dl.ac.uk*).
- *ChemWeb*: Access to a library of chemical journals, a conference diary and news service. Register free by visiting the site (see *http://www.chemweb.com*).
- *ChipCenter QuestLink*: Information on electronic components and information on semiconductor intellectual property. Register free by visiting the site (see *http://cmpmedia.globalspec.com*).
- *EEVL*: Links to engineering, mathematics and computing web resources. Free access via *http://www.eevl.ac.uk*. See also the other RDN services provided by JISC, ESRC and AHRC.
- *Institute of Physics*.
- *National Pipe Organ Register and Database of British Organ Builders*: Maintained at the University of Cambridge and Birmingham City Library (see *http://npor.emma.cam.ac.uk*).
- *OMNI*: Links to biomedical and healthcare information. OMNI offers free access to a searchable catalogue of internet sites covering health and medicine. Free access via *http://omni.ac.uk*.
- *Physics Web*: Links to physics news, press releases, events and jobs. Free access, but some resources are restricted to Institute of Physics members (see *http://www.physicsweb.org*).
- *Projects*: Most projects have their own websites of varying quality.
- *Regard*: Searchable database of UK research funded by the Economic and Social Research Council. Has in-depth information on projects, publications and other research tools (see *http://www.esrc.ac.uk/ESRCInfoCentre/index.aspx*).

Open access and web-based services

In June 2005, the UK Research Councils released their position statements supporting open access and the use of institutional and subject-based repositories (Jones, 2007). The statements mean that the UK's seven publicly funded Research Councils join with the National Institutes for Health in the USA and the international Wellcome Trust in supporting open access and the results of funded research being made available to the widest audience.

The principle that public funding of research should result in public availability of research findings is of undoubted benefit to researchers, the research process and the public good. The guidance that the Research Councils have given in supporting open access to funded research will increase the availability, dissemination and use of UK research with benefits to both individual researchers and institutions. Different Research Councils have slightly different requirements for their researchers to fulfil: some recommend open access deposition, while others require it as a condition of grant (Jones, 2007). All of them support the RCUK position statement (RCUK, 2007). The Wellcome Trust, which is an independent charity providing funding for research to improve human and animal health, recommends 'unrestricted access to the published output of research as a fundamental part of its charitable mission' (Wellcome Trust, 2007). STFC and Wellcome Trust are the two major shareholders in the Diamond Synchrotron, which will be considered in Chapter 12.

JISC endorses the RCUK statement and is providing funding for open access repository projects. There have been similar statements from organisations in other countries, e.g. SURF in the Netherlands and DEST in Australia (now DEEWR). For further information on open access, see Okerson and O'Donnell (1995), Jones (2007) and Willinsky (2005). A report commissioned by JISC gives further background on feasibility and requirements (James et al., 2003).

For a description of tools developed by members of the Open Archives Initiative community, see *http://www.openarchives.org/tools/tools.html*. Tools are available for personal or public document management and are written in a variety of languages, such as Perl, PHP and Java. Registered service providers are listed online (*http://www.openarchives.org/service/listproviders.html*). Some of these services are described below. Services on this list have been cited by people we have interviewed or have been mentioned in previous surveys as being used by researchers:

- *Archimede*: Hosted at Laval University Library, Archimede is open source software for institutional repositories. It features full-text searching, multiplatform support, web user interface, and more. Archimede fully supports OAI-PMH requests version 2.0 (OAI, 2004).

- *The Allied and Complementary Medical Database (AMED)*: AMED is a unique bibliographic database produced by the Health Care Information Service of the British Library. It covers a selection of journals in three separate subject areas: several professions allied to medicine, complementary medicine and palliative care (see *http://www.bl.uk/collections/health/amed.html*).

- *Arc*: Hosted at Old Dominion University, Arc is released under the NCSA Open Source License. Arc is a federated search service based on OAI-PMH. It includes a harvester and search engine together with a simple search interface and an OAI-PMH layer over harvested metadata. Arc can be configured for a specific community and enhancements and customisations by the community are encouraged.

- *Association of Research Libraries (ARL)*: Based in Washington, DC, ARL has an Office of Scholarly Communication (see *http://www.arl.org/osc/index.html*).

- *arXiv*: arXiv is a free e-print service for physics, mathematics, nonlinear science, computer science and quantitative biology (see *http://arxiv.org*).

- *BIOSIS*: Information solutions for the global life sciences community are provided by Thomson Scientific. Their databases are arguably the most complete resource for finding life sciences information quickly and efficiently. They select documents from thousands of sources worldwide, index and abstract them into citations that describe their content, and maintain databases for searching citations, adding more than 600,000 new entries each year (see *http://www.biosis.org*).

- *British Library*: For instance, the Research Information Centre (Barga et al., 2007) (see *http://www.bl.uk*).

- *Callima*: From InfoBall is a search engine for scientific articles from various subject areas and sources. It provides a single point of access to a significant number of open access archives (see *http://www.callima.com*).

- *CERN*: CERN is where the web came from. The organisation also has a preprint server and supports various tools such as CDSWare (see *http://weblib.cern.ch/share/hepdoc/*).

- *Citebase Search*: Based at Southampton University, Citebase Search provides users with the facility for searching across multiple archives with results ranked according to many criteria, such as creation date and citation impact (see *http://www.citebase.org/search*).

- *Cochrane*: The Cochrane database hosts a collection of clinical trials results and an associated library (see *http://www.cochrane.org*).

- *Connotea*: The free Connotea online reference management service from Nature Publishing Group aims to integrate repositories with Web 2.0. It enables users to publicly bookmark and tag articles from within GNU ePrints repositories with the potential to expand the visibility and findability of those articles (see *http://www.connotea.org/*).

- *Community of Science (COS)*: This service provides a full range of internet-based services for the world's researchers, enabling universities, corporations, societies, private institutions, government agencies and individual researchers to find funding, promote their work, identify experts, manage resources and collaborate with colleagues. It is run from the University of Maryland, Bethesda, and is free to register (see *http://www.cos.com*).
- *CYCLADES*: From the European Research Consortium for Informatics and Mathematics, this system is designed to provide an open collaborative virtual archive environment that supports users and communities with functionality for: (i) advanced search in large, heterogeneous, multidisciplinary OAI compliant digital archives; (ii) collaborative work; and (iii) filtering and recommendation of records, users, communities and collections. CYCLADES allows users to register any OAI archive, which will then be automatically harvested and indexed (see *http://www.ercim.org/cyclades*).
- *DSpace*: DSpace is an open source digital asset management software platform from HP Labs and MIT Libraries that enables institutions to capture and describe digital content. It runs on a variety of hardware platforms and supports OAI-PMH 2.0 (see *http://www.dspace.org*).
- *ePrints*: The GNU ePrints software is being used to support a worldwide community promoting open access to academic publications (see *http://www.eprints.org*). Related services based on ePrints include CiteBase, ROAR, ROARMAP, ROMEO, OAA Bibliography, Open Citation Project. For an example of an ePrints news service, see *http://www.eprints.org/news/features/connotea.php*. See also the SHERPA project (*http://www.sherpa.ac.uk*).
- *ESP@cenet*: This is the European Patent Office gateway for online access to full-text patents worldwide, from 1920 to within the last few weeks. Access is available from desktop PCs with no password required (see *http://www.epo.org/patents/patent-information/free.html*
- *Fedora*: Fedora is an open source digital repository architecture from Cornell University that allows packaging of content and distributed services associated with that content. It supports OAI-PMH requests on content in the repository (see *http://fedoraproject.org*).
- *Google Search*: This facility offers caching, archiving and conversion of source to HTML (see *http://www.google.com*).

- *Google Search Engine Appliance*: This is a search engine for institutional intranets (see *http://www.google.com/enterprise/search/gsa.html*). Can be purchased or, in special instances, hosted. Yahoo! offers similar services.
- *Google Scholar*: A service that enables researchers to find scholarly literature, including peer-reviewed papers, theses, books, preprints, abstracts and technical reports from all broad areas of research (see *http://scholar.google.com*).
- *Google Maps*: A map service which can be 'mashed' with other information (see *http://maps.google.com*).
- *Google Earth*: a geographical information system combining satellite images, maps and Google search (see *http://earth.google.com*). It requires client software to be downloaded.
- *Google Books*: This facility can search the titles and contents of books. It provides a preview service if content is online and also citations. It encourages reviews and purchases (see *http://www.google.com/books*).
- *INSPEC*: INSPEC provides references to literature in physics, computing and engineering research. Access is restricted to further and higher education institutions (see *http://edina.ac.uk/inspec*).
- *JSTOR*: JSTOR has converted the back issues of paper journals into an electronic repository in order to allow savings in space while simultaneously improving access to the journal content. This was originally a Mellon Foundation project and is now a not-for-profit organisation (see *http://www.jstor.org*). Institutions must subscribe to use it.
- *National Museums of Science and Industry*: See *http://www.nmsi.ac.uk/index.asp*.
- *Open Archives Initiative Information in Engineering, Computer Science and Physics*: See *http://g118.grainger.uiuc.edu/engroai/*.
- *OAIster*: A worldwide search service based on OAI metadata harvesting which is hosted at the University of Michigan Digital Library Production Service (see *http://www.oaister.org*). OAIster can currently search 20,310,591 records from 1,096 contributors worldwide (as of 3 April 2009), including STFC's ePubs and Southampton's ePrints repositories. OAIster allows the searching of many digital resources, including text, image, audio, video and data sets. There is a Firefox toolbar plugin for OAIster. OAIster also handles repositories from multiple languages.

Managing and using digital information

- *OpendOAR*: The OpendOAR project provides a gateway to a very large number of open access repositories worldwide (see *http://www.opendoar.org*). OpendOAR is part of the SHERPA project.
- *Perseus*: From Perseus comes a system which harvests registered OAI repositories and incorporates the information into its search interface (see *http://www.perseus.tufts.edu/cgi-bin/vor*).
- *Public Knowledge Project (PKP)*: The PKP offers an open archives harvester (see *http://www.pkp.ubc.ca/harvester*).
- *Researchers' Guide to Screen Heritage*: This is a comprehensive directory of the publicly accessible sources of material related to the history of moving images and sound in the UK from the British Universities Film and Video Council (see *http://www.bufvc.ac.uk/databases/rgo.html*).
- *SAIL eprints*: Coming from CNR – Area della Ricerca di Bologna, Italy, SAIL eprints (Search, Alert, Impact and Link) is an electronic open access service provider for finding scientific or technical documents, published or unpublished, in chemistry, physics, engineering, materials sciences, nanotechnologies, micro-electronics, computer sciences, astronomy, astrophysics, earth sciences, meteorology, oceanography, agriculture and related application activities. SAIL eprints has been designed primarily to collect information on scientific documents (metadata) authored by CNR researchers and deposited as preprints or postprints in CNR institutional open access archives. In addition, SAIL eprints collects metadata from other data repositories all over the world publishing materials in the same scientific domains (see *http://eprints.bo.cnr.it*).
- *Scientific News*: Science news bulletins from a variety of UK and US sources with free access (see *http://www.scicentral.com/*).
- *Scirus*: This offering distinguishes itself from other search engines by concentrating on scientific content only and by searching both web and often proprietary databases. Scirus' aim is to provide scientists with a single comprehensive search platform covering both the web and normally 'invisible' databases. Scirus now harvests open archives data. At the time of writing its interface can access some 450 million items (see *http://www.scirus.com*).
- *Scopus*: The Scopus abstract and citation database for scientific, medical, technical and social science literature covers some 15,000 titles from 4,000 publishers. It is provided by Elsevier and integrated with Scirus (see *http://www.scopus.com*).

Virtual Research Environments

- *TORII*: From the International School for Advanced Studies, Trieste, Italy, TORRII provides unified access to various open archives in physics and computer science with filtering, advanced searching and personalisation. For more information, see the TIPS consortium web pages (see *http://tips.sissa.it*).
- *Web of Knowledge*: The Institute for Scientific Information's Web of Knowledge Service for UK education provides a single route to all the Thomson Scientific products subscribed to by one's institution. One can connect to the ISI Web of Knowledge Service and select individual products for searching from the list on the homepage (see *http://isiwebofknowledge.com*).
- *Xreferplus*: This service offers online access to many reference books including dictionaries, thesauri, encyclopaedias, books of quotations and atlases. Desktop access for internal use is available with no password required. For offsite access, Xreferplus uses Shibboleth authentication and there is a JISC deal for academics (see *http://www.xreferplus.com/search.jsp*).

Commercial services

There are a number of important commercial sources of information, particularly from academic publishers of books and journals, some already mentioned above. Digital services rather than sales of books and journals are leading to a huge change in the way access to content is managed. We have to be aware that new business models are still emerging and are likely to be in a state of flux for some time, see for instance discussion in Jones (2007). Existing commercial sources include the following:

- *British Standards*: An online catalogue is available, containing the full text of British and ISO Standards. Shibboleth is used for desktop access. The standards are expensive, but there is a JISC academic deal (see *http://www.bsonline.bsi-global.com/server/index.jsp*).
- *Cinahl*: Online healthcare information (see *http://www.cinahl.com*).
- *Elsevier*: Elsevier offers a portal-style interface to its publication lists. One can browse by subject or product type as well as search individual listings (see *http://www.elsevier.com*).
- *Embase*: This service, delivered via Elsevier, offers more than 17 million validated biomedical and pharmacological records from Embase and Medline (see *http://www.embase.com*).

Managing and using digital information

- *info4education*: This service has engineering and electronics product data, occupational health and safety and construction information. Shibboleth is used for desktop access (see *http://www.info4education.com*).
- *Knovel*: Knovel provides online access to ten engineering and science reference works with desktop access. No password is required for a free trial, but the main service is commercial (see *http://www.info.knovel.com/essentials/*)
- *LexisNexis*: LexisNexis provides authoritative legal, news, public records and business information, including tax and regulatory publications in online, print or CD formats (see *http://www.lexisnexis.com*).
- *Optical Society of America (OSA)*: The OSA posts information about conferences, publications and industry news. Many resources are free to access, but some areas are restricted to members (see *http://www.osa.org*).
- *PubMed*: PubMedCentral (PMC) is the US National Institutes of Health (NIH) free digital archive of biomedical and life sciences journal literature. A service of the National Library of Medicine that includes over 15 million citations from Medline and other life science journals for biomedical articles dating back to the 1950s, PubMed also includes links to full-text articles and other related resources (see *http://www.pubmedcentral.nih.gov*).
- *Safari IT ebooks*: Technical IT books are available online from O'Reilly, Addison Wesley and others. Institutions can subscribe to a 'bookshelf' (STFC currently accesses 150 books), with others available on additional payment. Desktop access is available with an institutional IP address. Users are strongly advised to familiarise themselves with the terms and conditions of use (see *http://proquest.safaribooksonline.com*).
- *Science Direct*: Science Direct is provided by Elsevier as an information source for scientific, technical and medical research. Subscription required for some sections but institutional access is provided in the UK via the Athens service (see *http://www.sciencedirect.com*).
- *SFX*: This is a library OpenURL resolver cross-search service. It is also available by institutional subscription and an appropriate institutional URL is provided (see *http://sfx4.exlibrisgroup.com*).
- *Talis*: Talis Information Limited (*http://www.talis.com*) is a provider of library management solutions for the UK and Ireland. It functions via a partnership programme, Talis Connexions. This connects

organisations providing library management solutions to academic, research, corporate and government institutions. Members are encouraged to share knowledge and technical assets, support open standards and develop complementary product strategies.

Special deals exist for making some of the above commercial services available to academic researchers. Some of these are brokered by JISC and some by Eduserv agreements covering both software and data (*http://www.eduserv.org.uk/chest*). There are a few differences in access rights for the different types of organisation that can make use of such services within a VRE complex.

E-mail archives and grey literature

JISCmail, the abovementioned national mail server and archive for researchers in the UK, will be described in more detail in Chapter 5. E-mail is an important, but largely unexplored source of information. There are many issues of confidentiality and ethics which prohibit open access to e-mail archives, even for research into social behaviour. Currently, such archives are moderated and available only to subscribers via simple textual search interfaces.

Grey literature is a term used to refer to unpublished documents, typically internal reports on investigations which are not widely circulated. In the context of e-research, we might extend this to cover items such as laboratory notebooks (often now kept online), personal information systems, and private blogs and wikis maintained by research groups. There is however an issue with the long-term maintenance of such information sources.

Institutional, facility or subject repository

The meaning of the term 'digital repository' is widely debated. Contemporary understanding has broadened from an initial focus on software systems to a wider and overall commitment to the stewardship of digital materials; this requires not just software and hardware, but also policies, processes, services and people, as well as content and metadata. Repositories must be sustainable, trusted, well supported and well managed in order to function properly (Abbott, 2006; see also Lord and MacDonald, 2003; Jones, 2007).

The Digital Curation Centre (DCC) is currently working with EU partners in proposing an ISO standard for digital archives, e.g. relating to the level of service provided, to include a guarantee of the longevity of the data. All data and information holdings that are expected to be persistent should be certified to a standard of this type.

We probably need a typology of digital repository services, possibly defined by the standards and interfaces they use for searching their content. Such a typology was developed by Heery and Anderson (2005). The following notes are based on their work, but expanded to include data repositories.

Digital repositories can be classified by content type:

- raw research data;
- derived research data;
- full-text preprint scholarly papers;
- full-text peer-reviewed final drafts of journal and conference proceedings papers;
- theses;
- full-text original publications (institutional or departmental technical reports);
- learning objects;
- corporate records (staff and student records, licences, etc.).

It appears there is some content largely missing from most deployed repositories. Within repository deployment, for example, there is little evidence of awareness of connections with archival management of courses as opposed to learning objects, what McLean and Lynch (2003) refer to as 'composite structures (such as entire courses – in various senses, including both course "frameworks" and actual populated "instances" of courses within such frameworks – exported from learning management systems)'. We think this would come under the heading of learning object repositories, which is outside the scope of the current study. There is however a similar debate beginning about 'research objects', such as at the heart of the myExperiment VRE project, which attempts to merge social networking with scientific workflow (*http://www.myexperiment.org*). In addition, the OAI Object Reuse and Exchange project (*http://www.open archives.org/ore*) is investigating issues around using compound digital objects, including versioning and linking.

A significant number of entries in institutional repositories are metadata-only, with no link to the full text. This appears to be due to caution regarding copyright and IPR. Repository administrators and authors are reluctant to come into conflict with publishers regarding copyright issues so will not include 'full text' when there is doubt about copyright or no assurance that the text is free from non-attributed third-party content. In addition, some repositories will only include links to full text for those entries published and/or authored while the author was employed by the institution. So, for example, only a percentage of entries within the Southampton ECS ePrints repository link to full text, while the STFC repository has a significant percentage of metadata-only records.

Entries can also be classified by coverage:

- personal (author's personal archive);
- journal (output of a single journal or group of journals);
- departmental;
- institutional;
- inter-institutional (regional);
- national;
- international.

By primary functionality of repository:

- enhanced access to resources (resource discovery and location);
- subject access to resources (resource discovery and location);
- preservation of digital resources;
- new modes of dissemination (new modes of publication);
- institutional asset management;
- sharing and reuse of resources.

By target user group:

- learners;
- teachers;
- researchers.

A variety of content is hosted, including:

- images, multimedia recordings;
- museum, library and archive artefacts;
- natural sounds, voice and music.

We have also found a practical classification which influences how researchers use these repositories, particularly for publication. At a workshop on digital repositories and portals, there was a discussion about the difference between subject-specific and institutional repositories and where researchers would deposit their final peer-reviewed publications (Allan et al., 2006b). It was considered that they would be unlikely to want to use a repository that belonged to a facility like Diamond because peer pressure plays a big factor and researchers consider themselves foremost a member of a research community or have a strong affiliation to their university or other host institution. However, the facility managers will want a record of science outcomes, or at least to be able to easily access all publications and reports produced by their user community, as would any other service. In the current financial climate this is an essential metric for sustainability and such information is included in annual reports.

We therefore determined that an important classification could be by:

- institution;
- research facility;
- research publisher (journal).

Web 2.0 and information discovery – broad vs. deep

The trend towards the proliferation of 'user-generated' content and commentary in Web 2.0 is not merely a fad or flavour of the week, but a huge trend that has produced completely new categories of products and services on the web (O'Reilly, 2005). Widely-used online tools supporting education and research include Google and Wikipedia. Most of what these tools return is user-generated content. The abovementioned myExperiment project is an example of this type, but for a particular kind of research community. Analytic Bridge is another one (*http://www.analyticbridge.com*).

Using 'hosted' Web 2.0 services today, nearly anyone can remix information with software in order to make it more valuable, e.g. blending, or mashing job vacancies and homes for sale, such as CraigsList in New York (*http://www.craigslist.org*) does with Google Maps (*http://www.housingmaps.com*). This is certainly useful, but does not actually constitute new information, just a different way of expressing it.

E-research requires deep search in addition to broad search. This requires sophisticated tools and some support from information professionals. The danger of broad search is that information is 'popularised'. Deep or 'obscure' information becomes less easily accessible, because relatively fewer people look for it. This tends to over-emphasise easy or popular research areas at the expense of more difficult ones.

The key differences between a Google-style search and an information environment deep cross-search has been explained by Powell (2004). He has also described a number of initiatives to provide more open search access to items in repositories which are not published as HTML documents.

While Google is very heavily used for both learning and research, many other information services could be provided with equivalent interfaces. Google is primarily a search engine, but its success is gained from the range of sources it can index and the personalised and specialised facilities it now provides.

Wikipedia (*http://www.wikipedia.org*) is a somewhat different general resource that has rapidly grown in importance. As its name implies, this is an online encyclopaedia developed using wiki technology. It is an example of 'folksonomy' in action, where anyone in the world can add text on any subject. Its scope and accuracy are assured simply because there are a very large number of contributors and editors, so that errors and inappropriate entries are quickly removed. Its interesting entries include, for example, 'Digital Repository', 'Web 2.0' and 'Portal'.

Arguments for self-generated content and folksonomies have been produced by Surowiecki (2005), Anderson (2007), Tapscott and Williams (2007), Shirky (2008) and Leadbeater (2008). Arguments against are articulated by Carr (2007) and Keen (2007) among others.

Web 2.0 participative environments are probably more about sharing the knowledge that we (the human race) already collectively know rather than creating new knowledge. According to the infinite monkey theorem (commonly attributed to Emile Borel, 1913), by hitting random keys on a typewriter for an infinite amount of time, a monkey will almost surely type a given text, such as one of the works of William Shakespeare. Crucially, however, we do not have an infinite amount of time to do business or research, as most projects are bounded by funding and delivery deadlines. Simply recruiting more monkeys does not solve this problem.

Do you expect that the predictions and decisions regarding aspects of policy would be better made by many collections of independent individuals using research data than by professionals and experts?

According to Tapscott and Williams (2007), 'the winning organizations (and societies) will be those that tap the torrent of human knowledge and translate it into new and useful applications'. While this is true, it needs to be done in an appropriate way involving innovators and experts.

Andrew Keen (2007) notes that Web 2.0 is delivering 'superficial observations of the world around us rather than deep analysis, shrill opinion rather than considered judgment'.

In his acceptance speech following his award of the Bruno Kreisky Prize for advancement of human rights, Jürgen Habermas said:

> Use of the internet has both broadened and fragmented the contexts of communication. This is why the internet can have a subversive effect on intellectual life in authoritarian regimes. But at the same time, the less formal, horizontal cross-linking of communication channels weakens the achievements of traditional media. This focuses the attention of an anonymous and dispersed public on select topics and information, allowing citizens to concentrate on the same critically filtered issues and journalistic pieces at any given time. The price we pay for the growth in egalitarianism offered by the internet is the decentralised access to unedited stories. In this medium, contributions by intellectuals lose their power to create a focus. (Habermas, 2006)

E-research and the wider information environment

By e-research we mean both e-science and research within the arts and humanities that is undertaken within a digital environment. Researchers require input from both e-learning and the information environment, mainly in terms of discovering and structuring background information to form and guide their research. Support for research is also important in bidding for, reviewing and managing projects. There is an important publication and dissemination phase by which researchers are sometimes judged, where published output or citations are quantifiable metrics.

Increasingly there is recognition that in using digital information, the e-learning and e-research communities have the potential to work together with common ICT solutions and even some common content. The Roadmap for a UK Virtual Research Environment Programme

(Allan et al., 2004a) identified resource discovery as an obvious common service. Activity within the resource discovery arena is however disparate. There is benefit in investigating the potential of how portals to the information environment could be enhanced to support the needs of e-research and how the resource discovery approaches currently in use within the e-research community might benefit the information environment more generally.

Andy Powell, formerly at UKOLN, has provided a number of reviews of and opinions on activities of the JISC Information Environment (Ingram, 2005; Powell, 2005; Powell and Lyon, 2001). We use this work as an example of what could be achieved in a wider information environment underpinning e-research.

The current information environment is focused on the provision of resource discovery and related services for digital libraries and other catalogues, e.g. museums and image collections as well as digitised reports, theses and books. There is some support for survey-based scientific data (e.g. for social science), geo-spatial data and data from the arts and humanities (e.g. music, digitised paintings, manuscripts). This is provided via services such as MIMAS, EDINA, UKDA and AHDS. There is a growing awareness of the importance of biomedical and legal sources, some of which are listed above, but there is currently little overlap with the natural sciences such as supported by the UK Research Councils and subject-specific services (mostly journals and learned societies) other than those of ESRC and AHRC. This of course needs to be addressed.

There is a growing recognition that archival of both publications and 'grey literature' and links to curated scientific data is important. Providing access to data used in publications is already done by some learned journals, such as those in the domain of protein crystallography, and is being investigated by open access projects such as CLADDIER (*http://claddier.badc.ac.uk/trac*), e-Bank (Lyon, 2003) and StORe (*http://www.jiscstore.com/WikiHome*). Among other areas, StORe has considered the needs of archaeology, biochemistry, chemistry and physics. Differences between the handling of data and information have been noted by Allan et al. (2006e), but Borgman et al. (2006) have begun to investigate how digital libraries might also manage scientific data. While the importance is recognised of being able to access underlying data to support how conclusions are arrived at in research, this requirement is not yet widely addressed.

A final type of information which is not yet being considered in the information environment is 'personal information'. This could be a strong focus of the ongoing VRE programme, which has already identified tools such as the wiki, blog and forum as being useful for collaborating teams of scientists. The sharing of personal information is likely to grow through the use of peer-to-peer systems. Currently these are mostly used for accessing popular music and video via systems such as Shareaza, FilePipe, Ares, LimeWire, BitTorrent, etc. These could nevertheless be adapted for scientific use (see *http://www.zeropaid.com*). There needs to be some way of including such information in discovery services but differentiating it from peer-reviewed content.

How to make information accessible

What is required to make all these services available in a single e-research portal or VRE? What are the gaps and impediments? Many of the technical issues and questions noted in this chapter are related to cross-searching and access. The abovementioned information environment from JISC is an important example.

We illustrate what can be done in a research-focused institution today. An example is an interface to online services provided by the STFC Library. This includes links to the following sources: arXiv, BS online, STFC ePubs, Daresbury Chemical Database Service, Esp@cenet, info4education, INSPEC, Knovel and K-Essentials, Library Electronic Journal Service, PubMed, Safari IT ebooks, Web of Knowledge and Xreferplus. It also provides access to a number of subject-specific gateways and other reference sources.

Another interesting approach is the information portal provided as an interface to the Australian Bond University Information Repository. This has a blog on its homepage (*http://epublications.wordpress.com/*) and links to the e-publication repository (*http://wpublications.bond.edu.au*) and also the university library services (*http://www.bond.edu.au/library/*).

Universities in Australia have developed a shared discovery service called ARROW: Australian Research Repositories Online to the World (*http://search.arrow.edu.au*). This currently includes Australian Digital Theses, Library and Information Association, Policy Online and the universities of Bond, Curtin, Flinders, Monash, Queensland Technology, Melbourne, Queensland, Southern Queensland, Tasmania and Wollongong.

Despite such advanced services which can be included in a VRE, there are many issues which still need to be tackled on a technical level:

- *Authentication, single sign-on and authorisation*: This is considered in Chapter 5.

- *Attribution*: Information providers wish to retain IPR. There are also issues of liability in hosting content which may contain third-party material. Digital watermarking has been considered, but is currently difficult to implement.
- *Cross-search services*: There have been discussions of cross-search services vs. union catalogues, e.g. Ingram (2005).
- *Location service*: OpenURL is used as a basis for full-text location of documents from any source to which a host institution is subscribed. This resolves a URL in standard format found from a cross-search based on a variety of factors, such as subscription, institution type, location of document, etc. In some implementations it can automatically create forms for ordering copies via interlibrary loan or other delivery service – see for example the OCLC WorldCat Registry (*http://www.oclc.org/worldcat*).
- *Personal information management*: It would be good if we could propose a facility for researchers to create their own digital repository from web-based content on the fly from a seed taxonomy. This extends the concept of social tagging used in folksonomies and would facilitate linking private and public information systems in Web 2.0.
- *Presentation*: Many of the deep search services listed above have their own diverse form-based web interfaces for searching by author, title, subject, etc. There are many issues to be faced in making all these available from a single interface, some of which are noted below. JSR 168 portlet technology is currently used for presentation in portals, but may not be the appropriate standard for this kind of functionality; is JSR 286 up to the job?
- *Publication tools*: While at UKOLN, Andy Powell wrote a useful paper comparing the JISC information environment and Google services and suggesting how Google could be used to find other services (Powell, 2004). Other Web 2.0 services such as Flickr and Facebook could be useful for publishing information. It is widely accepted however that the original copy of the information should be kept by the author or host institution so that multiple publication channels can be used. This also avoids potential loss of data as web-based business models inevitably change.
- *Search protocols*: We need to list and review all the deep search standards, OAI-PMH (OAI, 2004), Z39.50 (US Library of Congress, 2006), SRU/SRW, OpenSearch, etc. and develop tools so that a query in SQL (say) can be converted to each of them and then sent off to all

appropriate sources of information. Note that the output of these search protocols is typically a set of records conforming to Dublin Core or MARC metadata schema.

- *Service registries*: These support cross-searching by providing a catalogue of services together with definitions of their interfaces and access rights. For example, the JISC IESR (*http://iesr.ac.uk*) is a machine-readable registry of electronic resources. It contains information about these electronic resources, and details of how to access them. It aims to make it easier for other applications to discover and use materials which will help their users in learning, teaching and research.

5

Collaboration, trust and security

In this chapter we consider distributed resources, what we can access on the internet or refer to as a grid, and how to underpin collaboration as an essential part of any virtual research environment. Collaboration includes shared access to computers, instruments and data, joint working and other forms of communication. Human beings crave communication and use it in many forms for both work-related and social purposes. All of the above must be supported by a VRE and it is difficult to separate personal activities from work.

The nature of the universe implies that it is impossible for one individual to have total understanding of all aspects of a complex research problem. Researchers tend to specialise on some aspect of a problem or domain in order to make progress. We increase our knowledge incrementally, based on what we already know. The extent to which this approach can continue to work may be limited – by putting different aspects together, a bigger picture can emerge; this can change research priorities and make related endeavours, such as product development, more effective. However, given the competitive nature of research institutions and universities, it is very rare that all the expertise in even one domain is co-located. To be most effective, e-research systems must support collaboration among geographically distributed individuals and groups, peers and experts alike.

Collaboration is essential to any progressive organisation and increasingly sophisticated tools exist to facilitate it. As individuals depend more and more on these tools in their private lives, it is perhaps inevitable that they are seen as an integral part of a virtual research or business environment.

The value of collaboration was recognised early on in e-research. Since its origin in the mid-1990s, there have been a number of attempts to define the grid succinctly. Foster et al. (2001) refined their definition of a grid to 'coordinated resource sharing and problem solving in dynamic, multi-institutional virtual organizations'. This definition is the one now most commonly used to define a grid in an abstract way. More practical definitions and implementations relating to large-scale networked computational and data storage resources are considered in Chapter 8.

Broadly speaking, the grid is about sharing resources. Sharing is always conditional and based on factors such as trust, resource access policies, negotiation and how payment should be considered. Grid users aim to engage in coordinated problem-solving which is beyond a simple client-server paradigm. They are interested in combinations of distributed data analysis, computation and real-time collaboration. The grid concepts therefore include dynamic, multi-institutional virtual organisations (VOs), where these new communities overlay classical organisational structures and may be large or small, static or dynamic.

As an example, we cite the eMinerals project, in which from 2002 to 2008, a consortium of scientists and software developers combined their skills to study the effects of minerals, such as clays, on pollution from heavy metal poisonous waste and toxic organic materials, corrosion and weathering, radioactive waste encapsulation and disposal and other environmental processes from the molecular level (Calleja et al., 2005). At the start of this project it was realised that computation, data management and collaboration were all of equal importance in the research, which covers many length and time scales in its physics and chemistry. In particular, it was recognised that there was no single group that fully understood and could exploit all the different computational methods involved, from quantum chemistry, to molecular dynamics, to large-scale environmental modelling, each of which has taken many years to evolve.

The eMinerals team operated as a VO in terms of sharing resources and providing support for the scientists. Rather than have a collection of scientists working on separate projects, the aim was to enable the team to operate as a task-oriented VO that could pull together its personnel resources and shared infrastructure to collaborate on large-scale studies of environmental processes. The key point is that members of this VO had different experience and expertise in a broad range of simulation methods, types of pollutants and mineral surfaces. Pulling all this experience together meant that, collectively, the VO had detailed knowledge and expertise across the wide range of minerals and contaminants and equally across the wide range of methodologies employed in carrying out simulations at different levels of theory. Figure 5.1 illustrates areas of expertise within the eMinerals VO.

This chapter looks at how collaboration works, the role of technology in making it happen, and the factors to consider in making it succeed.

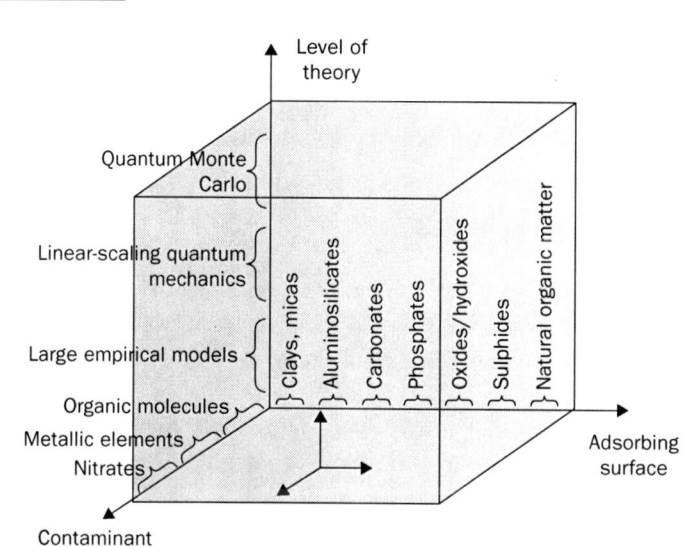

Figure 5.1 Areas of expertise within the eMinerals VO

Source: eMinerals project

Virtual organisations and their implementation

Human beings organise their activities around social groups – a great deal of literature, both fact and fiction, has been written about this. These groups can be short-term or long-lasting. A circle of friends is one type. A learned society with members accepted based on their years of experience, peer review and subscription is another. Other groups are less spontaneous, but still subject to normal social pressures and members such as 'my fellow students and teachers at college or university' or 'my peers in a research domain'. Social networking websites, referred to as part of Web 2.0, are trying to replicate these groupings in abstract online virtual worlds using ICT (O'Reilly, 2005). E-research is still catching up – at least it can now use ICT to support its own complex organisational structures.

Human groups are largely based on trust, but there is no such thing in a computer-based system, so access to resources has to be managed differently. I might trust my friend with the keys to my car, but if he crashes it I may have a lower level of trust afterwards. Whether or not we would still be friends is somewhat intangible, and potentially unlikely. Online research groups wish to share information and work together, but ICT systems used to facilitate such collaboration usually have fixed rules which can be encoded in software.

The idea of groups of people with authorised access to sets of resources is now encapsulated in the term 'virtual organisation' or 'virtual research community'.

Some definitions

The term 'virtual organisation' was coined in the paper 'Anatomy of the Grid' by Foster et al. The paper states:

> The real and specific problem that underlies the Grid concept is coordinated resource sharing and problem solving in dynamic, multi-institutional virtual organizations. The sharing that we are concerned with is not primarily file exchange but rather direct access to computers, software, data and other resources, as is required by a range of collaborative problem solving and resource brokering strategies emerging in industry, science, and engineering. This sharing is, necessarily, highly controlled, with resource providers and consumers defining clearly and carefully just what is shared, who is allowed to share and the conditions under which sharing occurs. A set of individuals and/or institutions defined by such sharing rules form what we call a virtual organization (VO). (Foster et al., 2001)

The paper goes on to give a number of examples, and to discuss the complex issues arising, particularly from the security standpoint.

The alternative but related phrase 'virtual research community' was coined and used in the UK's OSI document on e-infrastructure. The authors stated:

> A Virtual Research Community (VRC) is a group of researchers, possibly widely dispersed, working together and facilitated by a set of online tools, systems and processes interoperating to support collaborative research within or across institutional boundaries, typically described as a virtual research environment, or VRE. With collaboration across institutional, disciplinary and national boundaries becoming increasingly important to research communities, VRCs will become an essential component of the national e-infrastructure across all disciplines. (Dothen, 2004)

Or quite simply, as explained in the Australian VeRSI programme, a VO is 'a web-based online collaboration space where a group of collaborators can share files and data and access common tools without the encumbrance of institutional firewalls and compatibility problems'. This sounds very much like Web 2.0.

As a working definition in this book we use something close to the OSI definition, but include the concept that there might be non-human resources specific to the VO. This is a somewhat less dynamic picture than the one painted by Foster et al., however, it does not contradict it.

Why bother with them?

Collaboration in one form or another is driving the modern research culture, especially in the so-called 'grand challenges'.

The emerging characteristics of a VRE are increasingly overlaid with a requirement to provide support for the creation, further development, or enhancement of research communities in virtual space. The OSI report of March 2006 indicated that:

> VRCs have the potential to open exciting new opportunities to collaborate in research and thus realise significant gains at institutional, national and international levels. Support for a rich variety of such interlocking communities is likely to remain a significant national and international objective for e-research development for the foreseeable future, while noting that this will most likely be influenced by both planned and emergent developments. The increased use by researchers of social networking applications, for example, adds urgency to the requirement for VREs to adhere to open and published standards and specifications. (Borda et al., 2006)

What is involved?

There are four key concepts important to a VO which reflect human groups (Preston, year unknown):

- development of relationships with a broad range of potential partners, each having a particular competency that complements the others;
- mobility and responsiveness of ICT to overcome problems of distance;
- timing is a key aspect of relationships, with actors using responsiveness and availability to decide between alternatives;
- trust between actors separated in space for a VO to be effective.

There are a number of ways these concepts can be implemented. Foster et al. considered this from the standpoint of middleware, e.g. connecting a grid of worldwide distributed resources. Here we reduce the scope and consider how a VRE might encapsulate the VO concept, how it might be used to manage the organisation's membership, and how the members would access the available resources.

There are a number of challenges and issues in realising this goal. Collaboration can take many forms, not just the sharing of information via a web interface. Access Grid (AG), for instance, has potential where audiovisual communication is required. VRE interfaces involve not only portals, but others such as rich desktop clients, or in the case of AG, a whole room as a semi-immersive environment.

Because of their current importance in deployed infrastructures, we briefly describe the Virtual Organisation Membership Service (VOMS) and Shibboleth. Other ways to manage VOs are considered in the following sections where we describe Access Grid and Sakai.

The Virtual Organisation Membership Service

Most implementations of VOs for grid computing use VOMS, a service developed as part of the EU DataGrid project (2002). This software is implemented in Java and has additional security components.

VOMS is a system for managing authorisation data within multi-institutional collaborations. VOMS allows distributed collaborations to centrally manage members' roles and capabilities. The VOMS user credentials convey this role and capability information to service providers so that they can make more fully-informed authorisation decisions.

The VOMS database contains information about each VO member. A suite of administrative tools allows administrators to assign roles to members and manipulate capability information. Tools then allow users to generate a local proxy credential based on the contents of the VOMS database. This credential includes the basic authentication information that standard grid proxy credentials contain, but it also includes role and capability information from the VOMS server as attributes. Standard grid applications can use the credential as normal, but VOMS-aware applications can use the additional VOMS attributes to make authorisation decisions regarding user requests.

Shibboleth

Shibboleth is discussed in more detail in Chapter 7; here we consider its use in managing virtual organisations.

Shibboleth also provides attributes, in this case from the user's host institution direct to the service provider. Attribute information can be as simple as 'member of department X' or as complex as 'member of project team who has signed up to the project terms and conditions'. The decision to authorise the user as a VO member is based on this attribute information. Work is ongoing in the SARoNGS project to integrate Shibboleth more fully with a grid infrastructure based on VOMS.

Collaborative working

According to Wikipedia, a collaborative working environment (CWE) supports people in their individual and cooperative work. Research in CWE involves studying organisational, technical and social issues. It lists tools or services which may be considered elements of a CWE, including e-mail, instant messaging, application sharing, video-conferencing, collaborative workspace, document management, task and workflow management, wiki and blog. Access Grid is mentioned as being a particular type of CWE. It will be seen below that many of these tools have also been recognised as being important in VRE development and are now available in portal frameworks such as GridSphere and Sakai.

Wikipedia also describes that the term 'computer supported cooperative work' (CSCW) was first coined by Irene Greif and Paul Cashman in 1984, at a workshop attended by individuals interested in using technology to support people in their work. In 1987, Charles Findley presented the concept of collaborative learning. CSCW addresses how collaborative activities and their coordination can be supported by means of ICT. On the one hand, many authors consider that CSCW and groupware are synonyms. On the other hand, different authors claim that while groupware refers to real computer-based systems, CSCW focuses on the study of tools and techniques of groupware as well as their psychological, social and organisational effects. We consider CSCW to be a generic term, which combines an understanding of the way people work in groups with the enabling technologies of computer networking, and associated hardware, software, services and techniques.

When collaboration is not supported and rewarded, new ideas and innovations are slower to emerge, redundant efforts proliferate and practices tend to stagnate. On the other hand, deploying tools that support collaboration, such as chat rooms, threaded discussion and instant messaging, does not guarantee that the e-research activity will be more collaborative if there is no supportive knowledge and research activity culture – community building is important. It is hard to predict which tools will be used and how, as research teams differ in experience and preferences. There are obvious groups which could benefit from new technology to support collaboration, such as the CCPs in the UK. CSCW methodologies can help to untangle some of these issues.

The study of computer-supported collaboration includes the study of the software and social phenomena associated with it. In these systems, the concept of 'social networking' is recognised and implemented so that participants can dynamically form themselves into groups (VOs?), for instance 'friends' of 'user X'. Social networking is just one aspect of what is now referred to as Web 2.0 (O'Reilly, 2005).

Collaboration tools

Collaborative software is software designed to help people involved in a common task achieve their goals by enhancing online communication. Collaborative software is the basis for computer-supported cooperative work – in the context of e-research it is designed to achieve the goals of complex projects involving a distributed team and grid resources.

While not prescriptive, we have noticed, from the ways e-research tools are used, that they fall into three rather broad categories:

- *Generic*: Generic tools for shared resources, typically used for project, task, information management, collective decision making, admin, etc. May involve other internet resources.
- *Specific*: Specific research tools, data collection and analysis, simulation, etc. Almost certainly with restricted access.
- *Community*: Community-building tools, possibly based on social networking technology. Such tools are used for many purposes, not just research.

We contend that a successful VRE must have appropriate tools from all these categories.

Some of the most widely used forms of web-based collaboration involve fora, wikis and blogs. Indeed, there is another book in this series devoted entirely to wikis (Klobas, 2006). These all allow users to post up information, such as text, images or video clips, so that others can view the posts and add comments or even edit the original text, depending on their role and the permission given to them by the collaboration tool. A Google search involving a detailed technical question will nowadays almost inevitably throw up links to several such sites. These are usually populated with messages posted by geeks identified only by nicknames and avatars. What social pressure makes these people hide their true identity? Is this what separates normal life from other (work) activities? In these systems, all users tend to be grouped together and are distinguished by their role, e.g. 'user' or 'administrator'. In more advanced systems, the concept of 'group' is supported, but participants will have to be admitted to a group usually by an administrator or moderator. In a portal, such tools might all be available together as different interfaces to shared underlying data and selected according to preference. Indeed, one aspect of research into the use of portals is to determine the best combination of such tools for different purposes.

The more general term 'social software' applies to systems used typically outside the workplace, for example, online dating services and social networks like Friendster, SecondLife and Facebook. There are however a growing number of such systems destined for professionals and research focused communities. Examples include Analytic Bridge (*http://www.analyticbridge.com*) for people to share information about statistical analysis of data, OpenWetware (*http://openwetware.org/wiki/Main_Page*) for the biology and biological engineering community, and myExperiment (de Roure and Goble, 2007) for people to share research workflows, particularly from bio-informatics.

Groupware in portals

The Sakai framework (see Chapter 10) illustrates many of the groupware tools typically found in portals. These include, among others, chat, e-mail and archive, forum, threaded discussion, resource folders, wiki, blog, message of the day, RSS news, preferences, presentation tool, calendar, WebDAV and web content. In addition there are many tools customised for e-learning.

Access Grid

Access Grid was conceived as a logically shared space using audiovisual communication in a special-purpose room (*http://www.accessgrid.org*). The underpinning concept of AG is the 'virtual venue' (VV). Groups of users meet in a VV, either in response to some notification at a predefined time, or spontaneously in the hope of finding someone else to communicate with. In AG terms, the VV is the instantiation of a VO with dynamic membership. Typically, AG uses video cameras, projectors and loudspeakers, and one or more 'AG rooms' are set aside at each participating (real) site for users to occupy and use. A very common scenario with AG then is to book a virtual meeting, say to discuss progress on a project involving participants from several sites around the country or world. At the allotted time, the participants go to their rooms, activate the equipment and join the meeting in the agreed virtual venue. This is an open system inasmuch as it is implemented for e-research and there is nothing to stop 'intruders', but in practice they are rarely seen and usually only as a result of a mistaken VV.

Another underpinning concept of AG is the use of network 'multicast' technology. This reduces network bandwidth requirements, but is not universally implemented as it requires hardware in network routers (from a variety of vendors) to be correctly configured and interoperate using the multicast standard. Currently there are not many multicast applications so this is not guaranteed. Multicasting means that in a one-to-many transmission, a packet of data is sent out from the source and split if necessary at each network router into multiple packets, each then sent, possibly down further branches, to a list of destinations. In 'unicast' networking, the same packet has to be sent out multiple times to each destination. 'Broadcast' implies that the same packet is sent to everyone on a given sub-network, which is rarely useful. AG can use a 'bridge', so that the source sends to the bridge which then connects to the multicast-enabled network.

AG is built from a number of loosely-coupled software components:

- *VIC*: This video-conference tool from University of California, Berkeley and Lawrence Berkeley National Laboratory, is a real-time, multimedia application for video-conferencing over the internet. VIC is based on the draft internet standard Real-time Transport Protocol (RTP) developed by the IETF Audio/Video Transport Working Group. RTP is an application-level protocol implemented entirely within VIC; there are no special system enhancements to run RTP.

- *RAT*: The Robust Audio Tool is an open source audio conferencing and streaming application from University College London that allows users to participate in audio-conferences over the internet. RAT requires no special features for point-to-point communication, just a network connection and a sound card. For multi-party conferencing, RAT uses IP multicast. RAT is based on IETF standards, using RTP above UDP/IP as its transport protocol, and conforming to the RTP profile for audio and video-conference with minimal control.

Access Grid is available as both open source (see *http://www.accessgrid.org*) and commercial versions (see *http://www.insors.com/io/contact.html*). The VIC and RAT tools can be used separately if required, although the IP addresses of the video and audio-streams from the virtual venue must be known. Access Grid will also operate with VRVS (the Virtual Room Video conferencing System developed at CERN) over a suitable bridge.

We usually assume that for a meeting, all participants must be treated alike, i.e. they should all see and hear all others. This is not necessarily required, however. It is reasonable, subject to agreement, to hold meetings where some participants only send and receive sound, for instance over a telephone link. We have also considered the possibility of using AG in extreme conditions using wireless contact. For instance, an operator carrying out a delicate manoeuvre may require advice from one or more experts not physically present. The operator might wear a headset to communicate and use a head-mounted camera so that the expert can see what is going on. There is, however, no need for the operator to see the expert as this would be a distraction – only the spoken guidance is required. AG bridge technology would be used in this solution, which would be equally useful in industry as in research.

Access Grid was originally conceived as a collaborative way of using grid resources; however there are few grid interfaces which are actually integrated with AG. We have found that a useful procedure is to use a portal to access information during an AG session. A simple example of this is an online workshop. Here, participants will upload their presentations into a portal resource area. Participants in other rooms can then access the files and display them, or they can be displayed using the AG shared presentation facility. In any case, this becomes a useful archive for workshop attendees and notes can be added directly to the worksite wiki.

Portal Access Grid

Other interfaces for AG are available as the underlying software components are easily available. For instance, a desktop computer equipped with a webcam and headset with microphone can be used to join an AG venue. However, this tends to make the participant look like a 'space alien' and does not benefit from the sophisticated echo-mitigation used in room-based sound systems. In CSCW terms it does not work well.

Nevertheless, this is perceived as a useful way of enabling people to communicate. To make this easier to achieve, the Portal Access Grid (PAG) was developed in a UK project funded by OMII (see

Virtual Research Environments

http://www.rcs.manchester.ac.uk/research/PAG). PAG is a fully-functional portlet client for the open source Access Grid toolkit that also enables automatic and transparent switching to unicast when multicast becomes unavailable; allows the use of Access Grid behind restrictive firewalls and from low-bandwidth connections; and significantly simplifies the installation procedure for users.

The portlet client, which can be installed in any JSR 168 compliant portal framework, will connect to any AG server and allow navigation of virtual venues, communication using audio and video, access to a Jabber text chat, and access to shared applications and data within the venue. The portlet client will also introduce access to new forms of data storage in addition to those currently offered by AG by integration with grid technologies such as Storage Resource Broker and GridFTP-based services. These developments have the potential to benefit the significant portion of the academic community currently using Access Grid; will allow use of Access Grid within a familiar web-based environment from almost any location, e.g. internet cafés and hotel rooms; and will address the major perceived drawbacks to Access Grid compared with other collaboration environments. Figure 5.2 provides a screenshot of PAG in a GridSphere portal.

Figure 5.2 Screenshot of PAG in a GridSphere portal

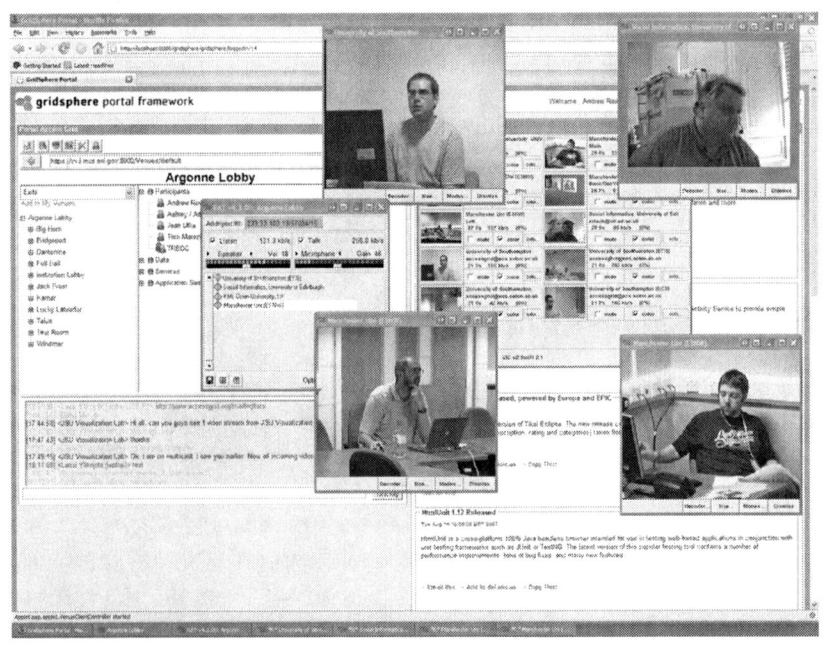

Source: PAG website

Agora

The Agora online meeting tool (*http://agora.lancs.ac.uk*) was developed at the University of Lancaster in the JISC funded Sakai VRE Demonstrator project to give research groups using a portal the options of desktop video-conferencing (many-to-many) with a wide range of additional functionality such as whiteboard, shared desktop, chat, recording and playing movies (Crouchley et al., 2007; Severance et al., 2007). Agora predates the previously discussed PAG. Agora and PAG both address the requirements of desktop-based video-conferencing mentioned in the definition of a collaborative working environment.

In Agora, a Sakai tool is used to create conferences and invite the participants, creating a dynamic VO rather than a virtual venue; this conference information is then passed on to the Agora client software. We have also considered linking Agora with Access Grid. This would involve the creation of an Access Grid bridge to allow simple lookup and connection of Agora VOs into AG venues.

Agora uses a central point for sending packets to and from clients. With this approach Agora can still support video-conferences with a relatively large number of simultaneous participants. Regardless of the number of participants, each participant uploads their information just once, and the server broadcasts this to the other participants. The bandwidth consumed is proportional to the number of participants, and is about 160 kb/s per participant. The bandwidth available to the Agora server typically determines the maximum number of participants with a connection of a 100 Mb/s being theoretically capable of serving up to 300 users.

Like Access Grid, Agora uses a number of UDP ports for the transmission of the RTP packets. A TCP port is also required as a message port for synchronisation of whiteboard, shared desktop and chat events. The institutional firewall of the Sakai server hosting Agora must allow communication to and from these ports.

Agora was developed on the principles that it should be easy, simple and useful, requiring only minimal installation and investment by the users themselves. Download of client-side software is therefore automatic at startup. The user interface of the tool also reflects this approach (see Figure 5.3).

Figure 5.3 Screenshot of Agora in a Sakai portal

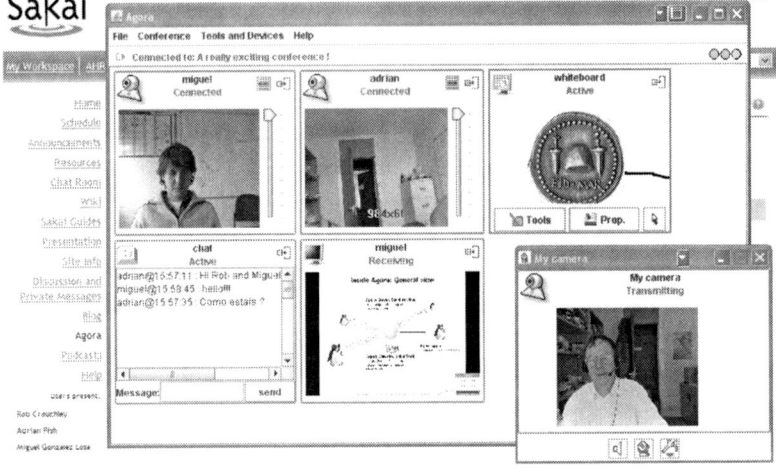

Skype

Probably the most widely used means of communicating over distance, as its name implies, is the telephone. Skype is software that effectively allows users to make telephone calls over the internet. Calls to other users of the service and to free-of-charge numbers are free, while calls to other landlines and mobile phones can be made for a fee. Additional features include instant messaging, file transfer and video-conferencing.

Skype as a service was introduced in 2003 and has been owned by eBay since 2005. There were 309 million registered users in early 2008, with some 13 million concurrent users online in September 2008.

Skype uses a proprietary voice over IP (VoIP) network protocol. Its applications are proprietary and closed source. The main difference between Skype and standard VoIP clients is that Skype operates on a peer-to-peer model rather than the more usual client-server model. This is based on the KaZaa P2P file-sharing system. The Skype user directory is entirely decentralised and distributed among the nodes of the network, i.e. users' computers, which allows the network to scale very easily to large sizes and reduces operating costs.

Concerns have been raised about using systems such as Skype over public academic networks (JNT, 2006). These concerns focus mainly on its use of bandwidth and its use of encrypted IP tunnels. Skype is not

Collaboration, trust and security

peculiar in this respect and the same concerns apply to other P2P software. Not all nodes are equal peers; a node that is connected to a high-bandwidth network may be promoted to a super node and will have network traffic directed through it even when not actually in a call. Clearly this is not tolerable in a research environment dependent on ICT, particularly as some of the traffic may be commercial and therefore should not be routed over a free-to-use academic network. All Skype communications are encrypted by default to ensure privacy. Unfortunately, this could be used as a way to bypass security for hacking attacks which would otherwise be detected in a firewall or other intruder prevention system. Such activities have also been historically observed with web browsers. It is unfortunate that many ICT systems used for academic, as opposed to commercial research, have rather poor security.

Currently the best policy for using systems of this type is to quit them when not in use. This implies that, just like Access Grid, a different mechanism such as e-mail (or a real telephone) must be employed to set up a collaborative session.

Instant messaging and chat

Instant messaging and chat are technologies that create the possibility of real time text-based communication (no sound or video) between two or more participants over the internet or an intranet. Chat and instant messaging are synchronous forms of communication, i.e. they happen in close to real time. E-mail, forum, discussion, etc. are asynchronous and it is not expected that messages posted will be received or answered immediately. Some systems do however allow offline working.

Standard free instant messaging applications offer functions like file transfer, contact lists, and the ability to have simultaneous conversations. These may be all the functions that a small research team needs, but larger communities will require more sophisticated applications that can work together. Enterprise-level applications include software such as Jabber, Lotus Sametime, Microsoft Office Communicator, etc., and can be integrated with other systems such as workflow. Such services have additional features, such as the immediate receipt of acknowledgment or reply, group chatting, conference services (possibly including voice and video), conversation logging and file transfer.

There is a long list of instant messaging applications; some widely used ones (with over one million users daily) include QQ, Windows Live

Messenger, Skype, AIM, Jabber, eBuddy, Yahoo! Messenger, IBM Lotus Sametime, ICQ, Xfire, MXfit, Gadu-Gadu, Paltalk, IMVU, Mail.ru Agent, Mettbo, PSYC and Bigant.

Sakai has a built-in chat tool. Members of a worksite can open the tool and join an existing chat thread or start a new one. Messages from different users are coloured differently to make it easier to follow a conversation. Access Grid uses a Jabber tool for text conversations 'aside' of the main AG streams; room operators often find this useful for discussing technical issues.

JISCmail and other list servers

List servers are very widely used and typically support bulk asynchronous communication such as e-mail. List servers could be used for other purposes, e.g. as a VO management tool. A research collaboration (VO) will often use a list server to broadcast information to all its members, one example being meeting invitations.

JISCmail is the UK's national academic mailing list service operated by STFC on behalf of the JISC. It facilitates knowledge-sharing within the academic community, using e-mail and the web, through the provision, support and development of specialist mailing list-based services, enabling the delivery of high-quality and relevant content. JISCmail is based on a LISTSERV system – the long-established commercial e-mail list software from L-Soft (*http://www.lsoft.com*). LISTSERV itself is used for managing many research-focused e-mail lists worldwide.

The bulk of JISCmail users are from higher and further education and research communities, both in the UK and worldwide. The equivalent for commercial users is called Mailtalk. JISCmail users by country worldwide are shown on an interactive map (*http://www.jiscmail.ac.uk/map.html*).

JISCmail has a web interface which is used for list, user and archive management. This does not currently interoperate with portal technology, but can be displayed in a separate browser window or iframe. Once logged into the web interface there are additional services for carrying out surveys, planning meetings, sharing files and holding online discussions (chat). These services use the list as a VO and are thus restricted to its subscribers.

Many such services maintain archives of the e-mails sent. There has been little research into how to use these archives for other research purposes, e.g. by text mining to organise or generate new information.

Security in a VRE: authentication and authorisation

Security could be the antithesis of collaboration. For an overview of the issues, see Neumann (1998) or Surridge (2002). Li and Baker (2006) offer more information about some security systems used in grids.

This section describes some general concepts relevant to VREs. Specific implementation details are described in Chapter 7.

This chapter has been somewhat back-to-front – we have already described virtual organisations, which are in the main concerned with authorisation. I have left the discussion of low-level authentication issues until last. However, these are pretty standard to any internet-based ICT system, so probably need less explanation and there is a great deal of specialist literature available.

Authentication

In ICT terms, this is often implemented as the act of responding with a secret password or other 'credential' to a 'challenge' from a security system, thus providing proof of 'trustworthiness'. Usually a credential or token establishes an identity, or another secret is used which can be validated against prior 'authentic' information. Authentication is really the process of obtaining this secret or credential required to validate during the challenge. It requires due diligence in assuring that the person or service given the key is who they say they are and will abide by the rules of the VO. Simply giving a password to just anyone is not very good security, and can be likened to giving your friend the keys to your car.

Public key infrastructure

Computer security is typically enforced using a public key infrastructure (PKI) (Sun Microsystems, 1998a). The effectiveness of public key cryptosystems depends on the intractability, both computational and theoretical, of solving certain mathematical problems such as integer factorisation. Public and private keys used as credentials in such systems are mathematically related, so the private key can only decrypt a message encrypted with a recipient's public key. To find a private key from a user's public key is computationally very time-consuming to solve, but usually faster than trying all possible keys by brute force.

Using keys means that the user does not have to manually log into every service they invoke; instead software can act on their behalf once the key is installed. The fact that the key is cryptographically signed by a higher authority also provides a trust mechanism by showing that the user has been authenticated. A service can accept or reject a request by checking which authority signed the requestor's key. Again, computer security is based on secrecy and trust has nothing to do with giving your private key to a friend, which must be strictly avoided.

The use of PKI is based on a handshaking procedure using secret tokens encoded using the keys. Details of this can be found in the many references to PKI and its implementations. PKI is at the heart of the internet standard secure socket layer (SSL), now referred to as transport layer security (TLS) (Sun Microsystems, 1998b). The keys are typically encoded in X.509 standard certificates. This will be discussed further in Chapter 7.

Single sign-on

This is met with in many discussions of VREs and will be further considered in Chapter 12. Single sign-on (SSO) is basically associated with providing the information required for authentication/validation just once to gain access to more than one component within a security domain.

The following is from Wikipedia, with some changes. SSO is a method of access control that enables a user to authenticate once and gain access to the resources of multiple software systems. Single sign-off is the reverse process, whereby a single action of signing out terminates access to multiple software systems.

The term 'enterprise reduced sign-on' is preferred by some authors because they believe single sign-on to be a misnomer: no one can achieve it without a homogeneous IT infrastructure – see further comments below. In a homogeneous IT infrastructure, or at least where a single user authentication scheme exists or where a user database is centralised, single sign-on would be beneficial. All users in this infrastructure would have a single set of authentication credentials, e.g. in an organisation which stores its user information in a LDAP database, all systems could use the database for validation, thus achieving SSO.

The following comments expand on the authentication issues of SSO. Possible steps to achieve fully automatic SSO are discussed here. A 'vision' for SSO within CCLRC/STFC has been around since at least 2004. What did this mean in practice?

The following notes assume the existence of a FedId/passwd pair for each component requiring authentication with any other component, e.g. a user wishing to log onto a computer. The FedId (short for federal identifier) is the username allocated centrally from STFC's corporate data repository. The passwd constitutes a secret key which, if disclosed, could imply a security compromise. Authentication systems therefore validate and/or manage key pairs typically using various kinds of encryption.

Step 1

A FedId/passwd login for each component verifies the information against an authentication service, e.g. LDAP, JAAS, Active Directory, Shibboleth, Vintela etc. Each component therefore accepts the same 'single FedId/passwd'. An authentication service needs to be developed appropriate for the security domain and namespace of interest. The passwd should have a 'strength' such that it cannot easily be guessed, e.g. from the FedId or other public information associated to it. Jensen (2007) refers to this as 'single passwd'.

Worry 1: There is a slight worry about this, that if a passwd, i.e. the primary secret key, is compromised then every component in the system is exposed. It is possible to achieve SSO like this for web-based applications using Firefox Password Manager as an abstraction layer.

Step 2

Login to any component or 'single application' generates a secure secondary token, i.e. a new key pair. This can be passed, via a token manager service (using encryption), to other applications requiring authentication. This does not need the user to type in the secure primary passwd each time, so needs some other way to recognise who the user is in order to access the relevant token. It does however enable the token to be used for one service to invoke another, potentially in a workflow or other machine-to-machine invocation. Services 'trust' each other by validating key pairs using the PKI handshake process. This is the basis of 'delegation'. Jensen (2007) makes a distinction between 'authentication forwarding' and 'delegated authentication'.

Note 1: We already do this kind of thing in projects like GROWL which use a UUID as a token. The client application passes the token on each function call. Cookies in a web or portal-based solution are equivalent. Jensen (2007) refers to this as 'single authentication'.

Comment 1: In response to Worry 1, we note that any such token must be time-limited. This time-limit period should be quite short in order to limit the amount of damage that can be done if it is intercepted. Clearly, it does not help if the primary passwd is compromised.

Question 1: Can this system work without a workflow or other protocol transferring tokens between components (delegation)? In any case this requires a secure communications infrastructure based on something like TLS. The grid research leading to the Grid Security Interface (GSI) has delivered a solution to this problem. We do not believe that other systems such as Kerberos or Shibboleth have working delegation mechanisms.

Question 2: How can this be made to work with the web services we are using for much of the current e-science middleware, e.g. via SAML? Even this machine-to-machine scenario does not have an obvious solution today.

Solution 1: A single user interface to all components, which could be a web-based portal, would have a primary authentication stack and use internal authorisation mechanisms for each service invoked. It would run on a secure server.

Step 3

The 'correct' solution would require us to re-factor most of the software to use grid middleware such as the Web Services Resource Framework (WSRF). Unfortunately, because the way the UK E-Science Programme has evolved, there are very few services currently using WSRF and there are also still web services issues with respect to SSO.

Question 3: There is still the same problem if multiple different user interfaces are used. How will we solve this?

Solution 2: We need a client solution which communicates some 'secret' credential to each service that is invoked. In Step 1 this is a passwd. In Step 2 this is a secure token, such as a GSI certificate, which can then be delegated to solve the N-tier authorisation problem. In Step 3 we propose a smart card mechanism, which means that the user can access the system from any card-enabled resource, including their home laboratory computer equipped with a card reader. The card could also be the basis of authorisation for physical access systems at a research facility.

6

Domain differences and usability

In attempting to consider the needs of e-research we identified some domain differences. We again cite the UK's Joint Infrastructure Systems Committee (JISC), which has examples spanning many domains.

E-research, e-learning and digital information

The 'domains' or 'silos' widely thought to demark current JISC (and other worldwide) activities are: (1) e-research as managed by the Committee for the Support of Research; (2) e-learning as managed by the Committee for Learning and Teaching; and (3) the information environment as managed by the Committee for the Integrated Information Environment. The latter is responsible for development of middleware and AAA services, core common services such as resource discovery and curation, core interoperability standards, IPR and activities like the E-Framework for Education and Research. There are overlaps with other committees and some share parts of this agenda. There are other JISC committees, but they are less relevant here. In fact, JISC is striving to develop programmes that bridge these domains for economies of scale and benefits in sharing of practice, tools and information. Some of JISC's work is jointly undertaken with the UK Research Councils.

Figure 6.1 illustrates the overlap of teaching and learning with a couple of examples from the research domain. JISC is working hard to identify commonalities to enable domains to be bridged and for software and resources to be reused. This is undertaken partly in developing actual services, such as digital repositories or the National Grid Service, and partly in the work of the E-Framework for Education and Research (*http://www.e-framework.org*) in developing service usage models and promoting standards. The driving forces of the main domains are summarised below.

Figure 6.1 Commonality of e-research domains

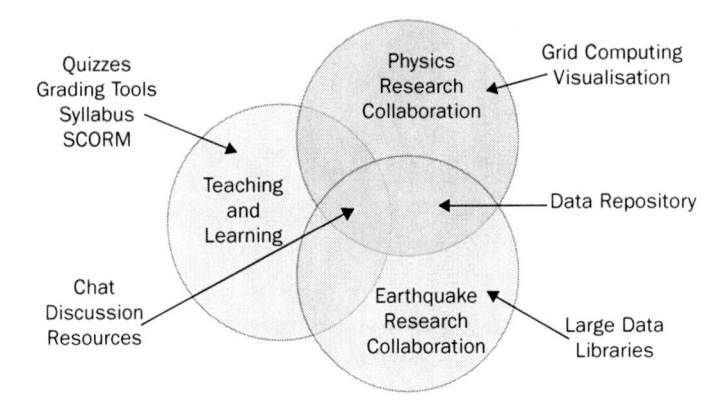

Quizzes
Grading Tools
Syllabus
SCORM

Physics Research Collaboration

Grid Computing
Visualisation

Teaching and Learning

Data Repository

Chat
Discussion
Resources

Earthquake Research Collaboration

Large Data Libraries

E-research

Many researchers are carrying out activities to generate new knowledge. They are active across a wide range of subjects and their procedures vary enormously from one to another, encompassing observation, experimentation, computer simulation and analysis of historical materials or discipline-related corpora. These activities are characterised as being diverse, complex, multi-organisational if collaborating teams are involved, and dynamic as they evolve rapidly as new hypotheses and procedures are developed. The actors involved tend to be peers. Access to scholarly publications is important to researchers, but so is access to existing scientific data as well as the creation and archiving of new data.

E-learning

This is characterised by being largely institution-based with established and relatively well-defined procedures including pedagogy, administration and assessment in various forms. The actors involved can be arranged hierarchically in peer groups, such as administrators, teaching staff and students. Access to digital resources explaining and outlining methodologies and their application to example studies is a cornerstone of this area.

Digital information

This is characterised by a body of specialists maintaining and making information available through services. Digital information has many forms, including text, sound and video material. It can include scholarly publications and scientific data in either raw or secondary forms and packaged with appropriate metadata explaining at least provenance, format and location. The focus of the wider information environment is to provide services for the publication, discovery, access and to a limited extent analysis of this material (the latter through 'generic' services such as mining or annotation). The information environment recognises that there is a need to deliver resources in a variety of ways and therefore to interface with different presentation services and systems such as those that support learning and research.

Differences between research domains

There are also differences between research domains, as discussed by Allan et al. (2006e). These are relevant to agencies funding research, such as the Research Councils in the UK. Again, a 'silo' effect occurs because each council is responsible for a specific area and, while a number of initiatives are starting to bridge them, there could be more reuse of technology. We will alternatively refer to such domains as 'subjects'.

Our examples in the later chapters are based on e-social science and large-scale experimental facilities, which clearly do not address all areas of research (e.g. mathematics, law, languages, history, medicine). Some differences between research domains have been described by Borgman (2005).

We have already mentioned the requirements survey carried out by the EVIE project in Chapter 2. Questions leading to their conclusions were asked in terms of the research lifecycle and focused on five activities: resource discovery, funding opportunities, collaboration, managing research outputs and 'other'. Researchers from every domain rated the activities surrounding resource discovery as the most important for a VRE to support, with 70 per cent of respondents rating it as essential.

Funding opportunity tasks were also rated as very important, with some domain researchers rating this as having the same importance as resource discovery. However, within the domains of medicine and health, education, social science and law, these tasks were not rated so highly. Indeed, one respondent pointed to the various existing information sources about funding opportunities already, as well as the support and advice networks, suggesting that such provision might fall outside of the VRE.

Collaborative activities were rated as very important or essential by over half of the respondents although this was very uneven across subjects. The arts, and medicine and health predominantly rated this aspect of the research lifecycle as important or somewhat important. It was surprising that the activities surrounding the management of research outputs received a low rating, as discussions with individual researchers had suggested more interest. In addition, this area of the research lifecycle was seen as not important by 12 per cent of respondents. These 'not important' responses came entirely from the domains of arts (performance, visual arts and communication); business; education; social science and law; and biological sciences. For these domains, the number of respondents rating the management of research outputs as not important was greater than the number rating them as essential. Nevertheless, some performing art groups are now investigating the use of advanced ICT, such as Access Grid, for distributed collaboration; consequently, the responses may change as familiarity grows.

At this point in the survey it would not have been obvious which activities might come under the catch-all aspect of 'other activities'. Consequently, this area of the lifecycle was only rated by half of the respondents.

The distribution of the five importance ratings across the activities, when broken down by the research level of the respondent, is proportionately representative of the overall ratings, with just one exception. Only 10 per cent of graduate students and postdoctoral researchers rated the funding opportunity activities as essential, while 30 per cent of respondents overall rated this aspect as essential. This was attributed to most graduate students having no involvement with funding applications.

Some general questions and statements have arisen during related work. These were originally in the context of the wider information environment (IE) but are generally applicable to ICT supporting information sharing and reuse across domains. Detailed domain differences in the following areas still remain to be understood:

- The IE architecture needs to be extended to accommodate components relevant to other research processes. What are the additional components and how can this be done?
- Researchers do not know what the IE is. According to JISC, the IE is not really a 'thing', but rather a wide range of resources, standards and protocols, services, and projects and programmes; it is more about delivering resources (and curating them) in a more standard

and seamless way that enables interoperability, diversity and rich use. It is unlikely that researchers (other than those funded directly by JISC programmes) will support or contribute to the IE or actively link its services into their own work. Consequentially, there is a danger of 'reinventing the wheel', rather than using outcomes of larger programmes of work, whether from JISC or the Research Councils. What can be done to improve this?

- Digital data curation is important, but probably not recognised as such by many researchers at present.
- Researchers do not use deep search facilities sufficiently, but tend to use Google and Wikipedia as their main tools. Google has largely replaced the use of citation indexes. Can Google be used to lead researchers to other tools?
- The IE needs to embrace the needs of researchers to manage and share personal information. Is this part of its remit, and if so what technology should be used?
- There must be more linking between publications and raw data from scientific studies. This is only appropriate when that data can be shared. Projects investigating this should be accelerated and the best solutions implemented in the IE. Providers of data archiving services need to be involved.
- Open Archives initiatives are growing in importance, such as ePrints and ePubs. JISC needs to be seen to be playing a leading or at least a strong role in this. Investment in activities such as the Digital Repositories Programme needs to be made more visible and its outcomes embedded in research practice.
- There are many sources of information which are external to programmes such as the JISC IE. The world wide web is a major source of information and knowledge. There are also many proprietary sources. Discovery services must embrace all these sources, which in turn may require bilateral agreements to be in place.
- What user interfaces do researchers want/need? Are portals sufficient or should services be provided which can link into applications and desktop tools?
- Tasks of accessing and publishing information are only part of research-related 'admin' procedures which are growing in complexity. It is desirable to tie different administrative systems together using open standards.

- Security, confidentiality and IPR are still major concerns.
- Metadata such as provenance is important, but currently very subject-specific.
- Electronic publishing leads to new business models, e.g. payment for individual download of journal articles rather than purchase of shared whole issues. The impact on the researchers needs to be understood and potential negative perceptions addressed.
- Persistent URLs, registries and link resolvers are key elements of maintaining an information infrastructure in addition to the underlying services.

Usability

Although usability focus groups and requirements-gathering exercises are a part of the work of developing institutional systems and larger e-research projects, for example in the design of portal user interfaces (Klyne, 2005; Allan et al., 2008), a coherent user-centred design methodology is challenging given the relatively small parcels of work focused on extending existing rather than developing new applications. Most projects do not include HCI or CSCW experts, although JISC for one puts an emphasis on formative evaluation in its funding of development work. The necessity of placing the user at the centre of the development process feeds into investigations into how to sustain project objectives and outputs.

Agile programming methods have been suggested for use, mostly in informal circumstances, to address issues of requirements and usability (*http://www.agilemanifesto.org*). In agile programming, small teams of developers typically work closely with users and functionality is added incrementally in a series of small code and review cycles. This is implemented more formally in eXtreme Programming (XP). I know of only one portal project that fully embraced XP, and that was for the successful development of the GridSphere portal framework.

We will consider usability again when discussing perceptions of lightweight vs. heavyweight software in Chapter 9.

There are historical parallels, where complicated systems have been developed and not taken up. One such example is the web vs. the Andrew File System (AFS). AFS did not take off widely because the client was complex to install. On the other hand, any browser can now access files on the web. Access and installation are both key aspects of usability. Despite this, AFS is now being considered in a grid context.

It is reasonable for resource providers to install middleware and provide a commitment to offer an e-research service. However, only one kind of middleware is likely to be installed on each resource. Considering the web again, a web browser is a complex application, but is packaged in such a way that it is easy to install (but not necessarily lightweight in other senses). Likewise, web servers like Apache2 are now easy to install and support complex functionality. They even come packaged with operating system distributions. E-research middleware and services are not yet at this level of maturity. Is a measure of maturity that they should be supported in a standard operating system distribution such as Red Hat? SuSe and Platform Computing have already offered support for Globus Grid middleware in this way.

It seems that we are really talking about usability in making these definitions and the underlying software might actually be quite complex. As noted before, the CSCW community might have something to say about usability.

There might be clear incentives for users to learn certain technologies, such as a sophisticated text editor or a parallel computing environment. Users will use technologies if these give clear and obvious advantages. Is this a general statement? There are currently not many VRE users, so we need to make it easy to use so that more are willing to try e-research and recognise the advantages. This limits the functionality that can currently be offered, however. So what are the potential 'wins'? There is a trade-off between effort invested and perceived gains.

When is complexity necessary? Perhaps if it gives desirable functionality not achieved in other ways. There is a spectrum of VRE solutions scaling up in functionality and complexity. Complexity might be on the client or the server side or in between. It seems that the definition of lightweight is less useful than one of usability. If the required effort is perceived to be rewarded, it is probably worth it, but there is an 'activation barrier'. Another definition could therefore be that, in a heavyweight system, there is a large up-front cost before there are any returns, whereas in a lightweight system, there could be an iterative process – it is a question of the shape of the learning curve.

7

VRE architecture: the technology

We now consider a service-oriented architecture (SOA) for developing a VRE, principally one with a web-based portal interface. In an SOA, core services are designed to be pluggable – this provides flexibility so that these services can be deployed or removed on demand, although normally core services are unlikely to be removed. The core services are those such as AAA, for example authentication and authorisation services, for keeping a system up and running. In a real system, more services may be added as core services for ease of development. For example, an abstract database service or inter-process communications (IPC) are very helpful for developers to manage database access and synchronise operations, but such services may not be essential. Further services, known as external services, are outside of the core services. Such external services are also pluggable, which makes it possible for the end user to customise their VRE system easily. An example external service may be one that provides users with the facility to chat using text messages. Such a service could have an interface built into the VRE (as does Sakai) or use a preferred client such as Psi or Jabber connected to a chat channel of the core IPC service. Generally speaking, with some core and external services already provided, users are encouraged to develop their own external services if they cannot find what they want, thus creating a community of practice. This is the philosophy of the US TeraGrid science gateways (*http://www.teragrid.org/programs/sci_gateways*).

As mentioned previously, an SOA gives us 'flexibility'. This is key to a VRE system because it is not possible to design a general-purpose system that meets the requirements of researchers from all domains. Indeed, in the JISC and TeraGrid programmes there is currently no recommendation for even a base framework or underlying component tool set. In our work, we have chosen the Sakai collaborative portal framework as will be discussed in Chapter 10. The international E-Framework for Education and Research is starting to identify how common services can be reused across domains (*http://www.e-framework.org*).

Don't reinvent the wheel

Some standards used

Some of the technical standards met with in developing VREs are listed below. There are many others, but these are the most common. For more detailed information, see the eReSS wiki (*http://www.confluence.hull.ac.uk*). For an extensive introduction to the issues concerned with security and dependency of web services and the standards and specifications developed to address them, see Periorellis (2007).

- *Java*: programming language technology, classes and standard patterns including JSR 168 (portlet-1), JSR 170 (repository), JSR 286 (portlet-2);
- *security*: SAML, X.509, GSI, Kerberos, SSL, TLS;
- *browser-based web technology*: JavaScript, AJAX, CGI, JSP, Portlets;
- *web services*: XML, SOAP, WSDL, UDDI, WSRP, pub-sub pattern;
- *metadata*: Dublin Core, MARC;
- *data discovery and access*: OAI-PMH, Z39.50, SRW/SRU, OpenSearch, OpenURL;
- *database management*: JDBC, Hiberbate, SQL;
- *workflow*: BPEL, SCUFL.

Many tools and packages use these standards; Chapter 10 will consider their use in Sakai.

Some packages used

Some of the application packages used in developing VREs are listed below. Although there are many more, these are just the few with which we have been most involved. For more detailed information and others see the eReSS wiki (*http://www.confluence.hull.ac.uk*).

- *Globus*: grid middleware connecting high-performance computers;
- *Condor*: middleware for campus grids;
- *SRB*: Storage Resource Broker middleware;
- *SOAP:Lite*: SOAP web services package for Perl applications;
- *gSOAP*: SOAP package for C language applications;

VRE architecture

Table 7.1 Some e-research projects and prerequisites

Project	Project and goals	Prerequisites
eMinerals and RMCS	Environment from the Molecular Level http://www.eminerals.org Dove et al. (2003); Calleja et al. (2005); J. M. H. Thomas et al. (2007); Walker et al. (2008)	Metadata, Condor, Globus, SRB, PostgreSQL
e-HTPX	E-Science Resources for High Throughput Protein Crystallography Allan et al. (2005); Wang et al. (2006)	Metadata, web services, workflow, Java, Tomcat
Sakai Demonstrator VRE	http://www.grids.ac.uk/Sakai Allan et al. (2007); Yang and Allan (2007) Severance et al. (2007); Crouchley et al. (2007)	Sakai, web services, Java
GROWL VRE	http://www.grids.ac.uk/GROWL Crouchley et al. (2005); Allan and Kewley (2007); Grose et al. (2006); Hayes et al. (2007); J. M. H. Thomas et al. (2007b)	Globus, web services
NGS Portal	http://portal.ngs.ac.uk http://www.ngs.ac.uk Meredith et al. (2006)	Globus, JSDL, Web services, Tomcat, Java, Pluto
NW-GRID	North West Grid: http://www.nw-grid.ac.uk Addison et al. (2008); J. M. H. Thomas et al. (2007a, 2007b)	Globus, GROWL, Sakai, RMCS, Oracle
CQeSS	Collaboratory for Quantitative e-Social Science http://www.ncess.ac.uk Grose et al. (2006); Crouchley and Allan (2008)	Metadata, GROWL, Sakai, Oracle

- *Sakai*: collaborative portal framework (see Chapter 10);
- *uPortal*: portal framework;
- *GridSphere*: portal framework;
- *Apache2*: web server;
- *Apache Tomcat*: Java Servlet and Java Server Pages server;
- *PostgreSQL*: relational database;
- *Oracle*: relational database;
- *MyProxy*: proxy credential repository;
- *Shibboleth*: federated security infrastructure.

Table 7.1 shows how standards and packages have formed the prerequisites of some of the projects we have worked on over the past six years. Outputs of these projects form the basis for the work described in Chapters 11 and 12.

N-tier architecture

The abovementioned technologies are complex to deploy and administer and, moreover, strict security must be enforced to protect the powerful end resources. While it would be possible to implement a two-tier client-server system in which the user directly invokes remote services via middleware, this is not easy to do, or even recommended. We refer to this as the 'client problem'.

To achieve maintainable, stable, lightweight, platform-independent client interfaces for accessing distributed resources it is necessary to reduce, as far as is practically possible, the amount of logic contained within the client system. There are a number of reasons for this:

- Middleware and services are not yet completely stable, which leads to continuing modifications to the implementation of SOA and grid-based solutions. Thus, to provide stable and maintainable client solutions, it is necessary to isolate the implementation from the interface.

- Clients can have access to different services offering the same or similar functionality. Currently there is no single well-defined API to these services and the client would have to deal with different ways of invoking them, which would be very hard in a dynamic environment.

- When a client has access to more than one resource or service, it is often necessary to decide how a task can be subdivided across these. As the resources are not well interconnected between themselves, it is necessary for decisions regarding brokering and task scheduling to take place elsewhere. The resources are shared, which makes this hard to do in any one client system.

Providing a common framework for VRE developers to work with is vital to enable a large, distributed development effort, shared across numerous research groups to provide stable, maintainable lightweight client interfaces to e-research resources. Developer tools and APIs need to be produced in advance of, or at least in parallel with, the development of applications.

It is well known that an appropriate solution for isolating implementation from client and service provider and adding multi-user capabilities is a three-tier (or N-tier) architecture (Foster and Kesselman, 1998). Such an architecture serves to minimise the amount of information each client requires about other resources and eliminates the need for them to communicate. It also prevents the growth of unmanageable 'stove pipe' solutions that are non-scalable. Complexity is moved to the intermediate tier, which can be provided as a shared service with a well-defined interface and one or more instances hosted on multi-client servers. Services of this type are at the heart of VREs and support application developers using well-supported language-agnostic tools with open APIs. Some such technologies already exist, including CORBA and web services. The use of these for VREs will be described in Chapter 9. We first describe the generic capabilities of web services.

Web services and service-oriented architecture

Services, in the sense of Chapter 1, can be advertised by a service provider and accessed by a client using a published interface (API) and agreed protocol. These are typically 'hosted' web services which have no state or session management but are persistent, i.e. always available. There may be competing hosts offering similar or identical services, such as a lookup service or voicemail service, and brokering could be done, possibly via an intermediate agent to guarantee lowest cost, best performance, etc. It is likely that a dynamic VRE would use a number of such agents. Services must therefore publish sufficient information about themselves to enable brokering to be done. Services may also negotiate contracts in more complex situations, also via agents, and should therefore publish how they do business, e.g. what charging mechanism they use and if there is any quality of service guarantee. UDDI, mentioned below, is one way to publish some, but possibly not all, of this information.

Web services are really nothing to do with the web, but a new breed of application accessed typically (but not always) over HTTP protocols. A web service is a self-contained, self-describing, modular application component that can be published, located, and typically invoked using standard HTTP over port 80. Web services can perform functions which can be anything from simple requests to complicated business or scientific procedures. However, like many other web protocols, they treat the user as anonymous, so that the VRE must manage access and session control.

The main difference between a normal remotely-invoked application and a web service is that the latter has an XML-based interface which enables it to be largely self-describing, i.e. it can be published. Once a web service component is deployed, applications (or other web services and workflows) can discover and invoke the published service via its interface. The technical literature on web services is enormous and still growing (see Allan et al., 2003; Graham et al., 2004).

In an N-tier application architecture, web services may in fact just be wrappers for programmatic access to existing services. This good practice separates the interface from the logic. In fact we have found that 'document-based' web services are the most portable, as they first exchange XML documents describing in more detail the service inputs and outputs (Meredith et al., 2006).

The basic web services platform (sometimes referred to as WS-I basic profile) uses SOAP consisting of XML plus HTTP. HTTP is a ubiquitous protocol, running practically everywhere on the internet. The protocol is largely responsible for the rapid spread of the internet because, in addition to a few simple methods, it provides a straightforward self-describing data format for browsers to use subject to their own interpretation. The eXtensible Markup Language (XML) is similar to HTML, but enables the user to write specialised tags. As HTML and XML are encoded as ASCII text they are easy to transmit between computer systems. For this reason, web services are neutral to programming language, programming model and system software. Most examples use Java, but there are currently also XML parsers and SOAP implementations in computer languages such as Ada, C#, C++, Java, JavaScript, Perl, PHP, Python, Ruby, Smalltalk, Tcl, Visual Basic, Delphi, Orchard, K, etc.

HTTP and HTTPS

HTTP is the accepted protocol for web server-to-browser client communication with rendering of ASCII text and graphics on receipt over port 80. HTTPS utilises a secure transport based on TLS. Communication from client browser to server is in the form of GET or POST methods with the inclusion of environmental variables, typically created by the browser from HTML forms and accessed on the server via the common gateway interface (CGI). CGI can be used in languages such as C, C++, Perl and Fortran, but not Java, which requires server page wrapping, e.g. with Tomcat.

XML

XML, like HTML and SGML, is designed to mark up documents, but has no fixed tag vocabulary. The tags are defined for each application using an extensible XML schema definition (XSD). A well-formed XML document is a labelled tree containing hierarchical definitions. Note that the XML schema addresses syntactic conventions and does not address semantics. XML schema are themselves valid XML documents. Many new formats are expressed in XML, such as SMIL, the Synchronised Multimedia Integration Language for online animations and presentations and SOAP (see below) for web services. Such XML documents are really specialised metadata describing the objects they represent.

XML is very powerful because it contains descriptive tags and can be transformed automatically to other marked up formats. This is accomplished using XML Stylesheet Language Transformations (XSLT). An example is in transforming XML input including textual data into HTML output for presentation in a browser with the addition of formatting and background information based on the tags used. It could at the same time be converted to a set of printable forms or database entries. This procedure requires an interpretation engine (parser) using methods such as SAX or DOM.

Thus, like HTML, XML is readable by humans, but is more appropriate for machine consumption using a parser and XSLT transformation. The most powerful feature of XML is that it provides a meta-language in which one can write specialised languages using the predefined tags to express complex interactions between clients and services or between components of a composite service. For instance, an XML message can be converted on the web server back-end to a middleware request and the results converted back to XML.

There are now specialised databases for storing and searching across XML documents such as eXist and Xindice. Oracle DB also supports the use of XML documents. We will not describe XML further here as there are a large number of textbooks on the subject; for a bibliography see Allan et al. (2003).

SOAP

Originally standing for 'Simple Object Access Protocol' or 'Service Oriented Access Protocol', SOAP is a protocol specification that defines a uniform way of passing XML-encoded data using an envelope, a bit like e-mail. It also defines a way to perform remote procedure calls. SOAP is written in XML with an envelope consisting of head and body and is therefore independent of the underlying transport protocol, meaning that it can be carried over HTTP, SMTP, FTP, Java Messaging Service (JMS) or others.

SOAP arose from the realisation that current middleware needed a wrapper to be used on the internet. Architecturally, sending messages as plain XML has advantages in terms of ensuring interoperability and for debugging. The middleware developers seem willing to put up with the overheads of parsing and serialising XML in order to scale their approach to wide area networks. It can also offer security advantages if the only messages that arrive through port 80 are encoded in XML and conform to the predefined publicly accessible schema.

WSDL

Web Services Description Language (WSDL) is another XML metadata schema describing how services can be invoked by clients. It provides a way for service providers to describe the basic format of web service requests over the different protocols or encodings acceptable to the endpoint services. WSDL is thus used to describe what a web service can do, where it resides and how to invoke it. While the claim of SOAP and HTTP independence is made in various specifications, WSDL is most widely used with SOAP, HTTP and MIME as the remote object invocation specification.

WSDL provides a machine-readable description of how a remote procedure can be invoked using a SOAP web service. It does not provide any semantics, so a separate mechanism is necessary to describe what operations the service can perform. For instance, simply invoking a service with a method called 'search (mysearchstring)' does not indicate what it will search, what kind of input it requires or what results it will return. It may not even be a search service at all. It is therefore likely that a VRE will include additional metadata about the services and methods it invokes or a hard binding to specific services which have known definitions and are reliable.

WSIL and UDDI

In the world of web services, access and invocation are only the bare bones. Additional support services, such as discovery, transactions, security and authentication, are available to make the basic platform useful. Minimal requirements for a full-function WS-I platform include XML plus HTTP, SOAP and WSDL. At higher levels, one might also add technologies such as WSIL, UDDI, SAML, XAML, XLANG, XKMS, XFS or any of the range of services based on newer XML languages – services that are not universally required, and also not yet all widely accepted as standards.

The chief extension to the basic platform is to enable service discovery. Web Service Invocation Language (WSIL) and Universal Discovery, Description and Invocation (UDDI) provide this functionality (Allan et al. 2004c). UDDI registries describe numerous aspects of web services, including the binding details of the service. WSDL can be used as an UDDI service description. However, as noted many times, additional semantics are needed, leading, in fact, to the concept of the Semantic Grid (Berman et al., 2003).

Security frameworks

Assuming they cannot be bypassed, authentication and authorisation are the basic aspects of computer security. We briefly describe some commonly used authentication methods as used in VREs. Authorisation methods and policies tend to be specific to each VRE implementation. VO management is also VRE-specific. An interesting overview of security issues for web and grid applications has been given by Mike Surridge (2002). More information about some security systems used in grids is given by Foster and Kesselman (1998) and Li and Baker (2006).

A number of potential primary authentication mechanisms exist; we list them below roughly in order of increasing sophistication (or complexity). Not all are relevant, but it is useful to know they exist and broadly what they do. Any VRE might implement one or more of these, with a software stack that tests for each method in turn, starting with the most sophisticated and attempting progressively simpler methods where this fails to work. Some of these methods are based on PKI, as discussed in Chapter 5.

Most security systems rely on a secret password or other token that must be sent over the internet. If this is done in 'clear text' it can be intercepted and recorded so that a third-party can gain access using the same token. To avoid this, an encryption mechanism must be used, typically TLS (see also discussion of single sign-on in Chapter 5).

Trust authentication

When trust authentication is implemented, the VRE system assumes that anyone who can connect to it is authorised to access it with whatever user name they specify (including super users). This is the case for a public web server or a worksite in a portal such as Sakai which permits 'anonymous' access. Of course, access restrictions on the visible content and tools can still be made. This method should only be used when there is adequate operating system level protection on connections to the VRE server, e.g. users can only access the VRE if registered on a trusted client machine.

Trust authentication is therefore only suitable for TCP/IP connections if you trust every user on every machine that is allowed to connect to the server. It is possible to implement 'blacklisting' to block connections which have been problematic, but this requires close monitoring and is not a scalable approach.

Password authentication

Often, application userids and passwords are separate from client operating system user passwords, and can be encrypted in various ways. When this is implemented, the users are given a special username and password to access the VRE, e.g. via a portal interface. This simple access control is implemented on many secure websites. It is often the first method of choice as it is relatively straightforward and passwords can be sent over an encrypted protocol such as TLS.

LDAP authentication

LDAP is typically used only to validate user name/password pairs. As such, the user must already exist in the VRE application before LDAP can be used for authentication. TLS encryption can be enabled for the connection, but encrypted LDAP is available only if the platform's LDAP library supports it.

PAM authentication

This authentication method operates similarly to the password method except that it uses pluggable authentication modules (PAM) as the authentication mechanism. Like LDAP, PAM is typically used only to validate user name/password pairs. As such, the user must already exist in the VRE system before PAM can be used for authentication.

Ident-based authentication

The ident authentication method works by obtaining the client's user name from their desktop operating system, then using a map file that lists the permitted user name on the VRE system. The determination of the client's user name is the security critical point, and it works differently depending on the connection type.

Simple ident authentication over TCP/IP

The Identification Protocol is described in IETF's RFC 1413. Virtually every Unix-like operating system ships with an ident server that listens on TCP and UDP port 113 by default. The basic functionality of an ident server is to answer questions like 'What user initiated the connection that goes out of your port X and connects to my port Y?' VRE systems can therefore interrogate the ident server on the host of the connecting client and theoretically determine the username on the user's desktop operating system for any given connection this way.

One drawback of this procedure is that it depends on the integrity of the client: if the client machine is untrusted or compromised, an attacker could run just about any program on port 113 and return any user name of his choice. This authentication method is therefore only appropriate for closed networks where each client machine is under tight control and where the database and system administrators operate in close contact. In other words, it is essential to trust the machine running the ident server.

Another drawback is that this system cannot be used for 'pervasive' access, as the desktop username could be different on different clients' systems.

Ident maps

When using ident-based authentication, after having determined the username on the client operating system that initiated the connection, the VRE application checks that the user is allowed to connect with that identity. The map file is a simple text file with one mapping per line.

In grid systems, a similar map file is used to map a so-called 'distinguished name' onto the local user name for each resource. This is however extracted from a digital certificate in X.509 format and a sophisticated handshaking procedure based on PKI is used as the authentication. This is described further below.

Kerberos authentication

Kerberos is an industry standard secure authentication system suitable for distributed computing over a public network. A description of the Kerberos system is far beyond the scope of this book; in full generality it can be quite complex (and powerful). The Kerberos FAQ or MIT Kerberos page can be good starting points for exploration (US Navy, 2003). Kerberos provides secure authentication but does not encrypt queries or data passed over the network; for that use TLS, as with the other methods.

GSSAPI authentication

GSSAPI is a protocol for secure authentication defined in industry standard RFC 2743. As an example, PostgreSQL (a popular open source database used in some VREs) supports GSSAPI with Kerberos authentication according to RFC 1964. GSSAPI provides automatic authentication (single sign-on) for systems that support it. The authentication itself is secure, but the data sent over the connection will be in clear text unless TLS is used as the communication protocol.

Grid Security Infrastructure

The Grid Security Infrastructure (GSI) is an important component of the Globus middleware. It is now widely used by other software relevant to VREs, such as SRB and GridSite.

GSI is closely based on PKI and uses X.509 format certificates. Users, services and resources are all identified by certificates which are issued to them by a trusted entity referred to as a certification authority. This follows a formally-defined and legally-binding authentication process. While it is possible to issue certificates without following this process, they will not be signed by the certification authority and therefore are unlikely to be accepted by grid resources. Many websites using TLS will have certificates issued by well-known certification authorities such as Verisign or a subsidiary certification authority. The organisation ultimately responsible for grid certification authorities is the International Grid Trust Federation.

GSI provides a delegation capability which is an extension of the standard TLS protocol. If a VRE accesses several resources, each requiring mutual authentication, or if there is a need to have agents (local or remote) requesting services on behalf of a user, the need to re-enter the user's password can be avoided by creating a proxy.

A proxy consists of a new certificate (with a new public key in it) and a new private key. The new certificate contains the owner's identity, modified slightly to indicate that it is a proxy. The new certificate is signed by the owner, rather than a certification authority. The certificate also includes a time notation after which the proxy should no longer be accepted by services.

As an additional security measure, proxies have limited lifetimes. The proxy's private key must be kept secure, but because the proxy is not valid for very long, it does not have to kept quite as secure as the owner's private key. It is thus possible to store the proxy's private key in a local storage system without it being encrypted, as long as the permissions on the file prevent anyone else from looking at it easily. Once a proxy is created and stored, the user, or an agent such as a VRE service, can use the proxy certificate and private key for mutual authentication without entering a password.

When proxies are used, the mutual authentication process differs slightly. The remote party receives not only the proxy's certificate (signed by the owner), but also the owner's certificate. During mutual authentication, the owner's public key (obtained from their certificate) is used to validate the signature on the proxy certificate. The certification authority's public key is then used to validate the signature on the owner's certificate. This establishes a chain of trust from the certification authority to the proxy through the owner.

Note that the GSI and software based on it (notably the Globus Toolkit, GSI-SSH and GridFTP) is currently the only software to support the delegation extensions to TLS. Full delegation of this kind is important in distributed systems as it enables such features as accountability and non-repudiation.

MyProxy authentication

MyProxy is a proxy certificate repository used to enable pervasive access to resources from web portals (Novotny et al., 2001). It is therefore useful for many services in a VRE that need to be invoked on a user's behalf. The MyProxy service will only respond to other services that present valid security tokens, typically via the GSI API. The proxy is unlocked using a password forwarded from the service on behalf of the user. Once a service has accessed MyProxy and downloaded a user's proxy certificate (another one is delegated for this purpose with an even shorter lifetime) it can be used as described above. Of course, the VRE must ensure that such proxies are kept secure while they are valid. GSI and MyProxy can be used to instantiate N-tier authentication.

Shibboleth

Shibboleth is an architecture that enables organisations to build single sign-on environments that allow users to access web-based resources using a single login (*http://shibboleth.internet2.edu*). Shibboleth uses open standards, such as the Security Assertion Markup Language (SAML), and was developed by the Internet2 middleware group.

Shibboleth defines a way of exchanging information between an organisation and a provider of digital resources. The information is exchanged in a secure manner, protecting both the security of the data and the privacy of the individual.

The user's host organisation is responsible for authenticating them – that is, for validating that the credentials the user presents are correct (typically with a username/password combination). The organisation is also responsible for providing information about the user; for example, whether the user is a student, lecturer, or member of a particular department. This information is called 'attribute information' and represents a digital identity. The organisation is therefore called the 'identity provider'.

Organisations that use Shibboleth to access resources must join or create a 'federation'. A federation is a group of institutions and organisations that sign up to an agreed set of policies for exchanging information about users and resources to enable access to and use of resources and services. When combined with identity management software within institutions and organisations, the federation can be referred to as 'federated access management'.

How authentication is carried out by the institution and how rights management is carried out by the service provider is left up to the respective parties. In doing so, Shibboleth depends on a certain level of trust. These trust agreements are managed by the federations, which are typically established at a national level.

The UK federation is the UK Access Management Federation for Education and Research. It is run by the JNT Association, which provides the UK's Joint Academic Network (JANET) and builds on the experiences of successful pilot federation projects. For more information, see their website (*http://www.ukfederation.org.uk*).

Before the uptake of Shibboleth, the UK had a widely used single sign-on system for scholarly resources known as Athens. This used a centralised Athens password server as its identity provider and was hosted by Eduserve (*http://www.eduserv.org.uk*). Since 2008 this is being replaced by the Shibboleth-based OpenAthens service.

Shibboleth and the Grid Security Infrastructure are being integrated for VREs in the UK in the JISC funded SARoNGS project, Shibboleth Access to Resources on the NGS (*http://jisc.ac.uk/whatwedo/programmes/einfrastructure/sarongs.aspx*), and in the USA in the National Science Foundation funded Grid-Shib project (*http://gridshib.globus.org*). The former is used in the NGS portal and the latter in the OGCE portal and TeraGrid User Portal.

Identity management

Provided there is a clear mapping between them and they can ultimately be traced back to one primary authentication source, a VRE user can have more than one 'identity'. A typical example is of a user who belongs to more than one VO. Selecting and using these is referred to as identity management. Each identity has a separate series of attributes, probably including a security token of some kind. The identity to be used is typically decided by a 'context'.

Within a more complex VRE which may have multiple services and resources on offer, there will probably be more than one authentication mechanism implemented. From a user perspective, single sign-on is desirable. The VRE must then mediate between the different systems, accepting whatever security token is provided.

Some implementations, such as MyProxy used for SSO, are capable of generating 'on-the-fly' tokens so already carry out some of the tasks required for identity management.

VRE service definitions

Work is ongoing worldwide to define standards and reusable abstract services in all domain areas. We attempted an initial classification and description of some details of these services appropriate to research based on the work of groups such as JISC and the Open Grid Forum (OGF). A schematic of the initial classification was produced and is shown in Figure 7.1. Further work is required to identify how services can be broken into methods (functionality) and, if appropriate, where existing middleware and actual services provide such functionality. An initial attempt has been made (Allan, 2005).

The following sections further describe the classes and some of these abstract services. The differences between the domains these classes might represent were previously discussed in Chapter 6.

E-collaboration application services

Collaboration is about people working together, either as peers or in some more formally-defined relationship, such as student-tutor. Collaboration, as discussed in Chapter 5 includes various 'exotic' technologies such as Access Grid and Agora. It might extend to social networking services as implemented in applications such as MySpace, LinkedIn, Facebook, etc. There are moves to integrate such services with portals for VRE use. Services in this category might include the following:

- collaboration management;
- group and VO management;
- peer-group management;
- peer-service location;
- user registration;
- peer review;
- calendar;
- asynchronous e-mail, message board or discussion forum;
- resource sharing;
- audiovisual conferencing;
- other synchronous services, such as online chat.

Figure 7.1 E-research service classification

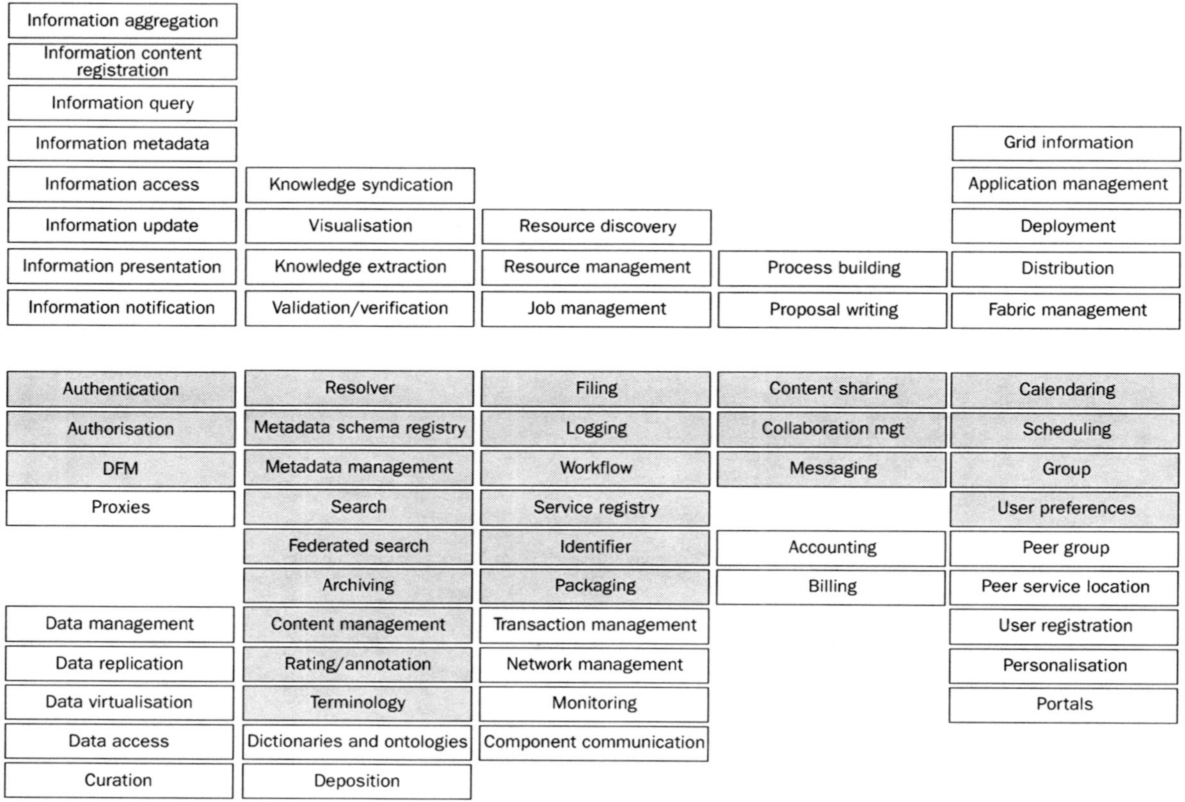

E-research application services

E-research is characterised by small communities of collaborating researchers in multiple institutions seeking to carry out complex processes jointly to create new knowledge. This is also often linked to personal learning activities and electronic publication. E-researchers are using the grid to create and analyse data from experiments, observations and computer simulations, as further discussed in Chapter 8.

Research services are therefore specific to supporting research processes and tools, including the grid. They should include collaboration with experts and peers, encapsulation of complex procedures for non-experts (possibly using some form of workflow technology) to facilitate growth of interdisciplinary sciences and aids for results publication and proposal writing. Research services might include:

- application management;
- e-publication;
- executable building;
- executable management;
- grid information;
- job management;
- job scheduling;
- knowledge discovery;
- knowledge syndication (join);
- process building;
- proposal writing;
- research resource discovery;
- research resource management;
- software deployment;
- software distribution;
- steering;
- validation and verification;
- visualisation and interactive services;
- workflow management.

E-learning application services

E-learning is characterised by providing electronic access to learning materials and well-defined activities, typically within a single institution. This involves large numbers of learners either working as peers or in hierarchies with teachers and tutors. In a managed learning environment, assessment and grading would also be included as part of the review process.

Learning services are about supporting a managed learning environment with particular relevance to teachers and students supporting both peer groups and organisational hierarchies. A variety of approaches to teaching can be included, embracing self-learning and assessment. A training and awareness environment might be distinguished from a more formal teaching environment because the former may not require assessment but could have more interactive demonstration material (e.g. via the grid). There should be the ability to walk through material in various ways, log activities and pay attention to accessibility issues. The aim is to provide a holistic approach, but there must be access to humans if a student runs into difficulties, whether of understanding or personal. An electronic system cannot completely replace tutors.

Not all these services are required in a personal learning environment as part of a VRE, where it is assumed that the learners are already experts in some domain and are self-motivated to learn about something new. Learning services include:

- activity authoring;
- activity management;
- assessment;
- cheat-o-meter;
- competency;
- course management;
- course scheduling;
- course sequencing;
- course validation;
- curriculum;
- e-portfolio;
- glossary;

Virtual Research Environments

- grading;
- help;
- learning flow;
- learner profile management;
- learning resource management;
- marking;
- personal development;
- quality assurance;
- reporting;
- resource list;
- tracking, trails and personalisation;
- user agent;
- view.

Digital information services

In the wider information environment, service providers in multiple institutions wish to make their resources available online for both learning and research processes. Resources are of many types. They include databases of survey results or other research material such as experimental and simulation data. Other resources may contain textual and pictorial data related to social or historical events or the arts, including literature. Music and speech are also special cases. Services for annotation, markup, publication, cataloguing, provenance tracing, format conversion and cross-searching are all important.

Services for digital information and data management need to address issues identified by initiatives such as the Digital Curation Centre (*http://www.dcc.ac.uk*). Special attention is given to database servers and large collections, some content of which may be of a qualitative nature, e.g. records of art, museum or archaeological artefacts. Conversion to electronic format (scanning, digitisation and markup) and data or text mining may also be targeted.

Data and information are further discussed in Chapters 3 and 4 respectively. Digital information services include:

- annotation;
- archiving;

VRE architecture

- cataloguing;
- content management;
- content migration/adaptation;
- cross-search;
- data and text mining;
- data deposition;
- data management;
- dictionaries and ontologies;
- information management;
- information resource discovery;
- institutional profiles;
- markup;
- packaging;
- publication;
- provenance;
- rating;
- terminology.

Common services

We have identified a number of common services that may underpin many other services. In many cases they could be provided as part of the infrastructure and need not be directly visible to users. They could be accessible as 'agents' to other high-level services. Currently, however, they tend to be built as core services into the software framework that constitutes the VRE itself. For this reason they have occasionally been referred to as 'portal services', e.g. by Fox and Walker (2003). Session management in addition to AAA are examples of this.

As the grid evolves, such services may become part of the middleware. If common services were provided in this way, it would give scope for system optimisation, e.g. through aggregation or federation in special cases, and they could be encapsulated in workflows for various scenarios. Shibboleth is an example of middleware which attempts to provide a federal authentication service as described above. Common services include:

- accounting;
- agent;
- alert and notification;
- authentication;
- authorisation;
- billing;
- inter-process communication;
- context-sensitive linking;
- digital rights management (DRM);
- e-notebook;
- fabric management;
- filing;
- file, dataset and binary large object (BLOB) management;
- hierarchy;
- identifier;
- identity management;
- logging;
- messaging;
- metadata registry;
- monitoring;
- network management;
- personalisation;
- proxy management;
- resolver;
- search;
- security;
- service registry;
- session management;
- spell checker;
- SQL;
- transaction;
- user management;
- user preferences.

VRE architecture

What e-infrastructure is available?

As described above, a VRE should be build on and integrate with a set of actual services of interest to researchers. This would be too great a task to initiate from scratch, so will involve finding and using service interfaces to existing components. The following are among the resources and facilities available to the academic research community in the UK:

- Access Grid nodes (mainly at e-science centres);
- course content (at universities and training institutions);
- Condor pools of workstations (at universities and teaching institutions);
- Resource Discovery Network resources (*http://www.rdn.ac.uk*) – see the RDN internet resource catalogue (*http://www.intute.ac.uk/services.html*), noting that RDN is now known as Intute;
- Arts and Humanities AHDS (AHRC) and e-Social Science (ESRC) and related training and awareness material, e.g. ReDReSS;
- catalogues and directories, such as Z-Directory (UKOLN), Z39.50 target directory (Index Data), RSS-Express (UKOLN), OAI data providers (OAI), IESR (JISC), text-mining service (NACTeM), Digital Curation Centre (DCC) and any other specific research resources funded in partnership with the Research Councils;
- tools referenced in JISC Collections list, including high-quality online research tools, learning materials and digital archives for UK HE and FE institutions (*http://www.jisc-collections.ac.uk*) – these cover seven subject areas (arts and humanities; engineering, mathematics and computing; geography and the environment; health and life sciences; hospitality, leisure, sport and tourism; physical sciences; and social sciences) and also include resources such as bibliographic, reference and research information; publications online; subject gateways; data services; learning and teaching; and support services;
- National Grid Service compute and data nodes (*http://www.ngs.ac.uk*);
- supercomputing facilities such as HPCx and HECToR (managed by EPSRC) (see *http://www.hpcx.ac.uk* and *http://www.hector.ac.uk*);
- UK Data Archive and MIMAS (ESRC);
- Protein Data Bank (hosted at the European Biomolecular Institute, near Cambridge);
- large-scale facilities such as SRS, ISIS, Diamond (some managed by STFC) and associated scientific data collections;

- LHC Data Grid (e.g. GridPP, EGEE);
- NERC Data Centres and Centres for Environmental Hydrology;
- telescopes, e.g. via eSTAR services;
- British Library, national museums, etc.;
- others such as British Geological Survey, UK Met Office, Hadley Centre, ECMWF.

To this, one can add the range of digital library and institutional information services mentioned in Chapter 4.

There is an issue of combining global services and local services for a distributed research community. Global services are developed and intended to be consumed by researchers from more than one institution. Local services are typically based in an institution or facility and restricted to its members. For the latter type, e.g. an information catalogue, there might be more than one source of information available, issues of access rights, API and representations. These are being addressed for online publications by activities such as open access (Jacobs, 2006), but issues remain in other areas, particularly processes of research management where there are no widespread ICT standards.

There are other issues which need to be addressed in the longer term; some are already the focus of funded projects, but typically each is only working with one or a small subset of the services required. Service providers have to work together to see the bigger picture. The following are required:

- an appropriate open machine-accessible API for online services in addition to web access;
- a common security infrastructure for web services permitting single sign-on and delegation;
- access control via an authorisation mechanism which can differentiate classes of user, e.g. academic or commercial;
- a new licensing model, e.g. 'on demand' for data and software;
- a new pricing model for computational and experimental resources and possibly data and publications.

To help with such issues, JISC also funds a range of advisory and support services, which are listed in the JISC Collections Catalogue (*http://www.jisc-collections.ac.uk*). These services include:

- HE Academy Academic Integrity Service (*http://www.heacademy.ac.uk/ourwork/learning/academic_integrity*);
- British Universities Film and Video Council (*http://www.bufvc.ac.uk*);
- Census Dissemination Unit (*http://census.ac.uk/cdu*);
- Centre for Educational Technology Interoperability Standards (*http://www.cetis.ac.uk*);
- Digital Curation Centre (*http://www.dcc.ac.uk*);
- E-Research Interoperability and Standards (eReSS; *http://www.confluence.hull.ac.uk*);
- Economic and Social Data Service (*http://www.esds.ac.uk*);
- Netskills (*http://www.netskills.ac.uk*);
- OSS Watch (*http://www.oss-watch.ac.uk*);
- Procure Web (*http://www.procureweb.ac.uk*);
- SUNCAT (*http://www.suncat.ac.uk*);
- Technical Advisory Service for Images (*http://www.tasi.ac.uk*);
- TechDis (*http://www.techdis.ac.uk*);
- Techwatch (*http://www.jisc.ac.uk/whatwedo/services/services_techwatch/techwatch*);
- Text Mining Centre (*http://www.nactem.ac.uk*);
- UK Access Management Federation for Education and Research (*http://www.ukfederation.org.uk*);
- UKBORDERS (*http://www.edina.ac.uk/ukborders*);
- UKOLN (*http://www.ukoln.ac.uk*);
- InfoNet (*http://www.jiscinfonet.ac.uk*);
- Internet Plagiarism Advisory Service (*http://www.jiscpas.ac.uk*);
- JANET (*http://www.ja.net*);
- JISC Legal (*http://www.jisclegal.ac.uk*);
- JISC Monitoring Unit (*http://www.mu.jisc.ac.uk*);
- Regional Support Centres (*http://www.jisc.ac.uk/whatwedo/services/as_rsc/rsc_home*).

8

E-infrastructure and grid resources

In this chapter we discuss grid resources, in other words the distributed computers, instruments and data sources linked by middleware which can be used for research. We focus mainly on computational and data grids.

What is grid computing?

Grid computing (Foster and Kesselman, 1997) is a form of distributed computing in which use is made of a 'grid' composed of networked, loosely-coupled computers, data storage systems, instruments, etc. Resources are known to each other in some way, and able to transfer data and requests for actions using agreed protocols encapsulated in 'middleware'. Grids have been used for academic research since around 1995 (e.g. the I-WAY Project in USA and UNICORE in Germany) and also in commercial enterprises for such diverse applications as drug discovery, economic forecasting, seismic analysis and back-office data processing in support of e-business and web-based consumer services.

What distinguishes grid computing from typical cluster computing systems is that grids tend to be integrated from loosely-coupled, heterogeneous and geographically-dispersed resources. A grid is differentiated from a simple set of distributed resources because the end user should not have to access the individual resources in different ways, but rather the collection of resources provides a set of services (applications and data) with common access modes. While a computing grid may be dedicated to a specific application, it is often constructed with the aid of general-purpose software libraries and middleware.

Typically, but not necessarily, a grid has multiple providers, often in different organisations, and covers a diverse range of resources and services which are advertised in some way. Many of the ones described in Chapter 7 still need to be grid-enabled. In this book, the term 'grid' is used to refer to this set of resources (computers, instruments and data sources). Examples discussed will include the UK's National Grid Service (NGS; *http://www.ngs.ac.uk*), the North West Grid also in the UK (NW-GRID; Addison et al., 2008), TeraGrid in USA (*http://www.teragrid.org*), the Pacific Rim and Grid Middleware Assembly (PRAGMA; *http://www.pragma-grid.net*), the Distributed European Infrastructure for Supercomputing Applications (DEISA; *http://www.deisa.eu*) and Enabling Grids for e-Science in Europe (EGEE; *http://www.eu-egee.org/*).

For a light-hearted introduction to grid computing, see the CERN Grid Cafe website (*http://www.gridcafe.org*).

Grid deployment requires many things, all necessary but no single one sufficient: hardware, networks, middleware, users, policies. This should enable researchers to do things they could not do before using the combined resources. User requirements have to be taken into account, as do local policies to encourage participation and collaboration. To make a grid work across multiple organisations is very hard. Shipping large quantities of data requires high bandwidth and quality of service, but this is only part of the picture. The middleware has a central position in facilitating the integration of all these parts and providing common services. Middleware such as Globus was designed specifically to address these issues, but is complex and not widely understood, requiring specialist intervention to deploy and manage. One thing we have learned is that grid-based projects do deliver skilled teams of geographically-dispersed individuals willing to work together. This benefit deserves more recognition.

Cloud computing

Cloud computing is a general concept that goes even further than the grid in incorporating software as a service. It also aims to exploit Web 2.0 and other recent technology trends, where the common theme is reliance on internet-based services for satisfying the computing and information needs of users. The users typically do not own the resource, so instead of capital costs there might be a flexible recurrent charge for usage. For example, Google Apps provides common business applications online that are accessed from a web browser, while the software and data are stored on Google's servers. It is remarkable that the number of providers of cloud computing services doubled in just four months from 1 May to 3 September 2008, and continues to grow.

According to the IEEE Computer Society, cloud computing 'is a paradigm in which information is permanently stored in servers on the internet and cached temporarily on clients that include desktops, entertainment centres, tablet computers, notebooks, wall computers, handhelds, etc.' The cloud is a metaphor for the internet based on how it is depicted in typical computer network diagrams and is an abstraction for the complex communication infrastructure it conceals.

Cloud computing is nevertheless often confused with grid computing, utility computing (the packaging of computing resources, such as computation and storage, as a metered service similar to a traditional public utility such as electricity) and autonomic computing (computer systems capable of self-management). Indeed many cloud computing deployments are today powered by grids, have autonomic characteristics and are billed like utilities, but cloud computing can be seen as a natural next step from the grid or utility model. Some successful cloud architectures have little or no centralised infrastructure or billing systems. These include peer-to-peer networks like BitTorrent and Skype and philanthropic computing systems such as Berkeley Open Infrastructure Network Computing (BOINC).

For current information about cloud services see the Cloud Computing Portal (*http://cloudcomputing.qrimp.com*).

Campus grids

Campus grids provide the exception to the rule that grids traverse multiple organisations. Nevertheless, they often provide access to some wide-area grid resources. The reason why they are currently successful in research-based organisations (both commercial and academic) is that they integrate all available resources in that organisation (possibly across geographically separate sites) with one or more familiar user interfaces. Thus, a corporate information system (contacts, admin, publications) may be linked with pools of desktop computer systems, high-performance research clusters, repositories, data stores and research instruments. Campus grids should simplify the concept of user and VO management, as all users are in some sense members of the host organisation. Chapter 12 will illustrate how this was proposed on a large scale for a national experimental research facility. We describe it further below on a smaller scale, focusing on the Condor middleware. Other resource management systems like Sun Grid Engine, Platform Computing's LSF and Concurrent Resources Moab should also be considered.

With the current interest in cloud computing, but the pressure to enhance data security, we are beginning to witness the emergence of the 'campus cloud' as a solution to local e-research requirements. This cloud will have all the required ingredients of a VRE accessible within the researcher's host institution. It may also have external links enabling collaboration with fellow researchers from other institutions.

Philanthropic computing

Philanthropic computing is also referred to as volunteer computing and is almost the opposite of the campus grid concept. In this case, computer owners donate resources (typically PCs) to one or more projects. They do not know each other and accept simple terms and conditions, including security assurances, from the remote application provider.

While philanthropic computing can be useful for e-research, and software such as BOINC can be deployed on campus grids, projects using public resources (i.e. personal computers in people's homes) are typically the ones of widest public interest. These include climate prediction, finding cures for diseases such as AIDS, heart disease and cancer, searching for extraterrestrial intelligence, etc.

There is a basic, but often unarticulated worry that 'deep' research topics (those which are hard to understand and solve) are being ousted by themes of 'wide' appeal (which may be easier to understand or at least better publicised). This has already been discussed in the context of information in Chapter 4. If not conducted with due care, endeavours such as philanthropic computing and 'folksonomies' could exacerbate this problem.

Incentives and education are therefore required to encourage people to contribute resources to significant research themes. Who decides on the themes and who provides the incentives? Clearly, research needs to be better explained for non-specialists and the model of peer review would equally need to widen to non-specialists if this model is adopted (people will want to decide for themselves which projects to support).

A novel use of philanthropic computing software is to deploy it in a campus environment, e.g. a campus cloud. In this case it is no longer purely philanthropic, as the owner of the resources will also install the software and decide what runs on them when other users are inactive. Thus, a university teaching pool could have BOINC running research applications overnight.

Berkeley Open Infrastructure Network Computing

BOINC is available as open source software from University of California, Berkeley (*http://boinc.berkeley.edu*). It was developed originally at

Berkeley to support the Search for Extra Terrestrial Intelligence SETI@home project. There is now a large list of other projects using BOINC with public participation (see *http://www.boinc-wiki.info/ Catalog_of_BOINC_Powered_Projects*).

Univa UD

Univa UD was formed from a merger of Univa and United Devices in 2007. Products include the Uni-Cluster resource management software and GridMP platform. More information about Univa UD applications can be found on *http://www.grid.org* and *http://www.univaud.com/ about/resources/case-studies.php*.

Grid applications

The range of applications used on the National Grid Service and TeraGrid includes advanced scientific computing, astronomical and atmospheric sciences, biochemistry, biophysics, chemistry, seismology, earthquake studies and geophysics, earth sciences, nanotechnology, cosmology, genetics, geography, neuroscience, language, cognition, social behaviour, materials research, physics, stellar astronomy and astrophysics, visualisation and image processing. Many science and engineering applications in these categories have been developed over a long period. We cite the 30-year experience of the UK Collaborative Computational Projects (CCPs) and other similar initiatives worldwide. Here, these are referred to as 'heritage' applications as they encapsulate the research over this period in working computer software as a kind of knowledge base. We need to continue to use and adapt these applications, run sequences of related tasks, do computational steering, etc. Scientists typically have a mix of their own analysis codes and open source applications developed by communities such as the CCPs. Grid computing should provide a simple but more powerful extension of what can already be done using desktop and supercomputing resources. For instance, some of the applications have their own well-developed graphical user interfaces which scientists wish to continue using. This will be further discussed in Chapter 9.

Some Grid usage patterns

Combining distributed components for a complex computational process is carried out by all researchers using ICT as a matter of course.

Such processes (workflows) can be partly automated on a computational grid. One approach to doing this is to identify typical application scenarios (patterns) which can benefit several communities. An initial attempt to produce a taxonomy for grid applications was given by Allen et al. (2003) and included community centric, data centric, computation centric, and interaction centric patterns. A few examples are given here.

- *Data computed on-demand*: This pattern illustrates the integrated use of computational resources and databases. For example, data about atomic and molecular physics processes (typically chemical reaction rates) computed on demand or looked up in databases from a range of applications with different properties (e.g. accuracy, time to solution, etc.) can be fused with experimental data to extend the parameter space covered. The various data may be retrieved from existing, possibly international, databases and used together in modelling processes, such as for properties of stellar atmospheres or in combustion and pollution studies, e.g. production of NOx.

- *Analysis of data from experiment and observation*: This pattern also requires the ability to compare partial results obtained using different data-capture techniques on large-scale facilities. Examples include a synchrotron radiation source (Diamond at Harwell, Australian Light Source in Melbourne, Advanced Light Source in Chicago); a neutron spallation source (ISIS at Harwell); telescopes (Jodrell Bank, Arecibo, Hawaii, Hubble); earthquake simulation facilities (such as in NEESit). Repositories of data from previous work such as the Protein Data Bank held at European Biomolecular Institute in Cambridge can be used in this type of procedure. The existence of grids of telescopes (such as in eSTAR) makes it more likely that rare events like supernovae will be captured and studied, leading to improved understanding of our universe.

- *Parametric computing*: This involves course-grained parallelisation of meso and micro-scale systems to investigate multi-parameter behaviour at different length and time scales. Examples include drug design on the grid using computer-aided molecular design studies, and computation of multidimensional potential energy surfaces for chemical reaction studies. Philanthropic computing has been tried to facilitate such research, e.g. cancer drug screening. Post-genomic studies using docking procedures are also important examples requiring parametric search procedures on the grid. A third example is from eMinerals (J. M. H. Thomas et al., 2007a), in which properties of glasses and clays are studied under different conditions of temperature and pressure such as exist inside the Earth's crust. Information about such minerals is important in the study of pollutant transport and potentially for encapsulation of nuclear waste.

- *Computational steering*: Optimisation algorithms typically use mathematical criteria to converge to optimal solutions, such as the lowest energy conformation of a three-dimensional protein structure. In some complex systems, however, there are many possible solutions and a scientist might want to explore their properties. Novel computational steering techniques use visualisation or virtual reality to allow researchers to 'push' the system into different states rather than carrying out a full but costly exploration of configuration phase space. An example from the Realitygrid project (*http://www.realitygrid.org/AHE*) even used virtual-reality haptic devices to enable researchers to 'feel' the materials being simulated, and used Access Grid rooms for them to collaborate and 'see' the results of steering their simulations.
- *Data grid*: Data grids have had some clear successes. Rather than users requesting data sets via a web interface and receiving them on a CD up to a week later, they can now discover and download data directly online into their analysis applications. Examples include atmospheric and earth systems modelling (e.g. BADC, ESG); astrophysics (e.g. AstroGrid for virtual observatory data); biomedical research (e.g. BIRN, caBIG); social sciences (Census, BHPS, NOMIS, etc.); and high-energy physics (LHC data soon to be coming from CERN via national Tier-1 centres).

Middleware

There must be ways for all the resources to work together in a VRE. Some grid resources share core middleware to provide a range of services. NGS and TeraGrid have the Globus Toolkit, while DEISA has UNICORE. For more detailed information about grid middleware, see Berman et al. (2003), Abbas (2004) and Li and Baker (2006).

There must be ways for users to interact with the grid. The idea of lightweight middleware has emerged to make the grid more attractive to application developers for the following reasons:

- easy to use and install – no super-user access required and no special firewall ports open;
- provides transparent access to resources;

Virtual Research Environments

- small learning curve for application developers and users;
- easily wraps heritage applications, such as those from the CCPs.

Globus

With Globus, the emphasis is to connect high-performance computing resources (*http://www.globus.org*; Foster and Kesselman, 1997, 1998; Berman et al. 2003). It arose from the I-WAY project in the mid-1990s, which linked supercomputing centres in the USA (Berman et al. 2003). Globus is therefore often chosen for building wide-area compute grids.

The Globus Toolkit (GT), originally from Argonne National Laboratory and University of Southern California, is designed to integrate resources to form multi-institution grids. Its basis is a strong security model using the X.509 digital certification standard with delegation over TLS as described in Chapter 7. Globus handles heterogeneous resources by adopting a set of well-known protocols and extending them where necessary. Packages implement functionality of the four 'pillars': authentication and security (GSI/OpenSSL); resource monitoring (MDS/LDAP); job submission (GRAM, DUROC); file transfer (GridFTP); plus communication (GASS and Globus I/O) as a core service. Globus is available as open source software (*http://www.globus.org*). Command line scripts and a conventional C programming library are provided. In addition, other languages such as Java, Perl, CORBA and Python are catered for with community grid (CoG) kits (see, for instance, von Laszewski et al., 2002; Berman et al. 2003).

In the early days, researchers noted that Globus was a toolkit rather than a grid application or VRE, and that it had few good usage examples and little documentation, especially for the C API. The software installation was complex, requiring super-user access on both client and grid resources – Globus components also had to be installed on desktop systems such as PCs. Resources needed many firewall ports opening for communication in both directions. Nevertheless, the functionality was limited to the four pillars and GT2 was monolithic rather than being object or service-oriented. With the exception of OGSA-DAI, there have been few additional contributions; in fact there has been divergence (gLite is an example). Many of the negative features have been addressed in subsequent releases (currently GT4, which includes an interface based on web services). While support has been officially withdrawn for GT2, it is still widely used.

Storage Resource Broker

Originally from the Data Intensive Cyber Environments group at the San Diego Supercomputer Centre, SRB offers a logically distributed virtual file system (*http://www.sdsc.edu/srb/index.php*). There is a single namespace for files and collections which can be physically stored on multiple servers, referred to as 'vaults'. SRB works with most, but not all, underlying storage systems and has a large range of user interfaces covering most platforms. It has been said that SRB had a poor security model, but it has since been made to work with X.509 certificates, so can integrate with Globus. It initially relied on a central metadata catalogue for locating files which was noted as a single point of failure, but this has been changed to a distributed model. SRB installation and management of servers is still complex. Poor performance has been noted in some projects where SRB did not respond well to large numbers of file updates or transfer of large data sets, but GridFTP can be used for the latter. The software is not fully open source and user interfaces are quite complex. There is also a poorly understood federation mechanism which makes it difficult to use SRB to share data between projects started with separate SRB instances. The current version of SRB will cease to be supported soon and will be replaced by the Integrated Rule-Oriented Data System (iRODS), which is radically different (*http://www.sdsc.edu/srb/index.php*).

Condor

Condor, from University of Wisconsin, is designed to utilise 'spare' CPU cycles on resource pools, such as desktop workstations left running overnight (*http://www.cs.wisc.edu/condor*; Foster and Kesselman 1998; Litzkow et al., 1998; Berman et al., 2003, Thain et al., 2005). It can target heterogeneous pools because of its 'matchmaking' model which makes monitoring and resource selection possible from scripts. There are multiple 'universes' for various operational modes, but these have to be configured into the system when it is installed. Some universes can checkpoint and restart jobs in a homogeneous environment. There are many additional software components, such as Condor-G which can submit jobs to grid resources via Globus, and DagMan for workflow management. Condor now also works with X.509 security.

A group of computer resources operating under Condor is referred to as a 'pool'. This consists of some execution hosts (where the jobs are run); one or more submission hosts, where users submit their jobs; and

Virtual Research Environments

a central manager that maintains information about resources available and jobs waiting for execution, and acts as a matchmaker to combine a waiting job with a suitable execution host. The job submission scripts required for Condor are relatively simple to write and can often be generated automatically from a simple application GUI or VRE.

Support for parallel computing (e.g. grid clusters) is available, but limited. Condor is not open source, but executable versions can be downloaded for most common platforms. The emphasis with Condor is on high-throughput computing rather than high-performance computing; however, variants of Condor have been used successfully in situations where both high throughput and high performance were required. Condor is often chosen for building campus grids.

There are a variety of policies under which Condor can operate. For instance, a job might always run in the background on an execution host, or it might only run when the keyboard or mouse have been idle for a fixed amount of time, or a job may only be allowed to run out-of-hours on an execution host. Out-of-hours scheduling might typically be employed on pools of PCs installed in university teaching centres as part of a campus grid, making them available when otherwise unused as a valuable resource for research purposes, particularly for parameter sweep studies.

Uniform Interface to Computing Resources

UNICORE was developed in two projects funded by the German Ministry for Education and Research starting around 1997, making it a contemporary of I-WAY and Globus (*http://www.unicore.eu*). UNICORE has now evolved into a full and well tested independent grid middleware system and is in production use at several supercomputer centres worldwide (mainly EU and Japan).

Like Globus, UNICORE is based on a strong security model using X.509 certificates and TLS. Unlike Globus, it is implemented as a three-tier architecture with client, server and grid target tiers. The client includes a GUI and command line interface. We will return to consider this architecture in Chapter 9. The latest version of UNICORE is service-oriented and has a web services API.

There have been attempts to make UNICORE and Globus interoperate, for instance in the EU-funded GRIP and UniGrids projects (see *http://www.unigrids.org*).

Virtual Data Toolkit

The Virtual Data Toolkit (VDT) is an ensemble of grid middleware. The goal of the VDT is to make it as easy as possible for users to deploy, maintain and use grid middleware, making it less challenging and time-consuming. Ideally, it should require just a single command to immediately access or share grid resources – if only it were so simple.

VDT comes bundled with Globus, Condor (including Condor-G) and VOMS, plus many other components. In practice it simplifies installation on grid resources rather than client desktop PCs used by researchers. The VDT is a product of the Open Science Grid funded by the US National Science Foundation and the Department of Energy (see *http://vdt.cs.wisc.edu*).

E-infrastructure, SOA and services

Middleware is constantly changing and evolving. The emergence of the Open Grid Services Architecture (OGSA) provided examples of such evolution (Globus GT3 was an implementation of the draft standard); see Atkinson (2003) and Foster et al. (2003). Serious difficulties were experienced by grid application developers as the original specification of OGSA was thrown out in early 2004 and replaced by WSRF, now implemented in GT4, UNICORE and other toolkits. There is a report describing our experiences in the UK OGSA Testbed (Baker et al., 2005). The OASIS standards organisation ratified the WSRF standard on 24 April 2006 (OASIS, 2003b). This is important as we now have a stable standard for middleware on which to base long-term application development and support in an SOA.

More importantly, the adoption of web services enables lightweight clients to be developed. The use of web services nevertheless represents a tension between what we have described as grid computing and distributed computing, where the latter is typified by web service invocation of anonymous and stateless remote methods. In Chapter 9 we illustrate how these approaches can be combined.

Web Services Resource Framework

WSRF (*http://www.oasis-open.org/committees/wsrf*) is a set of six web services specifications that define what is termed the WS-Resource approach to modelling and managing state in a web services context.

Web services, as defined in the WS-I basic profile, typically operate as simple remote procedure calls with no 'side effects'. In using such web services, the client invokes the remote procedure, sends input parameters to it, and then waits to receive a response. The web service is stateless, so keeps no memory of being called. Services on the grid, however, are likely to be long-lived, so must permit their state to be queried from time to time. They need to interoperate to enable complex functionality to be built from basic services; for instance, two streams of data might be processed simultaneously. They must therefore provide their users with the ability to access and manipulate their state, i.e. data values that persist and evolve as a result of web service interactions.

Until the introduction of WSRF, the state of such services was typically managed by a portal, gateway or workflow system which would be responsible for coordination. This might for instance be achieved through choreography described using something like Business Process Modelling Language (BPML) and executed using something like Business Process Execution Language (BPEL).

While this is possible, WSRF defines additional functionality within the context of established web services standards. The functionality then becomes part of the service deployment layer, rather than the portal or workflow layer in the architecture. The functionality of the Globus toolkit, UNICORE and others is now available through a WSRF API.

Overview documents and specifications for WSRF are available from the Globus website (*http://www.globus.org/wsrf*).

A series of draft tutorials written by Asif Akram is available from *http://www.grids.ac.uk/WOSE/tutorials*.

Finally, we note that web services should be language agnostic. A Perl implementation of WSRF has been written by Mark McKeown (see *http://www.omii.ac.uk/wiki/WSRFLite*).

gLite from EGEE

The gLite software distribution from the EGEE project pulls together components from other middleware such as VDT and uses it to provide different services which are easy to install, configure and use. There is a set of core services known as 'foundation services' which are typically deployed on all sites (security, accounting, compute elements, storage elements, information and monitoring). Above these is a set of external services known as 'higher-level services' (workload management, data replica management, visualisation, workflow, grid economies, etc.) which support applications (see *http://glite.web.cern.ch/glite*).

9

Desktop environments and the web

In this chapter we discuss how to access grid resources and others such as those from the web or that are locally available, all of which are used in e-research. We consider a researcher's main tool for doing this to be a desktop computer (PC) or laptop, but other 'mobile' options are possible, such as 3G phone, PDA, internet tablet, etc.

During this discussion we introduce the concepts of portals and gateways to e-research resources. These give the desktop computer, or other devices, interfaces to the virtual research environment. Together, these devices form an N-tier architecture which is designed to address the 'client problem' mentioned in Chapter 7.

Lightweight grid computing

Following a number of discussions with developers of scientific applications, we identified a need for easy ways to link existing applications to grid resources. At the time of the interviews (late 2003), there were many reasons why grid middleware was not considered appropriate for the purpose (Chin and Coveney, 2004).

This section summarises discussions at a workshop on 2–3 May 2006. The workshop primarily enabled developers and end users to compare experiences and formulate a common understanding of what was required. Representatives of several projects with similar goals shared information.

Lightweight vs. heavyweight – what is the difference?

Some definitions had been developed in the RealityGrid project (*http://www.realitygrid.org/AHE*).

- client-side software should be easy to install and use;
- it should provide transparent access to resources;
- it should be easy for new users to get started;
- it should be easy to wrap 'heritage' applications or plug in grid functionality.

The latter point is considered to be generic and does not distinguish heavy from light. Nevertheless, it is desirable to be able to deploy applications onto resources in a straightforward way and this is a feature of some of the software described.

Alternative definitions come from Beckles et al. (2006), who note the following:

> In the context of computational Grid infrastructure, we use the term 'heavyweight' to mean software that is some combination of the following:
>
> - complex to understand, configure or use;
> - has a system 'footprint' (disk space used, system resources used, etc.) that is disproportionately large when considered as a function of the frequency and extent to which the user uses the software;
> - has extensive dependencies, particularly where those dependencies are unlikely to already be satisfied in the operating environment, or where the dependencies are themselves 'heavyweight';
> - difficult or resource-intensive to install or deploy;
> - difficult or resource-intensive to administer;
> - not very scalable.
>
> We use the term 'lightweight' to refer to software that is not 'heavyweight', i.e. it possesses none of the features listed above, or only possesses a very small number of them to a very limited extent. Thus lightweight software would be characterised by being:
>
> - not too complex for end users, developers and administrators to use and understand in their normal work context;
> - easy to deploy in a scalable manner;
> - easy to administer and maintain.

It should be noted that many of the items listed are 'subjective'. Is 'heavyweight' always a negative thing? Not necessarily, but new users can get going more quickly with an environment that provides 80 per cent of the full functionality but which is easy to install and use. They are more likely to try it out and, following a positive experience, put time into learning to exploit it more fully. AHE (Coveney et al., 2007), GROWL (Allan and Kewley, 2007), RMCS (Bruin et al., 2008; Walker et al., 2008) and UNICORE (*http://www.unicore.eu*; Erwin, 2002) are examples of systems that are designed to be lightweight for end users. All these systems have evolved to fit the three-tier architecture model described in Chapter 7. The middle-tier (server) is used to abstract away the complexity for the user, but is not itself lightweight because it has greater functionality than the client tier and requires a system administrator. However, one server can serve a large number of end users and connect them to a large number of VRE resources – this is in common with portal solutions. As it is managed by an administrator, the server can be hidden from end users and made to be reliable and secure and thus acceptable to the resource providers as an access gateway. AHE, GROWL and RMCS are also non-intrusive with respect to resource providers, as they use what is most likely to be already installed on a grid, e.g. Globus, Condor and SRB middleware (see Chapter 8).

This makes the system usable for both providers and consumers, so we also need to define for whom it is meant to be lightweight. In this context, the issue of scalability is important, because there are likely to be many more consumers than resource providers and there are only a small number of middle-tier servers managed by 'grid experts'.

For application management, AHE is also lightweight (Coveney et al., 2007). Configuring it for a new application simply involves editing two files, which can be done with a graphical 'wizard'. It does however have limited functionality and at the time of writing does not support multiple jobs. The three-tier RMCS system (Walker et al., 2008) also provides a simple application deployment mechanism. In this case, executables are uploaded into logical collections using the Storage Resource Broker (*http://www.sdsc.edu/srb/index.php*) and are then available to the system for matching to known resource types.

Some applications can run also on individual PCs in high-throughput mode. Middleware such as BOINC or Condor is ideal for this. Campus grids using university teaching pools are growing in number and popularity. Many applications follow more complex patterns, however, some of which were identified in Chapter 8 and require medium-scale parallel computing resources. There is a danger (perhaps a long way in the future) that so many people will adopt the grid that the resources will be used up. However, the grid has access policies, e.g. to balance capacity vs. capability, and it potentially enables entirely new methods of working. We must however be careful that we are not just using the grid when we should be buying a more powerful computer – compute power is certainly not free and is only part of the VRE story.

Desktop e-research tools

In this section we compare some desktop tools which have been developed to make the grid easier for researchers to use. These are mostly command line or script-based and focus on data management and computational jobs.

SRB Scommands

Scommands are the client-side command line interface to SRB (Baru et al., 1998). Installation of the Scommands on a desktop PC is fairly straightforward – just download the source code on a Linux system and type *make client*. There are alternative interfaces to SRB, such as a web interface and InQ, a rich client for Windows.

Once installed and configured to point at a local SRB server, Scommands are similar to standard UNIX file commands. Further information is available online (*http://www.sdsc.edu/srb/index.php/Scommands*). A few examples include:

- *Sls*: list the contents of an SRB collection, analogous to the UNIX ls command;
- *Sput*: put a file into the SRB;
- *Sget*: get a file from the SRB;
- *Scd*: change the working SRB collection, analogous to the UNIX cd command;
- *Scp*: copy a file within the SRB, analogous to the UNIX cp command.

With the Scommands, SRB can be used as a virtual file system to access distributed resources (known as 'vaults') or to create shared areas for data sets or applications.

G-R-Toolkit – GROWL and RMCS

G-R-Toolkit combines software and functionalities developed in the GROWL VRE-1, eMinerals and e-CCP projects. The main components are GROWL, GROWL Scripts, RMCS, Rcommands and AgentX.

GROWL, the Grid Resources On Workstation Library, was a VRE designed to interact with a number of intermediate servers, which eliminates much of the complexity of using grids from the client's desktop PC (*http://www.growl.org.uk*; Allan and Kewley, 2007; J. M. H. Thomas et al., 2007b). It also avoids problems of complex software installations and firewall configuration issues. Underlying services are available for wrapping applications to make them available or for relaying to remote grid and data servers. GROWL is open source software. It provides a set of scripts for installation of other software dependencies and for simplified access to grid compute resources. It also provides a programming library interface, written in C/C++ which has a modular organisation comprising functions for authentication, file upload and download, third-party file transfer, interactive and batch job submission, the monitoring of jobs and interaction with the SRB (if used).

The most significant feature of GROWL is that it supports an implementation of the three-tier architecture. The GROWL server acts as the privileged gateway to grid services; it is managed by a system administrator, has the latest security patches, and is effectively part of the grid. GROWL will also link to local resources, such as the clusters on NW-GRID and university campus grid clusters.

The Remote My Condor Submit toolkit (RMCS; Walker et al., 2008) has also evolved to support the three-tier architecture. It uses the Condor middleware (*http://www.cs.wisc.edu/condor*) on the server to create a simple workflow for pre-processing, remote job execution and post-processing tasks. The Condor Directed Acyclic Graph Manager (DAGMan) tool is used to define such workflows in a relatively easy fashion.

Various tasks can be included in the pre and post-processing stages. RMCS acts as a broker to available grid resource for the job to be processed. Typically then, the pre-processing stage invokes Scommands on the remote resource to install an executable from a collection for that type of platform and downloads any necessary input data sets. The main stage invokes the executable to process the data. The post-processing stage invokes Rcommands on the remote resource to create metadata entries, runs AgentX to extract data or do semantic mapping, and then uploads the data sets created into SRB.

While Condor works well within a campus environment, there are instances when access to remote facilities is desirable or where the jobs to run require parallel resources and not simply sequential ones. One effective extension to Condor is Condor-G, which allows Condor style jobs to access grid resources using Globus middleware (*http://www.globus.org*). Authentication is via the X.509 certificates supported by Globus. DAGMan can still be used to schedule long-running jobs or jobs with acyclic dependencies.

It is also possible to upload the executables to be used. Generally, Condor-G is more flexible and reliable than conventional Globus submission methods.

One of the successful applications of Condor-G was in the NERC funded eMinerals project. Condor enabled eMinerals researchers to use facilities across the UK, including NGS and NW-GRID systems (Calleja et al., 2005; J. M. H. Thomas et al., 2007a). They have been able to incorporate commands to access files stored via SRB as well as commands to generate metadata about different compute runs.

Rcommands are the suite of web service methods developed in the eMinerals project to facilitate creation and manipulation of metadata describing a computer simulation. Rcommands and RMCS evolved alongside GROWL and share the same architecture, so they can be integrated in a straightforward way with minimal changes to the underlying database schema. The Rcommands schema is currently a subset of the iCAT schema (see Chapter 3).

AgentX is a library that allows users and applications to extract information from various types of digital data source independently of the way that data is stored or organised. AgentX is standards-based, being built upon technology developed as part of the Semantic Web effort (including SPARQL, RDF and OWL) and is written in C/C++. It is currently able to extract information from XML and plain-text documents. However, it is designed to be easy to extend to other sources of information through the development of plugins.

The complete functionality of the G-R-Toolkit is summarised below:

- *GROWL scripts*: these facilitate software installation, management of digital certificates and access to data sets on remote grid resources;
- *SRB client and Rcommands*: desktop tools to manage stored data sets and metadata;
- *RMCS*: this uses Condor DAGMan to create and enact workflows to integrate data management and remote computation;

- *R, Perl and Python framework*: scripting interfaces suitable for many research domains from bio-informatics to social science;
- *AgentX*: a sophisticated semantic toolset using domain-specific ontologies to link applications with ASCII, XML and relational database formats;
- *G-R-T C library*: web service clients appropriate for application programming.

Application Hosting Environment

The Application Hosting Environment (AHE) (Coveney et al., 2007) developed in the RealityGrid project (*http://www.realitygrid.org/AHE*) is a lightweight, general-purpose VRE based on WSRF:Lite. It is designed to provide the scientist with a simple, consistent, centralised way to control application instances running on distributed grid resources and provides a hosting environment for running unmodified applications such as NAMD, LB3D, LAMMPS and DLPOLY. The AHE provides resource selection, application launching, workflow execution, provenance and data recovery functionality.

The AHE uses a GridSAM server to provide a JSDL-compliant interface to a number of different distributed resource managers, including GT2, Sun Grid Engine and Condor. The Job Submission Definition Language (JSDL) is an OGF specification. Like RMCS, the AHE provides a uniform interface to access both local campus-based resources (e.g. running SGE) and grid resources (e.g. running Globus). The AHE is currently deployed at several sites in the UK and used to facilitate scientific access to the UK National Grid Service and US TeraGrid.

Simple API for Grid Applications

The Simple API for Grid Applications (SAGA) is an OGF specification which provides a well-defined API to a set of grid methods in functional areas such as job management, resource, data and access, logical files and data streams.

There is a likely mapping between these and subsets of functionality which have been implemented in G-R-Toolkit and AHE. There is already a convergence in the architecture for such software, and the SAGA API could be used to promote interoperability in the future. SAGA could also be used in portals where underlying grid services must be invoked as part of the VRE logic.

E-research portals

In this section we discuss web-based portals for e-research as a pervasive alternative to desktop tools (Yang et al., 2007a, 2007b, 2007c, 2007d).

What kinds of portals are met by researchers?

The researcher is likely to meet web browser-based portal technology in three work situations: (1) the institutional portal provided as a gateway to the services and information of an institution or large facility and maintained by central IT staff; (2) a project portal with all the resources of a particular multi-institution research project, i.e. a virtual organisation, probably maintained by project staff on a part-time basis; and (3) a service (subject-specific) portal provided for access to a specific service, e.g. a national data centre, maintained by paid IT staff as part of the service.

The following definition is from Wikipedia:

> Web portals are sites on the World Wide Web that typically provide personalized capabilities to their visitors. They are designed to use distributed applications, different numbers and types of middleware and hardware to provide services from a number of different sources. In addition, business portals are designed to share collaboration in workplaces. A further business driven requirement of portals is that the content be able to work on multiple platforms such as personal computers, personal digital assistants (PDAs) and cell phones.
>
> Many public access portals started initially as either internet directories (notably Yahoo!) and/or search engines (Excite, Lycos, AltaVista, infoseek and Hotbot among the old ones). The expansion of service provision occurred as a strategy to secure the user base and lengthen the time a user stays on the portal. Services which require user registration such as free e-mail, customization features, and chat rooms were considered to enhance repeat use of the portal. Game, chat, e-mail, news and other services also tend to make users stay longer, thereby increasing the potential for advertisement revenue.

Different types of portal are defined, including regional web portal, government web portal and enterprise web portal.

Institutional or facility portals

Wikipedia goes on to say:

> In the early 2000s, a major industry shift in web portal focus has been the corporate intranet portal, or 'enterprise web'. Where expecting millions of un-affiliated users to return to a public web portal has been something of a mediocre financial success, using a private web portal to unite the web communications and thinking inside a large corporation has begun to be seen by many as both a labour saving and a money saving technology. Some analysts have predicted that corporate intranet web portal spending will be one of the top five areas for growth in the internet technologies sector during the first decade of the 21st century.

We might also refer to these as 'institutional portals'. They could be designed for or provide views on common intranet services for a variety of purposes, such as e-learning, e-research, information management, administration, etc. A comprehensive book describes the state of the art in designing corporate portals circa 2001 (Collins, 2001).

In this context, Phifer et al. (2005) define 'higher education' portals as 'enterprise portals integrated with administrative, academic and other applications of interest to students, faculty and staff'. The authors placed them high up on the 'slope of enlightenment' in their 2005 HE hype cycle because, although budgetary constraints have slowed down adoption, they are emerging as key institutional interfaces for online resources and applications.

Many universities have started to develop portals, usually from a student portal and then moving on to other stakeholder groups, e.g. prospective students, staff, alumni. These can use portal software, e.g. Luminis, or can utilise the portal features of other enterprise software, e.g. Oracle or WebCT. Open source portals are also available, e.g. uPortal (*http://www.uportal.org*) and Sakai (*http://www.sakaiproject.org/portal*). Other organisations, such as the Research Councils, are developing their own portals, e.g. ESRC Society Today (*http://www.esrcsocietytoday.ac.uk*).

Two institutional research portal projects were piloted under the JISC VRE-1 programme: ELVI (Evaluation of a Large VRE Implementation) at Nottingham University (*http://www.nottingham.ac.uk/research-systems*); and EVIE (Embedding a VRE in an Institutional Environment) at Leeds University (Sergeant et al., 2006; Stanley, 2007). These sought to evaluate the embedding of research tools into institutional portals.

Outcomes of the requirements analysis from EVIE have already been mentioned.

Some features of enterprise portals are as follows:

- *single point of contact*: the portal becomes the delivery mechanism for all business information services – a one-stop shop;
- *collaboration*: portal (institution) members can communicate synchronously through chat or messaging, or asynchronously through threaded discussion and e-mail digests, fora and blogs;
- *content and document management*: services that support the full lifecycle of document creation and provide mechanisms for authoring, approval, version control, scheduled publishing, indexing and searching;
- *personalisation*: the ability for portal members to subscribe to specific types of content and services – users can customise the look and feel of their environment;
- *integration*: the combination of functions and data from multiple systems into new components, e.g. as portlets.

Most enterprise portals provide single sign-on capabilities to their users. Access control lists manage the mapping between portal content and services over the portal user base. This is facilitated by a corporate data repository within the institution.

Project portals (science gateways)

While an enterprise portal might be very good for business, e-learning and administration, it provides an outward-facing representation of the processes and community within a single institution or organisation. A project portal used for e-research will typically be used by people from many organisations so must be free of such institutional structure. We refer to this grouping of people and underlying resources as a virtual organisation.

The logic underlying a project portal must facilitate sharing of data and resources within the VO, which means across institutional administrative boundaries. This typically requires grid middleware to comply with differing standards, policies and procedures.

Service and subject-specific portals

Service-based portals are now very common. Examples include Google, Amazon and eBay, which are familiar to millions of people worldwide.

They share many similarities with project portals, but are focused on the end-to-end delivery of specific services or sets of services to their customers/users. They can therefore be based on published or proprietary standards.

There are many subject-specific portals to services mentioned in previous chapters, such as Cornell University's arXiv (*http://arxiv.org*), the NIH's PubMed (*http://www.pubmed.com*), and the UK equivalent, UK PubMed Central (*http://ukpmc.ac.uk*). Many experienced researchers prefer subject-specific portals which contain deep search and other facilities that they can use based on specialist vocabulary and subject knowledge.

Example Grid portals

Grid portals fall into the categories of service portal or project portal. The ones listed here are really service portals, but their functionality is cloned in some of the project portals listed in Appendix A.

The NGS Portal

The NGS Portal started as a simple web-based way to invoke the underlying functionality of the Globus Toolkit without having to install it on one's own desktop computer. The four 'pillars' of Globus were invoked from separate portlets, namely: authentication using grid certificates and MyProxy; resource status using MDS; job submission using GRAM; and file transfer using GridFTP. The functionality of these portlets could be embedded in any JSR 168 compliant framework such as GridSphere, LifeRay, uPortal or Sakai (Yang et al., 2006).

More recently the NGS Portal has become a vehicle for using and developing emerging grid standards such as JSDL. A job submission portlet was developed to use JSDL rather than the older Resource Specification Language (RSL) used in the Globus GRAM service. A repository was created so that JSDL documents for each application, once tested, could be made available for other users in a process of community building. Thus, a new user wishing to run an application on the grid can check the repository for existing descriptions which can be edited and used to simplify their work. More recently still, extensions to JSDL have been developed to support parameter sweep applications in addition to submission of single jobs. This is currently being tested and portlets will be supplied for the main usage scenarios.

The GridFTP portlet in the NGS Portal has also been extended to support multiple file transfer protocols including GridFTP, SCP, SRB, webDav, etc. using extensions of the Apache Commons Virtual File System.

The TeraGrid User Portal

While from the same origins, the US TeraGrid User Portal has taken a slightly different route. It still uses the original Globus pillars for its main portlets and its functionality is based on the Open Grid Computing Environment (OGCE), which provides portlets tested with GridSphere and Sakai (*http://www.collab-ogce.org/nmi/portal*). GridSphere is currently the framework of choice, but others could be used. The main portal is at *http://portal.teragrid.org*. In addition to the Globus pillars, portlets provide information about resources, documentation, training, consulting (helpdesk) and information about resource allocations.

Once logged in, it provides access to the full range of services, including grid computing, data management and scientific visualisation. The latter is achieved via the TeraGrid Visualisation Gateway which is a separate portal developed at the University of Illinois. TeraGrid encourages the creation of a separate community portal for each large participating project, as listed in Appendix A.

The NICE Portal

NICE Software, based in Italy, provide a commercial grid portal framework called EnginFrame (*http://www.nice-software.com*). Portlets in EnginFrame provide web-based access to the EGEE and DEISA grids in Europe and are used by a number of companies.

In addition to the usual grid functionality, an important feature of the NICE Portal is its visualisation capability. This is achieved in a web context by using virtual network computing so that images can be generated on the portal server or elsewhere and displayed on the user's desktop computer. IBM has adopted this technology as part of its deep computing visualisation solution. The NICE Portal is also able to work with Eclipse, Platform Computing LSF and Microsoft SharePoint infrastructures in addition to the Globus Toolkit.

The P-GRADE Portal

The P-GRADE Project at SZTAKI in Hungary and University of Westminster in UK has used the GridSphere framework to develop a variety of portlets supporting workflow functionality (see *http://portal.p-grade.hu*). Applications are integrated using the GEMLCA middleware, which offers application management functionalities similar to GridSAM and AHE. This in turn uses Globus or EGEE middleware to run jobs on grid resources. P-GRADE is focused on running parametric studies using its built-in graphical workflow system. The P-GRADE Portal is available as a user interface to many European grids, including those in the UK, Poland, Hungary, Turkey, Ireland, Baltic area, Croatia and Bulgaria. The P-GRADE portal is now open source software, so the portlets could be integrated with collaboration tools developed elsewhere for use in a VRE.

Portals of the future

There is currently no rich way to visualise data and information except through interfaces such as virtual network computing as used in the NICE Portal. New methods of relating information are needed to help us create knowledge, which is the goal of research. Concept mapping techniques helping us to explore and extend existing domain knowledge should be tried alongside more usual portal discovery interfaces – a wide and flexible view is required. Using Access Grid nodes and three-dimensional virtual reality caves could also be tried as visual user interfaces. Some projects in the JISC VRE-2 programme could help with the technology.

If we go to another extreme, the same sources of information and underlying technology must be provided to field workers or researchers in other 'extreme conditions'. Devices such as PDAs are relatively simple to integrate. What about a scientist involved in a complex and dangerous procedure, maybe underwater or in the canopy of the Amazon rain forest, wanting to get information? A tiny, but very precise view is required. Context-based audio control and delivery might be the only way to use the full range of human senses effectively.

There will always be more than one portal from various sources and a choice of portlets offering similar functionality. It is therefore useful to provide a repository of tested portlets which can access the more important resources, such as the NGS and national digital repositories. This portlet repository could be extended with contributions from the community, perhaps working with more experienced developers who have previously been involved in JISC programmes. The repository could also include open source portlets from independent sources and all could be tested in a variety of portal frameworks. There is a provisional list of

Virtual Research Environments

open source portlets on the eReSS wiki (*http://penfold.lib.hull.ac.uk: 8080/confluence/dashboard.action*); this is reproduced in Appendix B.

In addition to a repository of pre-tested portlets enabling projects to quickly create and deploy reliable portals, it is possibly useful to provide a personal portal providing similar functionality. This could be distributed on CD with a minimum set of portlets for the researcher to deploy on their own project server, giving the project team immediate access to a range of research services which could be extended. It is worth noting that a number of the popular portal frameworks come with a useful set of portlets 'out of the box' and therefore partly meet this goal.

Web 2.0

Despite what has been said about Web 2.0 (see Chapter 4), it is now delivering an enhanced web experience to many users because of the way it embraces client-side web technology (Yang et al., 2007a). This uses the functionality of JavaScript and Ajax (Yang and Allan, 2007b). Technologies like Google Gadgets make use of this, and some science

Figure 9.1 Yahoo! map mashup in Sakai

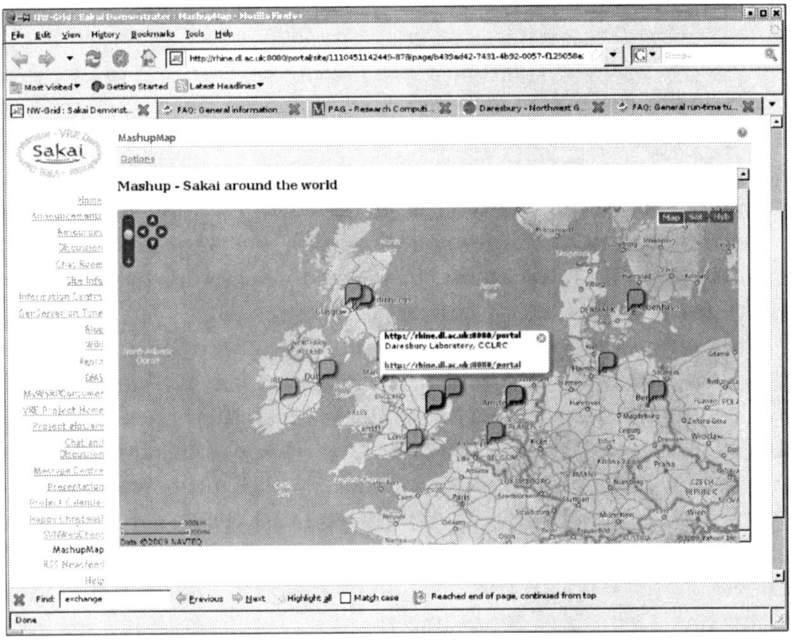

Desktop environments and the web

gateways have embraced it, e.g. Cyberaide.org. It is relatively easy to use JavaScript and Ajax code in portlets. Much less use has been made of Semantic Web technologies in e-research. This may be in wait for Web 3.0.

Another very important component of Web 2.0 is its mashup capability. This is being used in a number of research projects, one being MoSeS, as described in Chapter 11. Figure 9.1 shows a Sakai tool using a Yahoo! map service and mashup data stored on the portal, showing locations of Sakai servers in the UK. Users can upload and overlay geographical information using XML-based metadata such as GeoRSS. Other types of mashup are possible by merging different kinds of data sets facilitated by appropriate metadata.

10

The Sakai collaborative learning and research framework

Before giving examples of projects in which we have been involved, we first describe Sakai, which we have used as an example of a flexible Java framework for developing web-based VREs (Severance et al., 2007).

Sakai (*http://www.sakaiproject.org/portal*; Berg and Korkuska, 2009) was designed as an open source online collaborative learning environment. It has been deployed by many institutions around the world to support teaching and learning, ad hoc groups, portfolio management and research collaborations. Sakai provides a default set of generic collaboration tools together with other tools to support teaching and more.

The Sakai project is an open source and open standards project developing a Java framework and associated services. By focusing significant resources on building core capabilities, the project has provided a portal that is both immediately useful and which can be specialised for numerous domains through the addition of extra components. A few of the Sakai installations worldwide are shown on an interactive map (*http://www.sakaiproject.org/portal/site/sakai-community/page/d89dabbf-a033-412f-80c4-a38931056b26*).

The Sakai architecture consists of four layers: services, tools, presentation and aggregator. In general, the services layer manages data held in a database and can be called by other services or tools. The tools layer introduces logic that bridges data (service layer) and user interfaces (presentation layer). The aggregator works with the presentation layer to render interfaces in a way that is accessible and customisable by end users. While not service-oriented in the sense of SOA, Sakai matches well to our preferred N-tier architecture (see Chapter 7).

Default Sakai collaboration tools include: announcements, blog, chat, threaded discussion, e-mail archive, forums, mailtool, messages, resources (folders), schedule and more. Generic tools include: home, community links, glossary, link tool, message of the day, polls, preferences, presentation, RSS news, search, site info, site members, site stats, WSRP consumer, web content (iFrame) and more. Educational tools include: assignments, drop box, markbook, podcasts, post'em (feedback), syllabus, tests and quizzes and more. In general, these tools are pluggable, which makes Sakai highly customisable. By obeying a set of guidelines, developers can create new external services and tools to meet the requirements of their own research community. These new services and tools can then be plugged in or removed from the Sakai Java framework and configured on demand. The tools can be offered back as contributions to the source via the worldwide Sakai Foundation. This makes Sakai an ideal technical platform for a VRE system over which the developers and end users have complete control.

Sakai's detailed architecture is more complex but also more constraining than what is typically available from a web application using Java servlets, or from a standard portlet framework such as LifeRay or GridSphere. There are however a number of reasons that Sakai needed its own framework with core services:

- A Sakai installation must be dynamically configurable: with 20 or more tools typically running in Sakai, it is important that a problem in one tool cannot adversely affect the behaviour of any other component. Any tool can be added or removed without harming the system.
- Even though Sakai is assembled from tools that are independently developed, it must function smoothly with the natural feel of a single application. Sakai provides a style guide and a set of presentation widgets to help keep its tools looking consistent.
- Each Sakai tool must be produced with markup that can be used in a number of presentation environments including both HTML display in a browser and display within a portal.
- Sakai requires the code to support a capability (such as chat or discussion) to be broken into a presentation component and a service component. Among other things, the service component is responsible for the persistence of the data objects (chat messages, etc.). These components should be cleanly separated using an API. Providing a clean abstraction has made it possible to implement all Sakai functions as web services or as Sakai tools.
- Sakai tools and services should be production-ready and perform well at scale. There are educational installations of Sakai that must support 3,000 or more simultaneous users every day.

While these software engineering requirements may initially seem onerous to application developers used to writing Java servlets, the task is simplified by using the core services that Sakai provides to its tools through standard and published APIs. Overall, the framework provides the following:

- a rich set of administrative tools allowing the user to configure their environment;
- user identity and directory services with flexible plugin mechanisms allowing easy integration of technologies such as an authentication stack including Kerberos, LDAP, X.509, Globus, etc;
- a rich and flexible authorisation system that supports roles and fine-grained access control that is easily used by Sakai tools;
- an event delivery mechanism that allows one tool to subscribe to an event channel and receive asynchronous notification when another tool takes any action (this is a form of IPC mechanism); meanwhile, AJAX-like technology supports the delivery of these events right out to the browser;
- support for operating in a clustered application server environment to support large-scale deployments;
- a set of some 50 standard APIs to access the core and application services.

Sakai is therefore an ideal framework for the developer who wants to create a powerful set of tightly-coupled collaboration tools built on its core services. However, Sakai is not appropriate for the implementation of all tools and may be too heavyweight for some. Owing to this, and because many e-research projects are already using Java portlet technology but also want the power that the Sakai framework provides, it is very important that Sakai integrates closely with portals using JSR 168. We refer to portlets as 'loosely-coupled', because they do not use the Sakai core services to share information and synchronise events but are restricted to the JSR 168 API.

In brief, the JSR 168 standard was proposed to enable interoperability between portal frameworks and portlets written in the Java programming language. With the help of this specification, portal developers can use a set of standard APIs to develop portlets which can then be deployed under any JSR 168 compliant portal framework. The API is however limited in scope and the new JSR 286 API addresses some of the missing features. By using, adapting and integrating many pre-developed components from other sources into a flexible VRE, we can minimise deployment time and enhance uptake for many new communities and projects. Using pre-developed portlets can also ease problems associated with integration with institutional systems.

In summary, Sakai is an 'enterprise level' web-based tool integration framework with comprehensive underlying services, including role-based access control and database management support. Its major open source competitor as a framework for both e-learning and e-research is uPortal. Nevertheless, the two projects are closely aligned, with a common management board and shared input into JA-SIG (*http://www.ja-sig.org*). Small research projects have often adopted other portlet-compliant frameworks such as eXo Portal, GridSphere, LifeRay, Pluto, StringBeans, etc. Superficially these are easier to use. For a domain-specific project with only a handful of end users and if loosely-coupled JSR 168 portlets are sufficient, then any of these frameworks has been shown to be adequate. They do not however support the rich collaboration and integration capabilities and scalability that we expect in a VRE, which must simultaneously support many projects and hundreds or thousands of users.

Sakai was adopted by several UK VRE-1 projects, including the generic Sakai Demonstrator, the VRE for Research in Teaching and Learning and the VRE for the History of Political Discourse (see Appendix A). We continue to use Sakai as an e-research environment to support users in multi-institution VREs engaged in various kinds of research, e.g. Psi-k (*http://www.psi-k.org*), NW-GRID (*http://www.nw-grid.ac.uk*) and NCeSS (Daw et al., 2007). The latter is described in the next chapter.

Deployment and evaluation of Sakai for VRE-1 is described below. This tested and extended our understanding of practical ICT-based support for research, helping to answer the following questions:

- How can portal frameworks be configured to best suit the expectations and work practices of different research communities and institutional or organisational contexts?

- Can tools from multiple institutions and organisations be brought together coherently to enable sharing of information, processes and collaboration?

- Can community-specific tools be integrated meaningfully alongside generic and remotely-hosted web tools?

- Can a portal-based approach provide the flexibility to enable effective use by both researchers and administrators?

- At what points are desktop tools, or those provided by a mobile platform, more effective?

- How might these be best integrated within a meaningful user experience?

Working with Sakai

The Sakai open source framework was adopted as our framework of choice because its architecture is appropriate for agile development and deployment, it comes with a rich suite of built-in tools, and it is easy to use. The Sakai framework had already been used in the US Open Grid Computing Environment (OGCE; *http://www.collab-ogce.org/nmi/portal*) and in some TeraGrid science gateways, as mentioned in Chapter 8. In papers based on our work (Allan et al., 2007; Severance et al., 2007; Yang and Allan, 2007a) we have shared our experience of extending Sakai to fulfil the complex demands arising from all parts of the research lifecycle (Klyne, 2005). This was largely achieved by combining existing tools with new ones to give the required capabilities. Other technical deliverables included enabling access to 'hosted' services through WSRP, the Web Services for Remote Portlets (OASIS, 2003a) and illustrating how Web 2.0 style approaches (O'Reilly, 2005) can be used to enrich the interface and the user experience. We also evaluated how such a VRE system could be used simultaneously to support a number of related virtual research communities or VOs and to simplify management of research projects (Crouchley et al., 2007).

In the terminology of Sakai, a VO maps onto a 'worksite'. Through their worksites, bespoke tools can be configured to be available to the VOs that require them. Each worksite can be customised to have a specific look-and-feel with just the tools that are required by its members. There are a number of ways that tools can use remote services managed by a particular project or hosted as part of a grid resource.

We do not describe installation of Sakai here. *The Official Sakai Handbook* (Berg and Korkuska, 2009) begins with the history of Sakai and then moves on to how to install Sakai for the first time. It also presents a plethora of tools showing Sakai as a framework for easing the cost of developing extra features. Coverage also includes deploying and administrating a Sakai site and a section on how to build content. Case studies and experiences of getting management buy-in are presented, along with important strategies. Case studies include Michigan University's large-scale deployment, the University of Amsterdam's e-Portfolio, and quality control and commercial support.

Worksites and role-based access control

A virtual organisation represents a particular grouping of users with a particular set of requirements, in this case working together on a specific research question. Users will typically belong to more than one VO. Each VO can have its own 'worksite' in Sakai that provides easy access to the collection of applications, data and information resources required. The worksite provides a security 'context' or 'realm', which we will discuss below.

Sakai's internal VO management is through role-based policies. Users can be allocated different roles within each worksite. Roles can be extended by administrators from the small number of defaults, such as 'admin', 'member' and 'maintain' (Allan and Yang, 2008).

Clearly we need to manage large numbers of groups of users in a very flexible way. Figure 10.1 shows the process of accessing content in a Sakai worksite, which is described below.

Permissions allow users to access content from a tool configured into a worksite. As far as the user is concerned, roles are simply collections of permissions. For each tool, permissions can be set to allow or prevent users from seeing content or performing certain tasks depending on their roles. Some closely-integrated tools will share roles. Permissions apply to the tools rather than the content itself, as the tool always acts as the interface. Each tool can have a different available set of permissions affecting its perceived functionality, such as 'new', 'delete-any', 'delete-own', 'import', 'read' and 'revise-own'.

A 'type' is a broad user designation within Sakai. Each user can be designated to be of a specific type. There are a small number of default types such as 'guest' and 'maintain'; the latter includes the permission to create new worksites, which might, for example, be useful for a project manager who wishes to set up a related worksite for a conference or subproject. Worksites themselves can also have types, such as 'course' or

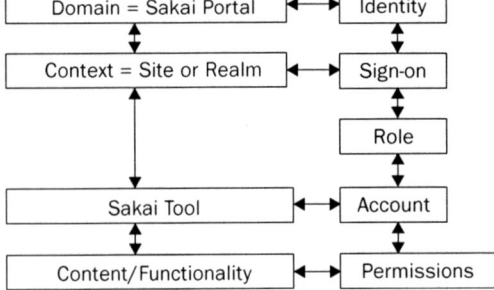

Figure 10.1 Context, role and account relationships in Sakai

'project'; this means they take on a specific template – we could, for instance, add one for 'conference'.

Sakai adopts the concept of 'realm'. A realm is a set of security definitions pertaining to the types mentioned above, defining roles and grants of roles and specific abilities to users. Grants in a realm do not apply to any particular content. Instead, a realm is programmatically associated with one or more tools (effectively their context). The grants of abilities to users in a realm apply to all the tools associated with the realm. A realm is really a set of default configurations stored in a template file. This gives sufficient flexibility to meet most of our requirements while being not too complex to manage.

Portal prototype: the Sakai VRE Demonstrator

The Sakai VRE Portal Demonstrator Project (Allan et al., 2007; Crouchley et al., 2007; Yang and Allan, 2007a) was one of the 15 projects funded by JISC under its 2004–07 VRE-1 programme (see Appendix A). The aim of the project was to create a working example of a generic VRE system based on the Sakai framework, which could engage with researchers and scientists and enable them to explore the benefits and capabilities of such a VRE in supporting their work.

This was a joint project led by Lancaster University, with three other partners, the E-Science Centre at Daresbury Laboratory, and the universities of Oxford and Reading. By integrating existing and new tools, the project developed a general-purpose VRE following an initial analysis of requirements (Klyne, 2005). While Sakai provides a base set of collaboration tools, several additional tools were developed to support geographically-distributed researchers, including the Agora audiovisual conferencing tool (*http://agora.lancs.ac.uk*). Other areas included: (1) management of grid jobs using Globus; (2) management of campus grid jobs using Condor; (3) management of research processes; (4) discovery tools and access to digital information repositories; and (5) data management.

Significant effort was put into solving the issues of interoperability between Sakai and web portals. Before the project was started, a web portal had been developed for researchers using computational and data grid resources provided by the UK National Grid Service (NGS; *http://www.ngs.ac.uk*). We wanted to reuse the JSR 168 portlets developed in this work to avoid duplication of effort. These would address the requirement for accessing grid resources from the user's desktop, as discussed in Chapter 9.

At the time the Sakai VRE Portal Demonstrator Project started, Sakai did not support JSR 168 but had its own API to core services as described above. As such, WSRP (OASIS, 2003a) was studied and a consumer based on WSRP4J (*http://portals.apache.org/wsrp4j*) was developed so that the grid portlets could be separately hosted and maintained but made accessible for Sakai VRE users. Figure 10.2 presents a screenshot of the unmodified file transfer portlet used from Sakai through WSRP.

At the end of the VRE-1 project and following some dialogue between developers in the UK and USA, JSR 168 support was finally integrated into Sakai. With the WSRP consumer also available, users could still consume portlets which were not deployed directly on the Sakai server. In this way, portlets can be plugged into and reused in the framework and remotely maintained portlets and services can also be integrated within the VRE. The WSRP consumer was developed as a Sakai tool and it has clearly proven the ease of extension of such a service-oriented architecture.

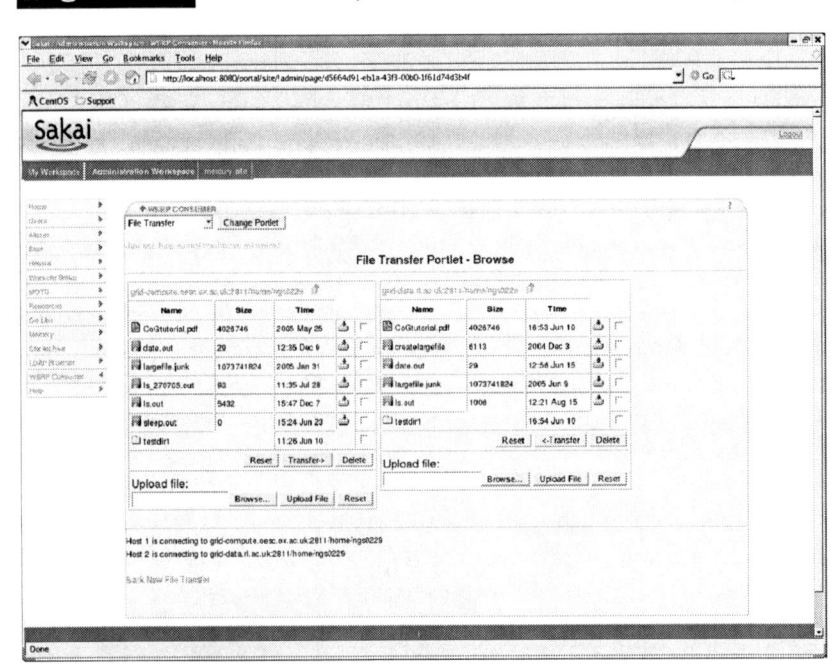

Figure 10.2 File transfer portlet accessed from Sakai using WSRP

Throughout the VRE-1 project, Sakai was heavily utilised to support project management, an essential part of collaborative research involving a distributed team. For example, a repository was set up within Sakai using the shared resource tool and nearly all project-related documents added. With the search tool enabled, this document repository has proven to be very useful. While users can log onto the portal to make use of the repository, it is also available through webDAV, which means that it can be accessed directly from desktop systems or exposed in a project website if anonymous access is permitted.

The success of the VRE-1 Sakai Portal Demonstrator attracted the attention of real users. In Chapter 11 we will show how it has been used in a large multi-partner VRE to support research in the social sciences.

Portal organisation and use cases

Here we provide some fairly generic examples of how Sakai worksites are used in a research context. These notes are based on actual experiences over the last five or so years.

It was found useful at the outset to define a small number of additional roles with appropriate permissions. 'Moderator' and 'member' were the most useful. Moderator has the ability to add or remove members from worksites and to set up new sites. These permissions were removed from the maintain role, which retains all other permissions concerning site content. Member is the same as maintain, but permissions are restricted to being able to add new content and modify or delete one's own content. Access is kept as a role for members who have read-only permissions, which is particularly useful for sites with non-moderated membership.

MyWorkspace and other worksites

When a user logs onto a Sakai VRE, they first see a number of tabs and the homepage of their 'MyWorkspace' area. Each tab navigates to a different worksite and shows its homepage or the last page visited plus a menu of other pages which have been configured with the required tools. Each worksite represents the resources of a VO, and the user only sees the tabs for VOs of which they are a member. Some VOs will be moderated as noted above, but others may be joinable. To see the list of joinable VOs and add them to the list of tabs, the user can use the membership tool in their MyWorkspace area.

As well as containing the help, membership and account tools by default in MyWorkspace, synoptic tools such as announcement and schedule are available. These provide a summary of information from all VOs of which the user is a member. Using the site info tool, the user can configure MyWorkspace by adding other tools and creating links to their favourite websites, RSS feeds, etc. I have found that web-content links to Outlook web client, JISCmail web client, Google, Wikipedia, etc. are useful, plus a private blog and private resource folder.

Project management

Large e-research projects usually have a large distributed team including project managers, technicians, researchers, members of a steering group, funders, reviewers, etc. Such a project might have one or more worksites configured with appropriate tools. The NW-GRID community has separate sites for project board, technical board and operations board plus other sites for specific research, workshops, etc. We have found the resources tool the most useful for posting meeting agendas, minutes and related documents. Schedule is useful for noting the occurrence of regular meetings and any reminders, such as who should take the minutes. Wiki can be useful for longer-running discussions related to the project or technical issues. The search tool is very useful, polls have been used in some cases, and site membership (the roster tool) can be useful for larger projects. A web content link to the project's public website is also useful.

Project management worksites are typically moderated. The NCeSS community decided that groups would be used in addition to worksites. In this case there is a general, joinable worksite for all members of the NCeSS programme, which has a moderated group for its strategy board. Only strategy board members can see documents belonging to that group in the resource folders. A group is an example of how different roles can apply within the realm of a particular tool context.

Project management worksites are typically accessed during formal meetings, often in conjunction with Access Grid. Documents can then be shared via the resources tool, and the wiki tool can be used to take minutes and notes online. Content from these tools can be projected onto the wall of the AG room alongside images from the other participants.

It is worth noting that, while useful in this context, Sakai is not actually a project management tool. We have found a couple of additional web or mail-based applications to be particularly useful as follows:

- *TRAC*: The TRAC project from Edgewall (*http://www.trac.com*) provides an open source Python application containing a combined wiki and ticket tracking system for web-based project management. It includes an interface to Subversion. Tickets can be assigned and progressed through various phases. They can be associated with the milestones shown in the project roadmap. In this way, a project can be driven as a series of milestones with tickets to ensure activities are carried out for their completion. A technical description of the work required for each ticket can be a page in the wiki.
- *Sugar*: The Sugar CRM (*http://www.sugarcrm.com*) is an open source web-based customer relationship management tool with commercial add-ons. This can typically be used to record contact details, notes of meetings and follow-on opportunities, including bidding for new projects. In a research context, it is valuable to share such information with colleagues. There are a large number of other CRM packages on the market, most of them commercial and designed for the requirements of large businesses.
- *JISCmail*: The use of JISCmail and other mail list servers has already been discussed in Chapter 5.

Integration with other web applications

There is widespread and heated discussion about web-based tools such as wikis and blogs; indeed, another book in this series is devoted to a discussion of wikis (Klobas, 2006). The Sakai RWiki tool was developed at the University of Cambridge in the VRE-1 project for Research in Teaching and Learning, while the Sakai blogging tool was developed at the University of Lancaster in the Sakai Demonstrator VRE-1 project. Both these tools are closely coupled with Sakai, and for this reason had to be written from scratch. Sakai also has its own threaded discussion and forum tools. So why were these written rather than using existing applications?

The answer comes down to the debate about lightweight and heavyweight solutions and also a consideration of what the VRE should be. We are of the opinion that a VRE should be a 'one-stop shop', offering a range of functionality from a single environment with single sign-on. This is what Sakai provides. Existing web applications which do not use JSR 168 duplicate much of the underlying functionality, for instance the security stack and the database management services. This makes it hard to integrate large self-contained (monolithic or stove-pipe) web applications. The applications are not exposed with APIs which would make them work in a service-oriented environment. The Portlet Bridge developed at the University of Reading in the Sakai Demonstrator VRE-1 project goes some way to making this possible.

It is of course also possible to use such applications separately. Indeed, if a fully-functional wiki is the only tool required, then an application like MediaWiki (as used for instance in Wikipedia) is likely to be more appropriate than Sakai. Unfortunately, there is currently no standard for the format of content in wikis or blogs, meaning that entries created in one cannot simply be exported to another.

Finally, it is also worth noting that Sakai is not a web content management tool and is not designed for building websites, even though it can permit anonymous users to view the content of certain worksites. For this purpose there are other applications which may be more appropriate, such as the following:

- *AlFresco*: AlFresco (*http://www.alfresco.com*) has a portlet interface and can be integrated into a VRE.

- *Magnolia*: JBOSS Magnolia (*http://www.magnolia-cms.com*) supports JSR 168 and JSR 170, has a portlet interface and can be integrated into a VRE.

11

Example 1: E-infrastructure for social science research

Social scientists form a large and diverse community and are engaged in many different areas of research. The work that we have done with this community since 2004 has been principally, but not exclusively, in support of those engaged in substantive problems of analysing quantitative data (statistical, text), as opposed to qualitative data (video, audio) (Crouchley and Allan, 2008). Another branch of social science is social anthropology. Here, researchers observe how people interact in groups and react to situations. In the present context it is relevant to understanding the drivers and barriers to uptake of new technology. The overlap of social anthropology and computer-supported collaborative working has been discussed previously in Chapter 5.

The UK's National Centre for e-Social Science (NCeSS) is supporting all these activities through its hub and research nodes and coordinates the ESRC e-infrastructure development (see *http://www.ncess.ac.uk*). The centre's investigations of the potential for the take-up of e-research in the social sciences has uncovered three distinct communities – the 'early adopters', who are keen to push to the limit of what is possible; the 'interested', who will adopt new tools and services if they believe these can provide (lightweight?) ways of advancing their research; and the 'uncommitted', who are yet to appreciate the relevance of ICT. This classification is fairly general and probably applies to many research domains. Early adopters from social science have been recruited into the NCeSS programme and are engaged in developing new tools or showing others how they can be applied. Seeing how these tools are used can convert the interested into adopters and research demonstrators can draw the uncommitted into the ranks of the interested.

We will see below that there is no single VRE for social science research, although there are some generic tools and some very specific ones. We will explain the reasons for this and illustrate some of the tools that are currently in use. We first go through some additional requirements, in the form of a scenario from just one of the areas.

A scenario from social science research

A scenario is a short story that elucidates the required functions in a context. We use a scenario that informs the necessary components of a VRE architecture and services for a social science researcher engaged in the analysis of quantitative data. This is based on the research lifecycle described in Chapter 2, enhanced with tasks peculiar to the statistical analysis of longitudinal data (Crouchley and Fligelstone, 2002; Crouchley and Allan, 2008). Similar illustrations could be done for scenarios from other research areas and this set could be widened, based on other reviews and studies in the domains of e-science and e-research. To illustrate requirements, we do not need full use cases as they are far too detailed for the broad picture we want to present here.

Our possible social science researcher (SSR) scenario is as follows:

1. Suppose we have a researcher (SSR) who could discover and access all the archived data sets from one or more national repositories and those used in related research publications in their domain and decide on the most appropriate data for their needs, without having to spend days reading through coding schedules and questionnaires.

2. Suppose the SSR could automatically access applications to re-estimate all the statistical models others have used on these data sets and see what happens if you drop variables from or add new variables to the analysis.

3. Suppose the SSR could quickly formulate, check the identification etc. and estimate any new models or combinations of existing models they thought might be relevant.

4. Suppose the SSR could redo this across multiple data sets.

5. Suppose the SSR could match their research questions to information held in existing digital resources and search for new explanations, perhaps in collaboration with researchers with complementary expertise.

6. Suppose the SSR could integrate multiple sources of data and text to help to fill in missing data and ideas and create publications.

Example 1: E-infrastructure for social science research

The kind of services or steps required in this scenario might include:

- discover and search publications and archived data sets;
- select, access and download data sets;
- reconstruct previously used models;
- recompute models on these data sets;
- recompute models with different parameter choices, possibly via a workflow engine;
- compare results;
- create new models or combine existing ones;
- repeat analysis across multiple data sets;
- match research questions to available information;
- integrate multiple data and text sources to identify missing data and ideas;
- create reports and publications.

What does this imply for the architecture of the required e-infrastructure? We attempt to explain this in the context of JISC's information environment architecture as shown in a diagram by Andy Powell as discussed in Ingram (2005). This focuses on information sources, principally libraries and repositories of publications, but is missing some of the key capabilities relevant to this scenario. These deal with actual data and its secure access and analysis on grid resources and are highlighted in Figure 11.1. In fact, broadly speaking, it links the information environment to the National Grid Service plus data repositories such as UKDA, ESDS and MIMAS, all of which are JISC services or have some JISC or ESRC funding. Many of them were listed in Chapter 7.

The original information environment architecture was designed to link providers to consumers via intermediate services such as brokers, aggregators, catalogues and indexes which might use standards such as OpenSearch and OpenURL. Other services provide registries for metadata schema and service lookup, and, of course, authentication and authorisation. Delivery mechanisms embrace portals (both subject-specific and institutional) and learning management systems. Many of these are as discussed in Chapter 4. Our vision for e-research is to enhance this with new data providers and computational resources, services such as grid brokers and specialist analysis applications, all delivered through VREs.

Figure 11.1 Extended information environment architecture

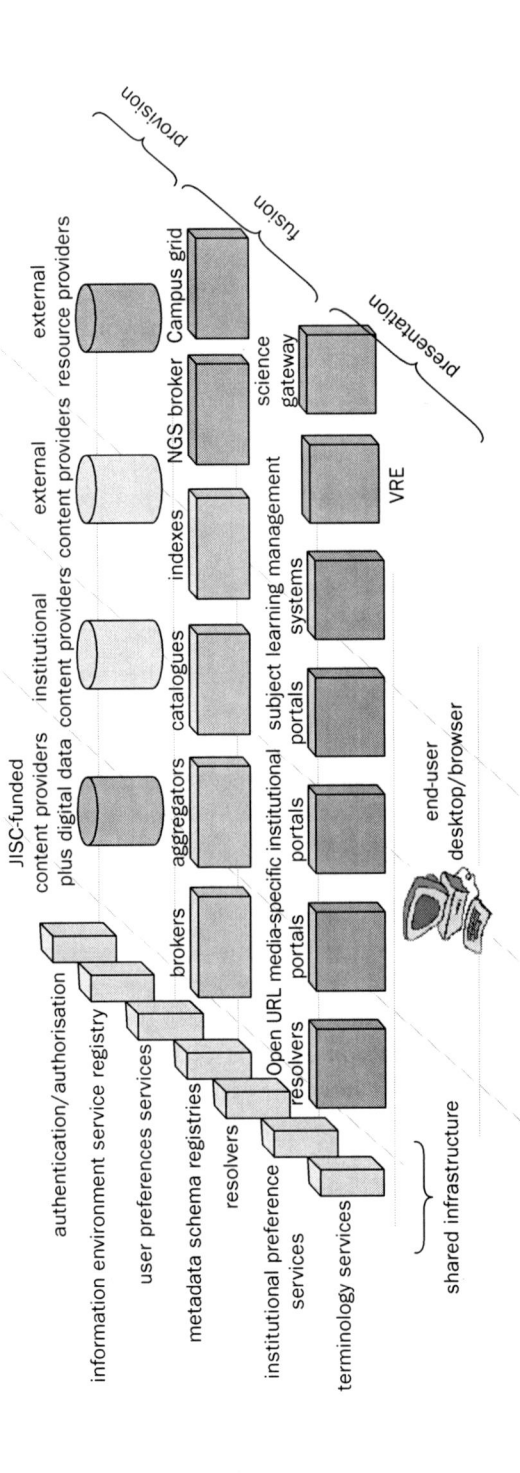

Source: Original by Andy Powell (UKOLN, University of Bath) 2005. This work is licensed under a Creative Commons License Attribution-ShareAlike 2.0.

Example 1: E-infrastructure for social science research

Step (1) of the scenario clearly highlights the need to link data sets to publications. JISC funded projects investigating this include CLADDIER (*http://claddier.badc.ac.uk/trac*), e-Bank (Lyon, 2003) and StORe (*http://www.jiscstore.com/WikiHome*). Institutional repositories of publications are discussed in another book in this series (Jones, 2007). At first inspection, the notion of content as used in the information environment may be different from the notion of archived data sets as in national archives such as MIMAS, EDINA and ESDS. The archives of online journals that contain copies of the data sets used by authors plus institutional research repositories also need to be included. So perhaps instead of 'content' we should simply use the phrase 'digital repository' to make it explicit. It is also not clear what presentation layer SSR would use. It could be a project VRE, or a social science gateway that is cross-connected to the digital repositories. One such gateway used for learning is the Intute Social Science Gateway, formerly known as SOSIG (*http://www.intute.ac.uk/socialsciences*). It could be just a browser to enable interaction with a web version of a catalogue, but that would lack functionality, such as the ability to cross-search, so we may need to add to the list of interfaces and underlying services.

JISC is also funding computational facilities for the support of research, e.g. the National Grid Service (*http://www.ngs.ac.uk*) which would be needed in Steps (2–4). Links to data, from MIMAS and EDINA, are being provided so that it can be accessible for analysis using applications running on grid resources. The infrastructure therefore needs to contain computational facilities such as these.

For Steps (2) and (5), we may also need new analysis tools which can run on the available computational facilities and new licensing models for the ones with which researchers are already familiar. For instance, commercial statistical analysis software must be made available with a licence supporting 'on demand' payments by grid users. We need to be clear that it is not enough to provide the physical infrastructure but that there has to be a set of tools and middleware augmenting what is available on the desktop. This has implications for the choice of service components. At this stage, we either want to use both the digital repositories and the computational facilities directly from a browser or as a plugin to a desktop computer application.

In Steps (5) and (6), the SSR will again want to use the journal literature, but will require the use of new discovery, content harvesting and synthesising services and tools. New tools must extend existing functionality by adding data and citations to the mix through cross-referencing with publications.

It is not sufficient for us simply to add elements to the original architecture diagram; we also need to look at the kind of service component diagram presented previously in Figure 7.1 and ensure components are accessible using appropriate standards. This will mean that the services are reusable and can satisfy requirements of the largest number of researchers and learners alike (see *http://www.e-framework.org*), not just those engaged in social science.

Social science research data

In the social sciences, perhaps more than any other domain except medicine, the sharing of data with other researchers or students and the reuse of data for new purposes is restricted by the terms and conditions outlined in repositories' end-user licences. This is similar for most data sources, such as ESDS, National Statistics, Neighbourhood Statistics and DfES. Strict control and licensing is indeed essential to protect the privacy of the individuals who are featured in the original surveys.

It is still current practice to obtain data on CD or DVD – the use of data grids is only just starting. There are still important data sets which are not currently available online. Registered users of the ESDS can however download and explore or analyse online a large and growing number of data sets in addition to ordering data on CD.

To illustrate the complexity of requirements, we cite the recent study performed by NCeSS to select data sets of primary interest in the ESRC e-infrastructure project (K. Miller, 2007). This mentioned the following data sources:

- administrative, retail, consumer, video CCTV and web usage data,
- data sets from the Medical Research Council and Natural Environment Research Council as required;
- British Crime Survey;
- British Household Panel Survey;
- British Social Attitudes Survey;
- ESDS International Service;
- Eurobarometer Data Series;
- European Social Survey;
- General Household Survey;
- Health Survey for England;

- International Monetary Fund;
- National Child Development Survey;
- Office of National Statistics (ONS) Omnibus Survey;
- ONS Millennium Cohort Survey;
- ONS Neighbourhood Statistics;
- Quarterly Labour Force Survey;
- samples of anonymised boundary data from the 1991 EDINA UK Borders Census;
- samples of anonymised records from the 1991 census;
- Workplace Employee Relations Survey;
- World Bank and Organisation for Economic Cooperation and Development.

Clearly data sets are from very diverse sources: local, national, international; open, commercial and confidential. The same survey mentioned the following requirements related to access and tools which inform the above discussion:

- access to data sets from other disciplines;
- availability of commercial tools such as SPSS, SAS, Stata for grid work;
- classification schema and variable mappings;
- controlled vocabularies and ontologies;
- geographical information system to utilise boundary data;
- linking between data and related publications;
- longer-term access to data via grid technology direct from provider;
- metadata registries;
- question banks;
- reuse of software and methodology from existing projects;
- Shibboleth enabling for access control;
- tools for geographic mappings;
- virtual safe setting for analysis of confidential data, e.g. Census Controlled Access Microdata Samples.

While this is illustrative of the broad domain of social science, many research domains have similar data requirements and diversity of sources.

A data gateway

To reduce the issues associated with privacy and licensing and to enable co-workers to collaborate, several research groups have considered the use of a secure digital environment to manipulate and combine data sets. An example configuration is shown in Figure 11.2. Using a secure server to do this and to submit large-scale computational analyses to run on more powerful grid resources enhances the ability to collaborate, but is at best an intermediate solution pending a full social science data grid. There is also research into virtual safe settings, but this is at a very preliminary stage.

The intermediate architecture implies use of a dedicated server as a secure science gateway, using middleware to interoperate with data sources and the National Grid Service. Client access to this server from users' desktop machines could be provided using a variety of methods, as described in Chapter 9. We are not aware of any plans for the large-scale data providers (e.g. ESDS) to allow this yet, although MIMAS is doing it on a trial basis. One project in Australia hosts a remote access data laboratory as a gateway service (see *http://www.abs.gov.au*), but this is not yet grid-enabled.

Groups using a data gateway need a shared file area plus a dedicated area for their users' own files. A range of applications, plus a programming environment such as R (see below) could be provided on

Figure 11.2 Grid hosted data gateway

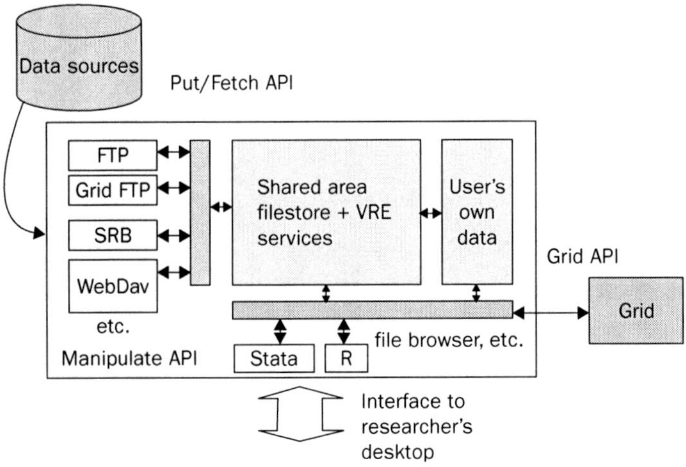

the server and also made accessible from the user's own desktop PCs via a portal interface or extensions such as MultiR (Grose, 2009), which is similar to GROWL. Software such as Stata, SPSS and SAS could be provided pre-installed on the shared server with appropriate plugins, but requiring appropriate licences. Certain data sets could be shared between researchers so that the server would be used as a cache for this data, again subject to the original source licences. Two issues require longer-term investigation: (1) how data will be moved from the source onto the server for manipulation prior to running the computational model or analysis; (2) how more flexible client access can be provided from desktop PCs.

Current solutions to issue (1) are: (i) obtain data on CD or DVD and upload it to the server. FTP or GridFTP can probably be used for this purpose. SRB or WebDav are other options. It is also possible to download data directly from the web if its URL is known and the user has, for example, a valid Athens or Shibboleth account. (ii) Some servers only permit direct use of client software via protocols such as ODBC to access data from its original source. It appears that our preferred solution of having all data grid-enabled is not currently possible.

Current solutions to issue (2) are: (i) a web interface such as RWeb or a portal; (ii) GROWL or RMCS client toolkit or similar; or (iii) GROWL or MultiR plugins to R, Stata, etc. running on the desktop (Grose, 2009). The latter would require some software installation and is currently far from trivial with Windows systems. Security probably requires use of Shibboleth authentication services, as these will be used on some data and information servers soon. Grid certificates may also be required.

Data management through E-Science

The DAMES node of NCeSS aims to deliver three linked portal interfaces: GEODE for occupational data, GEEDE for educational data, and GEMDE for ethnicity and migration data. These will link into the CESDA-PPP and UKDA/ESDS service providers. The portlet interfaces are being developed using GridSphere, but will ultimately be hosted by the e-infrastructure Sakai VRE. The project also addresses generic services for cross-searching of data sources using appropriate metadata and linking to analysis software such as Stata and SPSS. Clearly authorisation is an important area in this project for access to data and licensed software and Shibboleth will be used, as in the SARoNGS project.

High-performance modelling and software development

As noted above, high-performance computers are required for some aspects of social data analysis, particularly quantitative data analysis (Crouchley and Fligelstone, 2002; Crouchley and Allan, 2008). Here, we present two examples which are part of the NCeSS programme.

Collaboratory for Quantitative e-Social Science

The main objective of the Collaboratory for Quantitative e-Social Science (CQeSS) node is to allow people to collaborate in the understanding of quantitative social data and its underlying causes and effects mainly through statistical analysis and related computational modelling. CQeSS aims to facilitate statisticians, economists, educational experts and planners to work together to assess the causes of differences in educational attainment, the kind of jobs taken up by students, the effects of new school policies, finance, etc. CQeSS uses two approaches: one is to provide a portal for sharing data and collaborative working; the other is to grid-enable statistical analysis and modelling software to enable a larger and more complex class of research problem to be tackled.

CQeSS delivered open source middleware and a statistical analysis application called Sabre available on platforms ranging from Windows desktop PCs to the NGS. The project recorded experiences of using grid-based methods and working with other NCeSS nodes. This helped define the ESRC e-infrastructure project coordinated by the NCeSS hub.

The Sabre software is used on the grid for the analysis of recurrent events (longitudinal data). There are several alternative approaches that address explicitly the issue of temporal dependence between survey responses (Crouchley and Allan, 2008; Crouchley et al., 2009). Unfortunately, there is no comprehensive review of the relative merits of the different approaches for disentangling complexities such as state dependence, heterogeneity and non-stationarity in longitudinal data. In the presence of both state dependence and heterogeneity, different approaches can lead to completely different substantive conclusions about the causes of social behaviour. This is why high-performance computers are required (Crouchley and Fligelstone, 2002) to use the more sophisticated but computationally-intensive approaches.

One approach is the marginal likelihood method as implemented in Sabre (Crouchley et al., 2009). Sabre uses Gaussian quadrature for the numerical evaluation of the likelihood integral which arises from the mathematical treatment. Such techniques require the sort of high-performance computers that are available on the NGS. The deployment of such open source software on the NGS also removes the difficult licensing problems that can occur with the development of e-infrastructure. Sabre can also be accessed from widely-used licensed desktop software such as Stata and SPSS using a grid-enabled plugin.

R is a functional programming language designed for statistical computing. The GNU R Project provides many open source packages based on this language and a complete environment for statistical computing and graphics (see *http://www.r-project.org*). R can be provided on a data gateway and access can be provided via a browser from the desktop. R can facilitate the manipulation of quantitative model data using its built-in features which may require large amounts of memory, e.g. for handling multi-gigabyte spreadsheet data sets. Sabre has been adapted to yield a package, SabreR, which allows the user to model data using Sabre from within the R environment. All these plugins use GROWL web services which were developed for wrapping applications to make them available on the grid or for relaying data to remote servers (Crouchley et al., 2005; Grose et al., 2006).

The primary advantage of using SabreR (Crouchley et al., 2009) is that it makes all the extremely rich data analysis functionality of Sabre available from within R. Thus, R can be used for the pre and post-processing of longitudinal data and results associated with Sabre analyses. This allows a researcher to quickly and effectively define workflows (encapsulated as R scripts) for automating repetitive and time-consuming tasks, resulting in greater efficiency for the user and helping in ensuring the reproducibility of results.

To implement the required security means there are, of course, certain hurdles for users. To access the server to pre and post-process data and to submit and manage parallel Sabre jobs, a user initially requires a valid X.509 certificate as issued by the UK E-Science Certification Authority. In the future we will migrate to Shibboleth as a primary authentication mechanism with support for managing certificates generated using a local certification authority as part of the UK Certification Authority hierarchy. This will constitute a single sign-on mechanism.

For collaboration in CQeSS, the Sakai portal framework was deployed with a range of tools, some of which came from the previous JISC funded VRE-1 project. Sakai was also used in combination with Access Grid for a range of project management and educational purposes and is now also adopted by other NCeSS nodes.

Modelling and Simulation for e-Social Science

Modelling and Simulation for e-Social Science (MoSeS) is another NCeSS node, this time focusing on development of a national demographic model and simulation of the UK population specified at the level of individuals and households. MoSeS helps town planners to forecast trends in healthcare, business and transport in policy making by predicting demographic changes looking forward up to 20 years.

To make predictions, computationally-intensive agent-based simulation models are run on the NGS using a number of distributed data sources. MoSeS links into services such as the census for current and historical demographic information and the EDINA geo-linking service for mapping data on different regions such as electoral districts known as wards.

MoSeS offers users a number of different ways to interact with its simulations and scenarios. A series of JSR 168 portlets have been developed for the MoSeS portal, which uses the GridSphere framework. The same portlets will work in the e-infrastructure Sakai VRE. From this interface, PDF reports of simulation results can be generated via a simple workflow. These reports contain maps, tables, comparisons, etc. based on user-defined criteria. It is also possible to visualise simulation results using mashups with the Google Maps service to stream results into Google Earth.

Training and outreach

Training and outreach are very important in such a diverse research area where many traditional users are unfamiliar with the details of ICT. Staff at the NCeSS hub help to organise an annual international conference on e-social science which is a valuable event to demonstrate new research tools and the results they can produce. We briefly mention a number of other community engagement projects here as they are related to the activities of NCeSS.

ReDReSS

Resource Discovery for Researchers in e-Social Science (ReDReSS) was funded by JISC and ESRC and started around the same time as CQeSS in 2005. The goal was to provide a rich set of educational resources for social scientists to learn new skills related to ICT (see *http://redress.lancs.ac.uk*).

E-IUS

The E-IUS project is developing e-infrastructure use cases and service usage models which can feed into the international e-framework (*http://www.intute.ac.uk/socialsciences*). The areas studied initially are engineering, applied econometrics, computational biochemistry and corpus linguistics. Documents and video podcasts will be produced (see *http://www.engage.ac.uk*).

ENGAGE

The ENGAGE project is addressing issues that cause difficulties for users of e-infrastructure but which can be relatively easily solved. This is initially addressing work in four areas: high-throughput humanities for e-research, exposing bio-informatics programs as web services, protein molecule simulation on the grid, and enabling workflows in a shared genomics causality workbench.

E-Uptake

The E-Uptake project is attempting to widen the uptake of e-infrastructures in all branches of research. This project is jointly undertaken by NCeSS, the National e-Science Centre (NeSC) and the Arts and Humanities e-Science Support Centre (AHeSSC). It aims at a high-level approach by implementing a methodology to expose recurring, widespread inhibitors to the uptake of e-research technology. This is done through interview and questionnaire data which are transcribed and coded with additional metadata. Both inhibitors and enablers are identified. This will enable future training requirements to be targeted.

E-infrastructure for social science research

Since January 2007, the UK Economic and Social Research Council (ESRC) has been funding a three-year project to begin building an infrastructure to provide integrated access to a variety of data sets, tools and services for UK social science research, some of which have been described previously (Daw et al., 2005). This infrastructure is based on existing resources and uses software similar to that already deployed in other areas or via the extensive UK e-Science Programme which started in 2001. Many of the tools and services described above are being enhanced or repurposed to meet these requirements.

This part of the chapter describes the project, the aims of which are to:

- make available new, powerful, easy-to-use research tools and services to reduce the effort needed to integrate and reuse data sets, and simplify the way that research is currently carried out;
- make available research demonstrators to illustrate the capacities of the new research tools and the future potential of e-social science;
- enhance our understanding of issues around resource discovery, data access, security and usability by providing a testbed for the development of metadata and service registries, tools for user authorisation and authentication, and user portals and collaborative environments;
- increase e-social science capacity building by training end users and developing technical expertise;
- lay the foundations for an integrated strategy for the future development and support of e-social science infrastructure and services and produce a roadmap identifying the resources required to pursue the strategy;
- leverage the infrastructure investment being made by the UK e-science core programme and JISC for the benefit of the social sciences;
- provide exemplars of best practice and ready-made solutions to common requirements to support the plans of NGS, JISC and OMII to ensure that tool developers and service providers are led towards compatible and effective software and practices;
- promote synergies across NCeSS and other ESRC investments, coordinate activities, encourage mutual support and identify areas in which to promote the benefits of common policies and technology standards.

There are several challenging aspects of the project, which also tries to answer research questions such as:

- how to incorporate user requirements so that project outputs are appropriate, useful and highly usable to social scientists;
- how to move from research outputs to services for the support of social science research;
- how to incorporate this technology within the wider UK infrastructure as offered by the NGS, regional services such as NW-GRID, and the large UK data centres, MIMAS, ESDS and EDINA.

Research outputs

The e-infrastructure project supports all the NCeSS nodes and uses the software and methodology they are developing. It additionally provides a number of centrally-hosted services such as the Sakai VRE. The project outputs fall into three broad categories: research resources; support activities and materials; and investigations into the feasibility of technologies, technical standards, sustainability and project evaluation.

Research resources

As in all areas of e-research, resources comprise of software, grid-enabled data sets and the infrastructure on which these reside. They also comprise of people, i.e. the researchers, students and consumers of the research outputs. We again stress the importance of enabling people to access the software, data and computer systems and to be able to collaborate and interact in a rich variety of ways.

It is anticipated that the software outputs will provide straightforward access to the core of a UK e-social science infrastructure (computers and data), and will be used with sample demonstrator applications and tools presented on the infrastructure.

The user environment is comprised of a Sakai VRE plus other collaborative environments bespoke to the NCeSS research nodes, as described above (Daw et al., 2007; Yang et al., 2007a, 2008). The way Sakai is used has already been described in Chapter 10. Other portal frameworks such as GridSphere and Pluto are used for development purposes. The tools can be plugged into the VRE using recognised standards such as JSR 168, WSRP and JSF. In future, they could be discoverable via a social science service registry, from which the VO administrator can populate the corresponding portal worksite with the tools appropriate to their VO.

The project also aims to determine appropriate security mechanisms to meet the needs of all aspects of this emerging infrastructure and to grid-enable a number of data sets so that they may be subject to more flexible discovery, interrogation and integration ultimately through semantic services. Shibboleth is being considered for authentication.

Support activities

In order for the infrastructure to be usable by social scientists, the project is producing a variety of support materials, including documentation, learning objects for inclusion into learning environments (such as Sakai), and training materials, which are being delivered through workshops to introduce the tools and infrastructure to prospective new users. Some of the related projects focused on training have been described previously.

Investigations

The final category of project output consists of a number of investigations. Work to capture requirements for grid-enabling data sets (K. Miller, 2007) has been discussed above. This enables us to devise criteria for selecting data sets and recommending grid-enabling those data sets that offer the most value to the community at the start.

The project has also conducted a survey to assess the degree of awareness of ICT and e-social science to help inform policy and practice within ESRC as part of an ongoing, continuous process of engagement with social scientists on technical issues. This survey will be extended to act as a baseline to assess the future effectiveness of the UK e-social science programme.

A study to examine technical standards used in the project will facilitate an ongoing discussion of how the disparate technical elements of the social science e-infrastructure can start to converge. The study will take into account and feed into other activities in this area, such as work being done by eReSS (*http://www.confluence.hull.ac.uk*), the E-Framework (*http://www.e-framework.org*), the JISC Open Source Software Watch and the NGS in order to provide a cohesive approach to the adoption of standards by this and related communities.

Finally, the project is investigating issues related to sustainability and has examined the steps needed to take this initiative forward in order to provide an infrastructure that offers highly-effective and widespread support for many aspects of future social science research. In doing so, funding for a new project was announced at the time of writing.

The new project concerns social simulation, which is a relatively recent and rapidly expanding field with applications across the academic research community. Both micro-simulation and agent-based modelling have been widely adopted within economics, sociology and geography. Simulation models have also provoked high levels of interest in healthcare research, anthropology and political science. Policy interest is substantial within the public and private sectors. The project will build a production-quality e-infrastructure for social simulation (NeISS), covering the whole lifecycle. It will introduce social scientists to new ways of thinking about social problems and provide new services, tools and research communities to support them. The NeISS framework will be capable of being deployed for a diverse range of social research domains, not just limited to simulation. Tools within a Sakai VRE will enable researchers to collaborate, to create workflows to run their own simulations, visualise and analyse results and publish them for future discovery, sharing and reuse. This will facilitate development and sharing of resources, encourage cooperation between model developers and researchers and help foster adoption of simulation as a research method in the social sciences and as a decision support tool in the public and private sectors.

Research challenges

The main research challenges which we have identified are now discussed.

User requirements

We intend research resources produced by the project to be user-focused. They should be appropriate to the needs of social scientists, useful in increasing the productivity and effectiveness of social science research, and incorporate highly-usable user interfaces to reinforce and increase take-up. The realisation of these aims will enable the software outputs to have a significant impact on research practice and begin to realise some of the potential for e-social science. However, while desirable, these aims have significant resource and methodological implications that will be hard to meet in the context of this project, which has relatively meagre resources in relation to its ambitions.

From research to service

Much of the project's programme of work involves building on outputs from the NCeSS research nodes which have yielded many promising e-social science applications, some of which have been described above. One of the challenges for this project is to make the transition from tools that were initially research outputs to prototype services that can support a larger community and enable more effective social science research in the longer term.

This shift in emphasis has implications for academics involved in the original research when engagement in software development to create robust tools for others may not offer the same recognition as more traditional research outputs, such as academic papers. In the UK Research Assessment Exercise, by which universities are graded according to the quality of their research, software and service development are not highly rated. This leads to serious sustainability issues and poor career rewards for the more technically-oriented project partners. To exacerbate this problem, the investment required to develop robust and reliable software is high and may be beyond what a project of this size can achieve. This is one of the reasons why work to investigate the sustainability of project outputs is so important. There must also be management of expectations of what such a project can achieve that is commensurate with the resources available.

Embedding within a wider environment

The final challenge relates to embedding the infrastructure and associated tools and services within a wider environment as offered by JISC through the information environment and NGS (see Figure 11.1). According to its mission statement, the NGS aims to 'provide coherent electronic access for UK researchers to all computational and data-based resources and facilities required to carry out their research, independent of resource or researcher location'. While it is desirable for sustaining the project outcomes to embed the infrastructure within such an environment, the social science community is likely to have additional specific needs and present particular challenges to a model that has to date largely been focused on the provision of digital information and grid services for the natural sciences. Moreover, the NGS itself needs to address sustainability issues with a change of business model, perhaps linking into a larger European grid initiative.

Experiences with the NCeSS VRE

The principal vehicle to facilitate research collaborations in the ESRC e-infrastructure project is the Sakai VRE (Yang et al., 2008) established by NCeSS. It hosts a variety of Web 2.0 style groupware tools, some developed in previous JISC VRE-1 projects, plus tools for grid data management, job submission and monitoring. Use of the Sakai framework as a VRE was described in Chapter 10. The groupware tools which are used for collaboration include resources, blog, wiki, schedule, e-mail, discussion, chat, announcements, RSS news, glossary and Agora. Both the Sakai VRE and Access Grid are used by NCeSS for project management purposes and to support the research of its nodes, each of which constitutes a VO and has one or more worksites. Quite a few of the VRE users are members of more than one of these VOs. There are also several joinable sites where all users can share information.

A range of research tools has been selected for support from those being developed within the NCeSS programme, with selection criteria informed by ongoing consultations with the wider social science research community. Agenda-setting workshops have also enabled the project to identify a priority area: simulation and modelling. Building on the work of the MoSeS and PolicyGrid nodes, simulation and modelling tools have been deployed to enable researchers to run their own simulations on the NGS, visualise and analyse results, and archive them for future study and reuse. This facilitates development and sharing of social simulation resources within the UK social science community, encourages cooperation between model developers and researchers, and helps foster the adoption of simulation as a research method in the social sciences.

Portlets from MoSeS and GENESIS (Leeds and University College London) and DAMES (Stirling) are included for use by their VOs. Shibboleth-enabled authentication is currently being added to enable integration with online library catalogues and other scholarly information repositories. For direct use of Sakai to manage applications such as Sabre from CQeSS (Lancaster and Daresbury), the NGS Portal JSDL repository is being enhanced with descriptions of Sabre jobs. These job description templates will then be available for users to modify to meet their own requirements and to develop a community of practice. The same can be done for other grid-based applications.

In addition to Sakai, some NCeSS nodes have their own Web 2.0 style applications. These include ourSpaces from Policy Grid (Aberdeen) and MapTube from GeoVue (UCL). As noted in Chapter 10, it is difficult to integrate such self-contained web applications with a portlet framework unless their services can be exposed using an appropriate API and data interchange standards.

A set of generic tools and services, including workflow and visualisation, is also planned. This will include ones developed within the e-science community, such as Taverna used in myExperiment. The NCeSS approach to building e-infrastructure encourages community-level deployments of tools and services which can be included in the VRE. The programme is also uncovering requirements for usability, control and trust in qualitative research that are more appropriately served by a localised approach to tools, services and data, e.g. via project-specific gateways such as ourSpaces and MapTube. For example, there may be issues with the distribution of sensitive data to (and via) third parties or with the provision of new forms of data collected from participants who have agreed to its use only for studying a particular situation. Such issues will clearly take a long time to resolve.

12

Example 2: E-infrastructure for experimental facilities

The new Diamond Light Source (DLS) experimental facility built on the Harwell Science and Innovation Campus in Oxfordshire is the largest single investment in science in the UK for 40 years (*http://www.diamond.ac.uk*). DLS is a synchrotron which accelerates electrons to almost the speed of light. Steering the electrons around a nearly circular path with powerful magnets causes the emission of intense beams of light ranging in wavelength from infrared to high-energy X-rays. These beams are captured in equipment on 'beamlines' where experiments are performed as diverse as determining the structure of biological molecules to detecting trace materials, chemical analysis, medical imaging and forensic and materials science.

In 2005, this new facility was a 'blank canvas' for an e-science infrastructure to complement its otherwise standard and typically under-resourced IT provision. Such under-resourcing is sadly common at new-build experimental facilities, despite the fact that vast amounts of data are likely to be collected over a period of 20 or more years. No provision was made at the start to store, manage and analyse data at the facility. Effort and software to remedy this came from the STFC e-Science Centre at Daresbury and Rutherford Appleton Laboratories based on our experience in the UK e-Science Programme from 2001 onwards. The software which was developed and tested was also to be provided to other international facilities, such as the new Australian Synchrotron in Melbourne. The VeRSI Programme which is now supporting this synchrotron identified two principal issues around such shared infrastructures:

- researchers have to travel to use the facility, which is often expensive and inconvenient;

- researchers are confronted by the need to take huge amounts of observational data back to their laboratories.

We aimed to solve both these problems using ICT.

Requirements and prerequisites

There was an exercise to document requirements and develop a workplan for the rollout of e-science technology to support DLS (Gleaves and Ashtun, 2006). The early Diamond community identified two principal requirements: first, to manage access to beam time and the associated sample tracking and association of data collected with grant applications; second, to be able to manage the data they collected, to label it with metadata, store, search and retrieve it, and later to associate it with publications. The requirement to analyse the collected data using applications running on the NGS was added by others who saw the bigger picture of what could be achieved.

There were a number of reasons for initially focusing on data and metadata in this work:

- the need to preserve and make available data collected using public science funding;
- the need to repeat experiments in future, perhaps with slightly changed conditions, different samples or greater precision;
- the need to analyse and re-analyse data as understanding and methodologies evolve;
- the need to complement experimental data with computer simulation and modelling to enhance scientific value;
- the need to combine DLS data with data from other experimental sources, e.g. central laser facility (CLF) and ISIS neutron and muon spallation source, both also on the Harwell campus.

We visited and discussed requirements with representatives from different areas of work around Diamond. We illustrate the workflows recorded from two of the use cases here. Figure 12.1 shows activities of the Diamond User Office (DUO) staff. The user office is responsible for accepting proposals, having them reviewed and, if successful, scheduling beam time and associated resources on the experimental facility. The Magnolia web-based content management system (*http://www.magnolia-cms.com*) is used in this process with a custom-designed database.

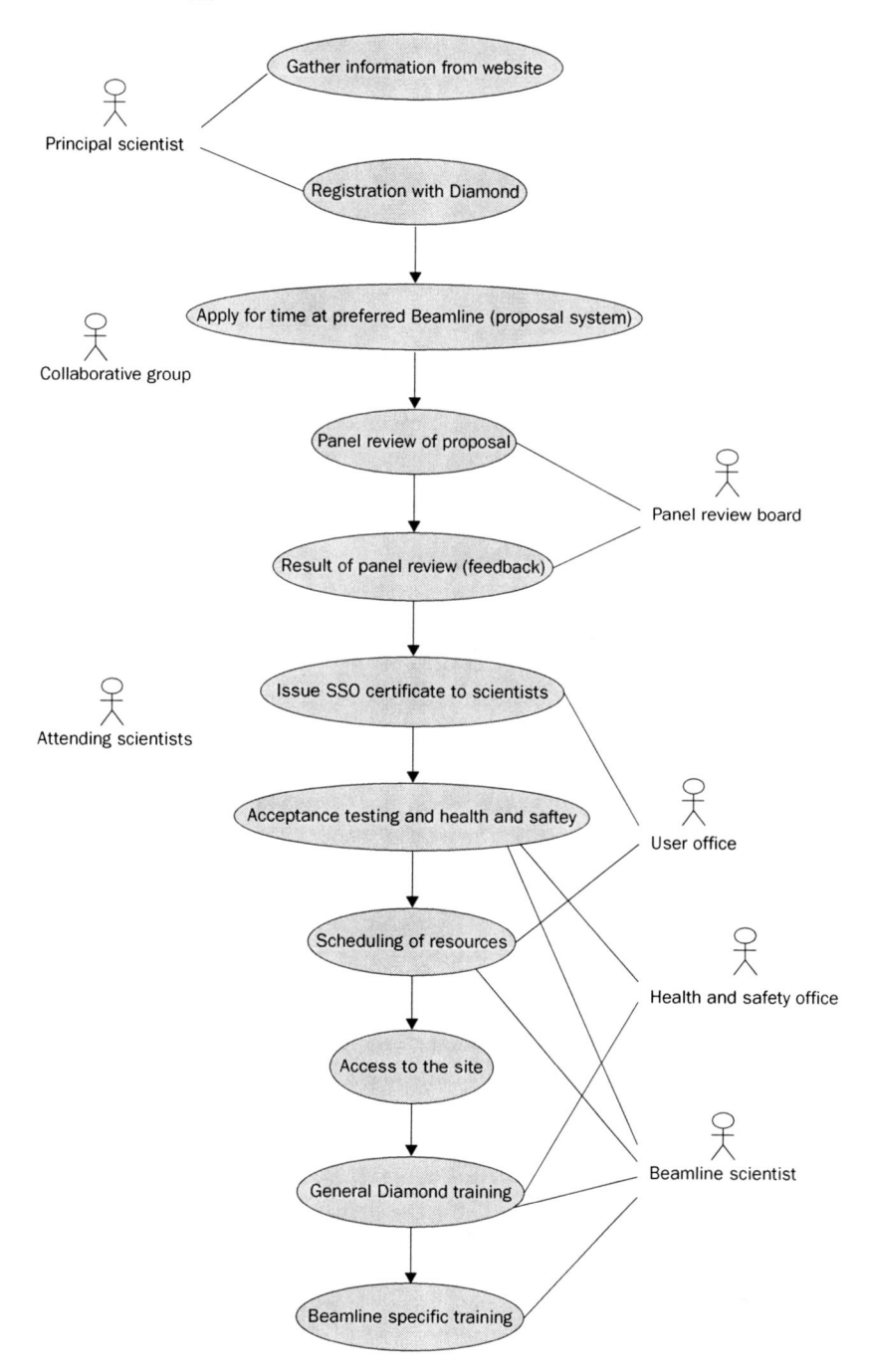

Example 2: E-infrastructure for experimental facilities

Figure 12.1 Diamond user office processes

Figure 12.2 shows activities around a protein crystallography (PX) experimental beamline. PX is also sometimes known as molecular crystallography (MX). A beamline is an area where an experiment is set up and data recorded, and it usually has one or more specialists working alongside researchers.

E-research, however, is about more than just data. One appealing idea was that research groups might want their students to visit the facility to carry out an experiment, say over a period of three days or so. As professors have other commitments and are less likely to spend this period away from their offices, some online communication would be necessary. As we were already using Access Grid in other projects, it seemed natural to experiment with it on the facility itself. All that was required was a camera on each beamline so that the professor could not only see his staff, but also the equipment they were handling, and use audio communication to discuss the procedure being carried out and the results being obtained. This worked well for demonstration purposes on the high-bandwidth UK academic network JANET, but less well on low-bandwidth connections, for instance in a test with researchers from Nigeria. Ultimately, we found that a high-resolution webcam with pan, tilt and zoom facilities and a Jabber text chat client for communication was all that was required to be effective.

There was a recurring discussion about single sign-on in this project. Even though it was not an explicit requirement, some of the more influential project members thought it was a good idea. There have been similar discussions in other large-scale ICT projects. A lot of effort was expended in this area, despite the lack of clear definition of the concept (see Chapter 5).

Following in-depth consideration of the user requirements and additional input from experts, a few guiding principles were established. The most important of these was to note that whatever we did in adding value using novel ICT should not adversely affect a user's primary ability to collect and store data. After all, the facilities are expensive to run and the samples being studied may be extremely fragile, so there is no second chance. This meant that, if all else failed, the data had to be collected and stored locally on a computer disk associated with the beamline control and data collection system. It was therefore decided that this should always be the first step in the data management process.

It turned out that the DLS IT infrastructure had already been designed with this in mind, which seemed very sensible. Unfortunately, at the time of writing this has been changed and we await to see the consequences. Each beamline, with a single source of intense X-rays emanating from

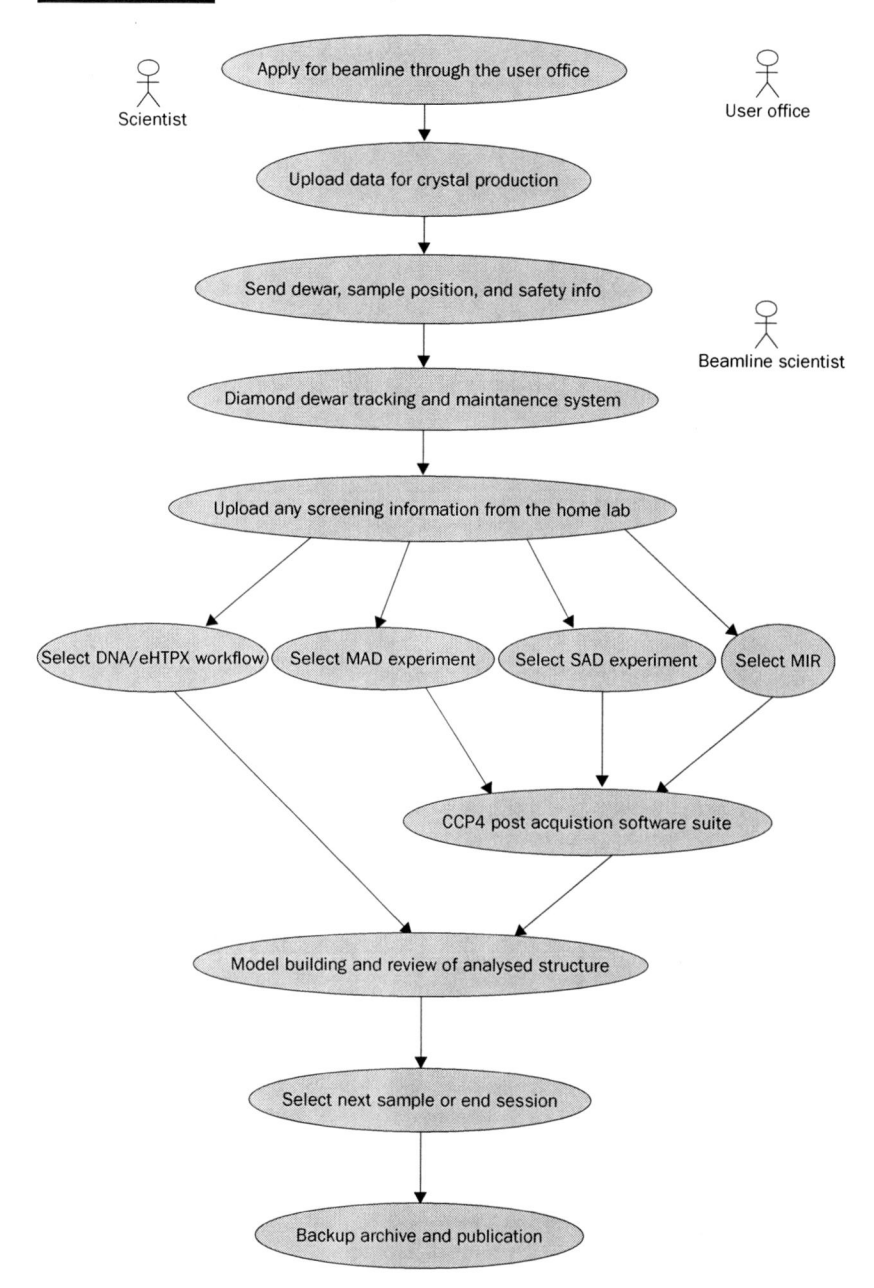

Example 2: E-infrastructure for experimental facilities

Figure 12.2 MX beamline processes

a bending magnet in the synchrotron ring, is essentially autonomous. It has a beamline scientist, a principal scientist and a range of equipment dedicated to a particular class of experiment. A relatively large number of these beamlines are designed for the important area of molecular crystallography.

Protein crystallography, itself a branch of MX, is of fundamental importance to the pharmaceutical industry and has evolved into a high-throughput technique for determining the three-dimensional structure of proteins following gene expression and synthesis and the crystallisation of sufficiently large samples of a given protein to enable an X-ray diffraction experiment to be performed. Of course, PX is not entirely straightforward as, even if the experiment is successful and a set of high-resolution X-ray images can be obtained, they still have to be interpreted and phase information inferred by a number of computational techniques before a candidate three-dimensional structure can be obtained. More fundamentally, not all proteins are amenable to crystallisation and those that are may crystallise in a conformation which is not like their shape in living cells, where they are under quite different conditions in aqueous solution. Any conclusions drawn by inferring protein function merely from the structures revealed in a PX experiment should therefore be taken with a pinch of salt. Nevertheless, the technique is widely used and the e-HTPX project had been funded by BBSRC and DTI from 2003 to develop an e-science resource for high-throughput protein crystallography (Allan et al., 2005; Wang et al., 2006). Staff at Daresbury, Oxford, York and the European Synchrotron Radiation Facility (ESRF) in Grenoble, had worked on this project for four years and delivered a range of software, standards and services linking data collection using samples in robotic handlers to semi-automated structure analysis using software from the Collaborative Computational Project No. 4 (CCP4; *http://www.ccp4.ac.uk*). Some of the staff who had worked on related PX projects on the previous-generation synchrotron radiation source (SRS) at Daresbury were now in leading positions at DLS, so we were fairly confident that DLS could benefit directly from this previous work.

The purpose of the e-HTPX project was to provide a single point of access for scientists, through the internet, to tools and resources for structural biology and drug design, including facilities for crystallisation based in biology laboratories such as the Oxford Protein Production Factory, and synchrotron beamlines at DLS and ESRF. These tools allowed the biologist or drug designer to track their project from inception through to realisation. e-HTPX also included new developments to allow remote access to the data collection procedure, in

Example 2: E-infrastructure for experimental facilities

particular expert software systems to control data collection and structure analysis.

Prior to e-HTPX, most scientists making use of synchrotron facilities had to visit in person to perform all data collection by hand, which was time-consuming. Thanks to the development of remote access protocols and automated data analysis it is now possible for the scientist to perform their experiments from their home laboratory, shipping the samples in cryogenic storage via a reliable courier. This brings savings in both time and money and allows for high-throughput experiments, leading to an overall reduction in time. Many of the standards and tools developed for e-HTPX have been made generally available leading to greater productivity for scientists carrying out drug binding and other studies in their home laboratories as well as national facilities (Winter et al., personal communication).

Figure 12.3 shows the general architecture we proposed for the DLS e-infrastructure. Some key components of the system include laboratory information and control systems (iCAT, ISPyB, GDA); data management and storage (SRB, Castor, DataPortal, ATLAS Tape Store); ePubs; and the ESRF proposal system. DLS users would also be able to access the computational services, such as the NGS, to run data analysis and simulation jobs.

Figure 12.3 Diamond Light Source e-infrastructure

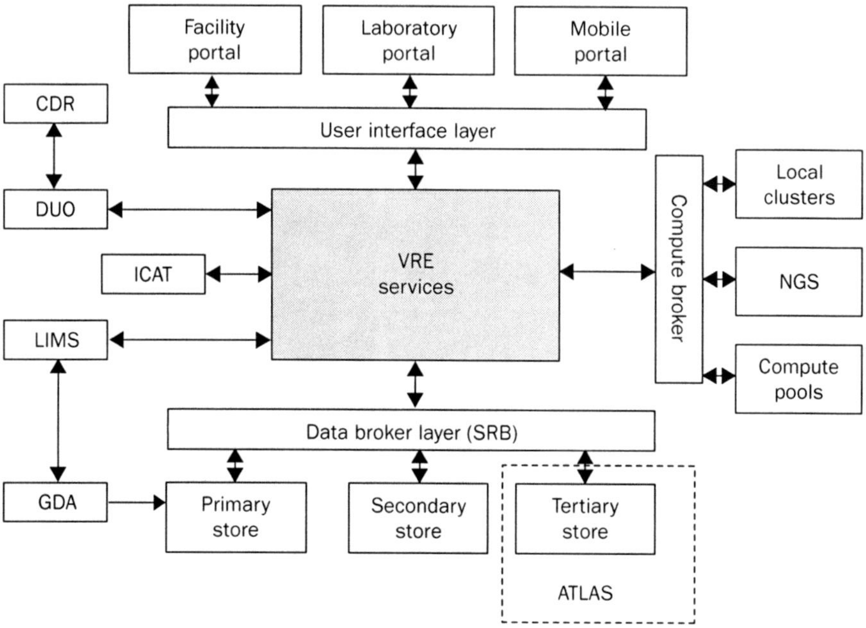

Mapping requirements to data flow, data models and analysis

The analysis of requirements led to a sophisticated model of how information and data was used on experimental facilities. In turn, this led to a design for implementation of an ICT system which could track data from beamline to storage, track samples, allow for discovery through a metadata catalogue and provide access and analysis via a portal interface and grid resources. Figure 12.4 shows the top process definition for part of the data and information flow at DLS.

Components of the infrastructure deployed to support this process are now described.

Figure 12.4 DLS data and information flow

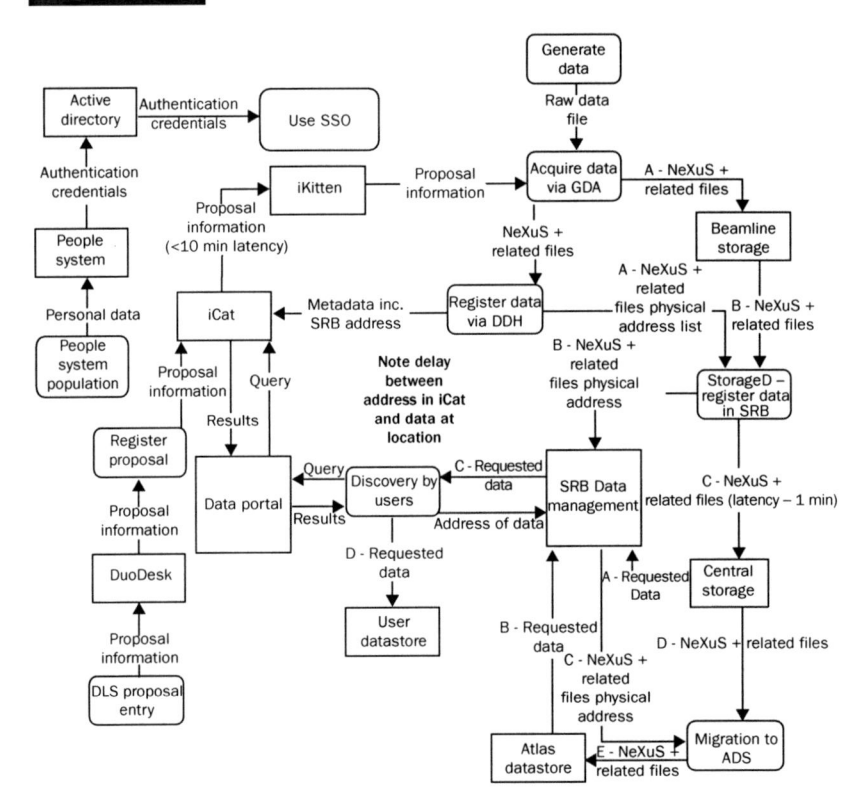

The facilities information catalogue

The iCAT software and DataPortal web interface were developed in the STFC e-Science Programme. iCAT is a realisation of a central metadata catalogue for experimental and diagnostic related primary (raw) data and secondary (processed) results. Wherever possible, metadata is gathered automatically through integration with existing software such as diagnostic, proposal or data collection systems. The catalogue and the data it references are accessible via a web services API for easy embedding into any access or analysis applications such as DataPortal, the browser-based metadata cross-search data discovery tool.

iCAT is currently being used on the UK Neutron, Synchrotron and Laser Facilities, ISIS, Diamond and CLF, and is being evaluated for the Spallation Neutron Source at the Oak Ridge National Laboratory in the USA and the Australian Synchrotron and Neutron Facilities.

ISPyB

The Information System for Protein crYstallography Beamlines (ISPyB) is a joint development between groups at the ESRF, e-HTPX and the EU funded SPINE project. This is a form of laboratory information management system (LIMS) for MX experiments. ISPyB provides users with a managed environment for keeping track of their experiments and is now available at Diamond, although not included in Figure 12.4. The available features include:

- submission of sample shipments;
- management of sample, crystal and protein information;
- real-time monitoring of data collections including diffraction images and crystal snapshots, harvesting of output from data reduction programs;
- view experiment-related information;
- create and edit laboratory reports about experiments;
- export metadata about experiments back to your home laboratory.

ISPyB is integrated with the Generic Data Acquisition (GDA) software used on the beamlines. GDA, developed on the Daresbury SRS, controls the positioning of samples in the beam and other elements, such as diffractometers, mirrors and cameras. Sample data is extracted from ISPyB, enabling GDA to run an experiment, perhaps scanning the sample over a range of wavelengths or rotating it or moving the camera and at the same time collecting data. Once the experiment is complete, the data is uploaded along with experiment metadata back into ISPyB.

Data management

Data and metadata collected during the experiment need to be managed and stored for further analysis, possibly using computationally-intensive techniques. Metadata from ISPyB is uploaded into iCAT and data is uploaded into SRB. SRB can then stage this data from the beamline computer system to a central repository, the National Grid Service or the Atlas Data Store tape archive for long-term storage. It is also possible to record data and associated metadata directly onto DVD for commercial users who want to conduct their own post-experimental analysis.

DataPortal is the principal user interface which enables academic users and their collaborators to get rapid access to their current and past data, view related experiments, publications, etc. This can lead to improved interpretation through access to more complete information. Researchers working together are able to create a powerful, long-lasting scientific knowledge resource relevant to their communities.

DataPortal offers secure external access to the data itself using single sign-on (FedId and passwd). DataPortal uses iCAT web services, is available as a portlet and has been integrated with portal frameworks such as Sakai.

The Australian Synchrotron currently uses the VBL Storage Gateway, which offers a range of file transfer protocols so that data can be transferred back to users' home laboratories. This includes GridFTP, SRB and SCP. Data transfer can be immediate or scheduled for a period when networks are lightly loaded. There is a similar file transfer portlet available on the UK NGS.

Computational framework

A great deal of value can be added to experimental facilities if data can be analysed as soon as it is collected. Results can steer the actual or future experimental work as conclusions can be validated and modelling can suggest other experimental procedures or even identify problems with samples or equipment. We proposed using e-science technology to do this, including RMCS and AgentX and using the NGS with a suite of analysis and modelling applications from the CCPs.

This part of the programme has not yet been realised, but similar work on the Spallation Neutron Source (SNS) at the US Oak Ridge National Laboratory and Institut Laue-Langevin in France has been successful in demonstrating the benefits. A portal for SNS connects world-class neutron science instruments with the TeraGrid cyberinfrastructure. The Neutron TeraGrid Science Gateway has enabled researchers to show for the first time that computations can predict experimental results in virtual neutron scattering experiments. It also allows interpretation of diffuse scattering data measured by single crystal diffraction, computer simulations in molecular biophysics, combining neutron scattering and bio-energy and rapid reduction of experimental data.

Publications

The dilemma facing researchers in choosing between institutional or facility repositories has already been discussed in Chapter 4. STFC has developed and hosts the ePubs repository, which is also available to researchers using large-scale facilities such as CLF and ISIS (Jones, 2007). It was naturally envisaged that DLS users would also deposit reports, preprints and articles in ePubs, making them available for cross-linking with data via iCAT and forming a valuable archive of work carried out. This is now the case and publications since 2000 can be browsed via *http://epubs.cclrc.ac.uk/search?st=browse-by-orgunit&ou=78*.

Education, training and remote access

While not yet included in work for the UK facilities, education and training has been recognised as important in the longer term. VeRSI in Australia has developed a virtual beamline (VBL) for the new national synchrotron in Melbourne. VeRSI is developing 11 use cases illustrating the benefits of e-research to researchers, particularly in areas associated with the Australian Synchrotron facility.

The VBL portal links to a high-quality video-conferencing system for collaboration. This is currently used on one PX beamline and an optical diagnostics beamline and is being added to others. At Curtin University, the VBL has been used to involve scientists and students from Western Australia and Melbourne in live powder diffraction experiments for materials analysis.

La Trobe University is developing eVBL as a remote training laboratory and online classroom to teach synchrotron science and expose students to experimental capabilities and procedures. Among other things, this allows school children to participate in a simulated Young's double-slit diffraction experiment as part of their physics lessons. A view-only mode of this is available online (*http://vbl.synchrotron.org.au/BeamLineAccess/ eVBL/eVBL.php*). They can also control a live instrument to do the experiment when available, but this requires authentication to the system and allocation of real resources.

Project management and other issues

Clearly the programme of work outlined was large and ambitious; however, we felt that it was achievable given the availability of solutions from our previous work. After two years, it was however de-scoped for largely non-technical reasons. There are lessons to be learned here for all similar programmes.

What was proposed required some 20 staff in the CCLRC (now STFC) E-Science Centre, with some of them embedded in the facilities: CLF, ISIS and DLS. As a 'project' with nominal annual funding of over £1 million, it should have been monitored via the corporate project register. However, because it was internally rather than externally funded, this was not done and the required management structure as set out in STFC's Corporate Management Handbook (a subset of Prince2 (*http://www.prince2.com*) and British Standard BS6079) was not fully implemented, although an attempt was made to retro-fit this. With hindsight, what came to be especially critical for the project was the lack of an identified stakeholder group and ultimately lack of high-level buy-in, which seriously impacted sustainability when funding became an issue at the end of 2007.

The project started with only vaguely-stated goals based on the initial analysis of user requirements, no detailed task specifications, and no detailed understanding of the effort required and dependencies between the tasks. In particular, there was a lack of understanding of the time required for testing and making updates and changes to a complex software infrastructure on a live experimental facility – this had possibly never been done before. An attempt was made to remedy the project management and documentation using the TRAC wiki software and project management system (*http://www.trac.com*). We listed and grouped tasks, defined task owners and tried to capture as much information about them as possible. It was too late, however, and some tasks were never fully documented as they evolved. A last-ditch effort was made to document data management tasks by analysing the database schema which had been already implemented, which included aspects of the proposed security infrastructure.

Management was not the only issue. The overall programme was too ambitious and similar problems with other large software projects have been recorded. Despite the fact that we knew this and were aware of good practice in managing software projects, it happened again.

Staffing and communication

A large number of communication problems originated from the lack of project scoping and specification. People did not know what other people were doing and when they found out realised that they had conflicting goals or implementations. Examples of this were in the definition of the schema for the various databases which were to be deployed. This caused overlap of functionality, duplication of data, differences in naming the same data, and changes which broke interoperability or resulted in information not being available when required. These problems could have been resolved with better documentation and regular project meetings to agree the scope of related tasks.

There was a problem with availability of staff, particularly on the DLS side, where many high-priority tasks related to commissioning the new facility meant that installing and testing e-science software to 'add value' took longer than expected. This could only be done by the system managers responsible for the beamline equipment.

An incident that was particularly amusing, with hindsight, was the revelation that a senior manager had spent a weekend evaluating wiki technology. Neither his own staff nor the e-science staff were aware that he felt this to be an important requirement. It was therefore a surprise to be given a demonstration, out of the blue, during a project progress meeting and to be told that he was recommending a commercial fully-functional wiki for use at Diamond. This was viewed with scepticism from all concerned and somewhat undermined the goal of providing a VRE which would have contained an integrated wiki, albeit with somewhat lesser functionality. Given that a similar process had occurred for the choice of web-based user management system and DLS project blog, now resulting in three separate information systems, it was becoming clear that key staff at Diamond lacked an understanding of the goals of e-science and had not bought into the partnership with STFC despite earlier assurances.

Scalability and network issues

The network at Diamond was designed to be failsafe. It was hierarchical, with three levels. The first level linked computers, instruments and disk storage on an individual beamline which could therefore operate independently from other beamlines and central IT services. There was a synchrotron network which linked all 'science' services at DLS. Finally, there was a network connecting DLS services to external services, most importantly those on the rest of the Harwell Science and Innovation Campus, such as the Atlas Data Store, a petabyte tape robot storage system run by the e-Science Centre, which we were proposing to use to store experimental data generated at DLS via SRB, as described above.

What we were initially unaware of, was that there had already been a number of debates about networking at DLS. However, there had been no analysis regarding the amount of data which would be produced from instruments on the beamlines, when it would be produced and what network bandwidth would be required to cope with it. In the end, the STFC networking team implemented the 'admin' network, and DLS IT services implemented the 'science' network. The latter was never as specified – not only did beamlines affect one another, but large data transfers, for instance several gigabytes of PX images moving from beamline to central storage, could bring down the entire operation because of insufficient bandwidth. This was not a stable basis for deploying e-science services.

The Storage Resource Broker (SRB) software from San Diego Supercomputer Centre was recommended for the DTI e-Science Programme in 1999. It was used to manage distributed storage and presented a virtual file system to the user as described in Chapter 8. This had been used, with partial success, in several of the larger e-science projects, but suffered from a number of fundamental problems. The choice to use it for data management at Diamond, without further evaluation, was therefore questionable. Subsequent discussions indicated that a new class of instrument becoming available would dramatically increase the amount of data and speed of collection required, making a complete rethink of the data management strategy unavoidable in future.

During the DLS deployment, it became increasingly obvious that, not only would SRB not perform well enough, but it was in fact not required at all. A logical file system was not a requirement; however, a simple hierarchical storage system, able to stage data from beamline disk, to intermediate storage and to the Atlas tape store was required, and SRB alone could not do this, especially with the large volumes of data concerned.

Missed opportunities

It is arguable that if each software component and standard (e.g. security, web services APIs, database schema, data collection, data transfer, hierarchical storage, analysis) had been treated separately they would have been more successful. As outlined in Chapter 7, a service-oriented architecture is important for reasons of software engineering. This had been proven in the e-HTPX project, which was based around an agreed metadata model and set of communication services. Components could therefore be swapped in and out, e.g. a commercial organisation might use the data collection part of the pipeline but not the analysis part. Components developed in e-HTPX such as ISPyB are still in use, and its metadata model has been proposed as standard for the international PX community (Winter et al., 2008).

The lack of high-level buy-in to the overall programme led to staff issues and ultimately to software being taken 'in house', so that ESRF and DLS now have slightly different versions of ISPyB and ISIS and DLS have slightly different versions of iCAT, DataPortal and GDA. Opportunities to exploit the work at overseas facilities are therefore limited as the source code has been branched and there is no definable set of interoperating 'products'.

Since the end of 2007, there have been several related attempts to spin off commercial activities. Despite far-reaching academic innovation and clear potential, this is notoriously difficult. One, MetaTaxa, resulted in a further short contract for a piece of work on DLS, which was completed but unfortunately taken no further. Others which still survive at the time of writing are DSoFt Solutions based at Daresbury and Constellation Systems based at Harwell. Both are seeking customers for ICT and software products to enhance research processes.

13

Conclusions: lessons learned and limitations

ICT has come a long way in the last ten years with the emergence of the grid and e-science, the Semantic Web and Web 2.0, with technologies supporting advanced integration of distributed software, human–computer interaction, semantics, mashups and service hosting. Indeed, we have come a very long way since the 1980s when the internet did not exist and e-mail was still a new thing. Trying to guess in detail what the future will hold is probably futile. In July 2005, however, the 2020 Science Group, sponsored by Microsoft did think through many of the possibilities and illustrated how the latest developments in computer science might benefit research into the grand challenges of natural science and engineering. Their report (Microsoft, 2005) makes interesting reading, and most of their conclusions focus on policy and social rather than technological issues.

It is easy to dismiss e-research as just another flash in the pan. However, the technology that we are using for VREs is now available in everyone's homes via broadband and will soon become as commonplace as the telephone. E-research does not require researchers to buy and learn to use special-purpose and complex pieces of equipment. The challenge of an easy to use, universally available technology platform for VREs has essentially been met and e-research will benefit from it.

Top ten e-research requirements

At a workshop in June 2006 (Allan et al., 2006b), we explained a vision of the VRE as a 'one-stop shop' for researchers to access data and global information relevant to their studies with appropriate semantic support and contextual services for discovery, location and digital rights management.

Putting the outcome of the workshop together with the outcome of other surveys which we analysed (Allan et al., 2006a) and reported in Chapter 2, we have identified the following ten conclusions:

- e-research discovery services need to work alongside Google;
- e-research needs to provide mechanisms for discovering scientific data and linking between data, publications and citations;
- e-research needs to use protocols and standards to facilitate exposing its services to a variety of user interfaces, including portals;
- e-research needs to provide facilities to publish and make available content from personal and group information services;
- e-research should embrace such things as the JISCmail list server and archives;
- training for users is needed, as well as increased awareness of what is available;
- e-research needs to embrace Semantic Web technologies, including provenance and versioning;
- e-research needs to work with and provide enhanced access for commercial sources and interoperate with proprietary software;
- e-research interfaces (e.g. portals) need to be highly customisable and to treat users' activities 'in context';
- e-research should embrace collaboration technologies to facilitate joint uses of its services (multiple users and multiple services interacting).

Impact of e-research

Advances in ICT have had three important effects for researchers. First, faster and more widespread networks mean researchers are able to communicate and together undertake increasingly ambitious projects, by using geographically-distant facilities, accessing remote data stores and using available computing power. Second, the innovations of Web 2.0 make the wide distribution of information quick and easy with users in control. Lastly, researchers are able to do more with their own isolated computers, creating a large amount of data currently inaccessible to other researchers, even those within their domain or institution. Many of these advances are being driven by the use of ICT in the home for educational and leisure purposes.

Because of this, e-research can be seen both as the next step in the natural development of research methodologies and as an initiative requiring deliberate, conscious effort if it is to reduce costs, increase outputs and preserve valuable digital repositories, as it has the potential to do. While some research projects will of necessity be undertaken by virtual organisations – such as remote control of expensive equipment and utilising distributed computing power – it will take conscious, concerted effort to make e-research thoroughly widespread and useful while not deviating from the goal of research, which is to create new knowledge. Even where people are regularly using VREs to conduct research, management is required to make sure researchers can concentrate on their main goal, instead of spending time developing new VREs when perfectly good frameworks exist already, or undergoing training to use unnecessarily complicated software.

Despite the obvious opportunities, e-research will not thrive without careful attention to the four 'C's: culture of research embracing new methodologies; champions who will lead e-research efforts; communications to disseminate the values of e-research; and integrated change management to make it happen.

Future

I would like to end on an optimistic note. We are seeing tremendous adoption of all forms of wireless devices. At the time of writing, advanced 3G mobile technology, as available in the Apple iPhone, Google Android, BlackBerry Storm and other devices, is very popular, with Web 2.0 applications such as MySpace and SecondLife being adapted to work with them. There is no reason why e-research should not take advantage of such developments. Tools for managing the information overload created by the web will be developed, involving peer-to-peer technology and knowledge management. Personalised e-research environments will evolve as researchers work in ways that are not only optimised for their tools, but also for the way they work both online and offline. E-research will soon become commonplace, it will be integrated with e-learning and e-admin and there will be no need to distinguish 'e' from 'non-e'.

There have been numerous discussions regarding the use of social networking tools, such as Facebook or SecondLife to support research collaborations, but there is no clear consensus on how this should be achieved. It will probably be an evolutionary process, and projects such as myExperiment are beginning to explore this area. It is not yet known what effect emerging standards, brokers and tools such as Open Data Definition, OpenSocial and Elgg will have.

Other projects are exploring how to export portal functionality into other frameworks; for instance MySakai encompasses a set of widgets that have been tested in Facebook, iGoogle, Mac and Vista desktops. Meanwhile, Cyberaid.org is using Google Gadgets to enable a new way of using TeraGrid services.

The remaining challenge is to make existing research tools themselves easy to use and integrate with this new environment. Many of them were developed for bespoke purposes, they are domain-specific and demand specialised knowledge. They may not work 'out of bounds'. Agreed metadata models and semantics are required before mashups and expert systems can be put in place. There has been much discussion about the Semantic Web and Web 2.0, but we are still a long way from realising their full benefit in genuine leading-edge research, particularly that involving large-scale experimental and high-performance computing facilities. However, they are starting to pay off in helping with the classification and organisation of data and providing access to information.

We should at the same time not diminish our appreciation for the lengthy training, dedication, effort and knowledge required to do research of any kind. Academic research especially is about creation and doing something new – it can become an obsession. Yes, tools are useful, but they should not over-shadow the desire to understand the workings of nature, create new knowledge and find new ways of working that are the goal of a true researcher. We should also be wary of any technology which oversimplifies research as there is a danger of replacing deep knowledge with broad but superficial knowledge, thereby stagnating evolution. There is nothing to replace original thinking, philosophy or mathematics, but computers can help by automating the processes that enable us to check our theories against reality.

Appendix A: E-research portals and gateways

This section lists some existing e-research portals and gateways and some other VRE systems which have been developed or evaluated. Please note that this list is by no means exhaustive. A number of related activities, such as conferences and workshops, are also listed.

USA: TeraGrid Science Gateways

The TeraGrid Science Gateways website (*http://www.teragrid.org/programs/ sci_gateways/*) includes a section on how to turn your project into a science gateway using the Science Gateways Primer (*http://www.teragrid forum.org/mediawiki/index.php?title=Science_Gateways*).

Portals and Science Gateways

The main TeraGrid User Portal was described in Chapter 9. Table A.1 lists the TeraGrid Community Gateways and gives an indication of the technologies they were using at the time of writing.

Table A.1 US TeraGrid Science Gateways

Name	Domain	Technology
Open Science Grid (OSG)	Advanced scientific computing	
Special PRiority and Urgent Computing Environment (SPRUCE)	Advanced scientific computing	PHP
Massive Pulsar Surveys using the Arecibo L-band Feed Array (ALFA)	Astronomical sciences	ASPX

Table A.1 US TeraGrid Science Gateways (*Cont'd*)

Name	Domain	Technology
National Virtual Observatory (NVO)	Astronomical sciences	HTML
Community Climate System Model (CCSM)	Atmospheric sciences	GridSphere
High Resolution Daily Temperature and Precipitation Data for the Northeast USA	Atmospheric sciences	XHTML
Linked Environments for Atmospheric Discovery (LEAD) (Christie and Marru, 2007)	Atmospheric sciences	GridSphere
Chemical Informatics and Cyberinfrastructure Collaboratory (CICC)	Biochemistry and molecular structure and function	MediaWiki
High Resolution Modeling of Hydrodynamic Experiments	Biophysics	
Computational Chemistry Grid (GridChem)	Chemistry	Java app
Computational Science and Engineering Online (CSE Online)	Chemistry	TWiki
Science Gateway for Diffraction Facilities, Data and Methods	Chemistry	GridSphere
Network for Earthquake Engineering Simulation (NEES)	Earthquake hazard mitigation	XHTML+PHP
Cyberinfrastructure for End-to-End Environmental Exploration Portal (C4E4)	Earth sciences	
GEOsciences Network (GEON)	Earth sciences	GridSphere
Purdue Environmental Data Portal	Earth sciences	GridSphere
Network for Computational Nanotechnology and nanoHUB*	Emerging technologies initiation	Joomla
Dark Energy Survey Data Management (DESDM)	Extragalactic astronomy and cosmology	MS FrontPage
Indiana University Centralized Life Sciences Data (CLSD)	Genetics and nucleic acids	

Appendix A

Table A.1 US TeraGrid Science Gateways (*Cont'd*)

Name	Domain	Technology
TeraGrid Geographic Information Science Gateway (GISolve)	Geography and regional science	GridSphere
Science Gateway for the Geodynamics Community (CIG)	Geophysics	Plone
QuakeSim (QuakeSim)	Geophysics	GridSphere
The Earth System Grid (ESG)	Global atmospheric research	UCAR portal
National Biomedical Computation Resource (NBCR)	Integrative biology and neuroscience	PHP
Developing Social Informatics Data Grid (SID-Grid)	Language, cognition and social behaviour	PHP
Neutron Science TeraGrid Gateway (NSTG) (Cobb et al., 2007)	Materials research	SHTML
Virtual Laboratory for Earth and Planetary Materials (VLab)	Materials research	
Biology and Biomedicine Science Gateway	Molecular biosciences	PHP
Cancer Biomedical Information Grid (caBIG)	Molecular biosciences	LifeRay
Open Life Sciences Gateway (OLSG)	Molecular biosciences	Drupal
The Telescience Project	Neuroscience biology	GridSphere
Grid Analysis Environment (GAE)	Physics	
SCEC Earthworks Project	Seismology	Plone
Asteroseismic Modeling Portal (AMP)	Stellar astronomy and astrophysics	
Distributed Rendering Environment (TeraDRE)	Visualisation, graphics and image processing	MM+Flash
TeraGrid Visualization Gateway (Binns et al., 2007)	Visualisation, graphics and image processing	GridSphere

* NanoHUB has spawned a number of other projects using its HUBzero technology. According to Gerhard Klimeck of Purdue University, the technology is now hosting more than 130 computational simulation tools for over 90,000 users over the last year in over 170 countries. It is also used for teaching purposes. See *http://www.nanohub.org*.

Workshops and conferences

The Grid Computing Environments Research Group (GCE-RG) of GGF has organised workshops such as the Science Gateways workshop at GGF-14 and annual GCE Workshop at the International Super Computing Conference. There are many papers resulting from these workshops which describe portal and VRE projects and the technologies they are using. See, for instance, *Concurrency and Computation: Practice and Experience*, Vol. 14, Nos. 13–15 (2002) and Vol. 19, Nos. 6 and 12 (2007) which were special issues on grid computing environments and science gateways respectively.

Projects in Europe

This section does not contain a full list of projects, but just mentions some examples mainly from the UK. One interesting project not listed is the Neanderthal Studies Professional Online Service (NESPOS). This project was developed with EU funding under the Digital Culture Programme and has an international online database and a collaborative VRE based on MediaWiki. All research objects are linked into the wiki and a bespoke visualisation suite called VisiCore was written by a commercial partner to view and annotate maps and images of the context (GeoCore) and finds (ArteCore) (*https://www.nespos.org/display/openspace/Home*).

Table A.2 UK information portals

Name	Technology	Description and URL
Connect		Learning and Teaching Portal http://www.connect.ac.uk
CREE	uPortal	Contextual Resource Evaluation Environment http://www.hull.ac.uk/esig/cree
Go-Geo!	Perl	Geodata Portal: Phase 3 http://www.jisc.ac.uk/whatwedo/programmes/portals/gogeo3.aspx
Pixus		Image Portal Demonstrator http://www.jisc.ac.uk/whatwedo/programmes/portals/imageportal.aspx
SPP	Jetspeed	Subject Portals Project: Phase 2 http://www.portal.ac.uk/spp/

Appendix A

Table A.2 UK information portals (Cont'd)

Name	Technology	Description and URL
VSMPortal		Visual and Sound Materials Portal Scoping Study and Demonstrator Project http://edina.ac.uk/projects/vsmportal/
Xgrain II		Information Cross Search http://www.jisc.ac.uk/whatwedo/programmes/portals/xgrain2.aspx
HEIRPORT	Cold Fusion	Historic Environment Information Resources Portal http://ads.ahds.ac.uk/heirport/ Now included in CREE

JISC VRE Programme

eReSS, the JISC funded e-research Interoperability and Standards activity, provides more information about how JISC projects have adopted and used ICT standards and tools on its wiki.

Brief description of VRE-1 Projects

See *http://www.jisc.ac.uk/whatwedo/programmes/vre1.aspx*. Note that the video recordings which give an overview of this programme can be also obtained here.

Table A.3 UK JISC VRE-1 Projects

Name	Technology	Domain and URL
Sakai EduResearch	Sakai, DSPace	Social science teaching and learning programme http://www.caret.cam.ac.uk/projects/jiscvre.html
PolDis	Sakai, Access Grid	History of political discourse http://www.jisc.ac.uk/whatwedo/programmes/vre1/politicaldiscourse.aspx
Sakai Demonstrator	Sakai, Shibboleth, WSRP, JSR 168	Generic collaboration and research tools http://www.grids.ac.uk/Sakai

217

Table A.3 UK JISC VRE-1 Projects (Cont'd)

Name	Technology	Domain and URL
GROWL	Web services, Condor, Globus	Bio-informatics, chemistry, statistics http://www.grids.ac.uk/GROWL
IBVRE	uPortal, WSRP, JSR 168, Shibboleth	Integrative biology http://www.vre.ox.ac.uk/ibvre/
BVREH	Various	Humanities http://bvreh.humanities.ox.ac.uk/
EVIE	Bodington KVP	Institutional VRE http://www.leeds.ac.uk/evie/
ELVI	SunGard SCT	Research business processes http://www.nottingham.ac.uk/~bbzijw/elvi/
Memetic	Semantic Web (RDF), Access Grid, Compendium	Generical collaboration management http://www.memetic-vre.net/
Cheshire	Cheshire, Sakai, Kepler, JSR 168, JSR 170	Digital libraries http://www.jisc.ac.uk/whatwedo/programmes/vre1/cheshire3.aspx
CSAGE	Access Grid	Arts and humanities http://www.jisc.ac.uk/whatwedo/programmes/vre1/sage.aspx
CORE	Chandler, web services, JSR 168	Teaching in orthopaedic surgery http://www.core.ecs.soton.ac.uk/
OGHAM	GridSphere	Archaeology (Silchester Roman Town study) http://www.jisc.ac.uk/whatwedo/programmes/vre1/silchester.aspx
ISME	GridSphere, Access Grid	Materials science http://www.jisc.ac.uk/whatwedo/programmes/vre1/isme.aspx
IUGO	Metadata standards, Semantic Web (SWAD), WSRP, JSR 168, RSS, etc.	Conference organisation and content curation http://iugo.ilrt.bris.ac.uk/

Appendix A

Brief description of VRE-2 projects

See *http://www.jisc.ac.uk/whatwedo/programmes/vre2.aspx*. Information about all these projects can also be found from *http://www.jisc.ac.uk/publications/documents/bpvrev2.aspx*.

Table A.4 UK JISC VRE-2 Projects

Name	Technology	Domain and URL
CREW	XML, OWL, RDF, SKOS, AJAX, JSR 168, JSR 286, WSRP, RTSP, RTP, AVI, MPEG, WMV	Collaboration and research tools based on MEMETIC and IUGO http://www.crew-vre.net/
myExperiment	Web 2.0, social networking, HTTP, AJAX, Ruby, RDF, RSS	Sharing for science experiments online http://www.myexperiment.org/
VRE-SDM	XML, HTML, ECMAScript, JSR 168, JSR 286, WSRP, XMPP, RDF, OWL, Z39.50, SRW	Document research in humanities http://bvreh.humanities.ox.ac.uk/VRE-SDM
VERA	GridSphere, HTTP, CSS, SQL, RSS, JSR 168, JSR 154, JSP, scalable vector graphics, JDBC, Javascript, XML	Archaeology (Silchester Roman Town study) http://vera.rdg.ac.uk/index.php

VRE-3 projects

At the time of writing the VRE-3 Programme has just been announced. Watch the JISC website for news of new and exciting e-research projects. The VRE projects in Table A.5 are described online at *http://pims.jisc.ac.uk/projects/view/1293* to *http://pims.jisc.ac.uk/projects/view/1302* respectively.

Table A.5 UK JISC VRE-3 and related projects

Name	Technology	Domain and URL
NeISS	Sakai, Shibboleth, workflows, parallel and grid computing, Web 2.0, social networking	E-infrastructure for social simulation http://www.neiss.org.uk
NeuroHub		Neuroscience http://www.jisc.ac.uk/whatwedo/programmes/inf11/neurohub.aspx

Table A.5 UK JISC VRE-3 and related projects (Cont'd)

Name	Technology	Domain and URL
Video Conversion on PAG	CREW and Memetic	Video editing and playback
IBBRE	CORE and myExperiment	Research on internet-based behavioural interventions
CRIB	Sakai, Profile-2, BRII, CREE	Collaborative research in business
Cancer Imaging VRE	Microsoft Research Information Centre, Trident, SharePoint and Exchange Barga et al. (2007)	Linking university and hospital information resources for sharing information on cancer
One VRE	PAG, Sakai, portals	Bridging between VRE portals and PAG
BRAIN	myExperiment, Web 2.0, Cloud, Semantic Web, Pattern languages	Building research innovation networks
Linksphere		Cross-search library and museum resources plus social web for researchers
Text VRE	German Text Grid	Humanities and textual studies, annotation and retrieval
VRIC	CORE, myExperiment	Virtual research integration collaboration for orthopaedics
ISC VRE	REF bibliometrics, Sakai, social networking, DSpace-2	Institutional scholarly communications with integrated publication sharing

Other work on research portals

Older research portals

Some other projects in the UK are listed in Table A.6. This is also not a complete list and most of these projects have finished.

Table A.6 UK research portals

Project	Technology	Description and URL (if available)
HPCPortal	Perl and C	Generic Grid http://www.grids.ac.uk/HPCPortal
InfoPortal	Perl and C	Grid resource information
DataPortal	JSP	Scientific data collections
Bridges	WebSphere	Biomedical information delivered by grid-enabled services http://www.brc.dcs.gla.ac.uk/projects/bridges/
DAME	Struts and GridSphere	Distributed aircraft maintenance environment http://www.cs.york.ac.uk/dame
VOTES	GridSphere	Virtual organisations for trials and epidemiological studies
RealityGrid	GridSphere	Computational steering http://www.realitygrid.org/middleware.shtml
myGrid	Jetspeed-2, uPortal, GridSphere	Workflows in bioinformatics http://www.mygrid.org.uk
BDWorld	Mambo, PHP	Biodiversity studies
GeneGrid	GridSphere	A virtual bioinformatics laboratory
Discovery Net	Sharepoint	Knowledge discovery
NGS Portal	Pluto	Generic Grid portal for the NGS http://portal.ngs.ac.uk
GridPP Portal	Perl and GridSite	Portal for GridPP Applications http://www.gridpp.ac.uk/portal
e-HTPX Portal	JSP	Workflow management in synchrotron-based high throughput protein crystallography experiments
P-GRADE Portal	GridSphere	Generic portal for grid and parallel applications http://portal.p-grade.hu
GEMEPS	GridSphere	Grid enabled microarray experiment profile search http://labserv.nesc.gla.ac.uk/projects/gemeps/index.html

Workshops and conferences

The following workshops have been held in the UK:

- 14–17 July 2003: 'Portals and Portlets', international conference held at NeSC, Edinburgh (*http://www.nesc.ac.uk/action/esi/contribution.cfm? Title=261 e-Science Technical Report UKeS-2004-06* and *http://www.nesc.ac.uk/technical_papers/UKeS-2004-06.pdf*).
- 3–4 March 2005: 'GridSphere and Portlets', held at NeSC, Edinburgh (*http://www.nesc.ac.uk/action/esi/contribution.cfm?Title=549*).
- 22 June 2005: 'VRE and Portals Workshop' at 1st International Conference on E-Social Science, Manchester (*http://www.ncess.ac.uk/events/conference/2005/*).
- 20–21 September 2005: 'Portals and VREs AHM '05 Mini Workshop', Nottingham.
- 18–19 January 2006: 'JSR-168 and WSRP Developers' Workshop', Portsmouth (*http://dsg.port.ac.uk/events/workshops/VRE05/*).
- 17–18 July 2006: 'Portals and Portlets 2006', international conference held at NeSC, Edinburgh (*http://www.nesc.ac.uk/action/esi/contribution.cfm?Title=686*).
- 28 February 2008: 'Portal Developers' Workshop', Reading.

Information and research portals

Table A.7 European research portals

Project	Technology	Description and URL
MADEIRA	XHTML and JavaScript	Multilingual Access to Data Infrastructures for the European Research Area http://www.madeira.net
IReL	PHP	Irish Research e-Library http://www.tcd.ie/Library/Irel.php
Vascoda		German information discovery portal http://www.vascoda.de
Manuscriptorium	Z39.50, OAI-PMH with desktop tools	Historical book resources in several European countries http://www.manuscriptorium.com/Site/ENG/default_eng.asp

Appendix A

Table A.7 European research portals (Cont'd)

Project	Technology	Description and URL
DEISA (Soddemann, 2007)	Apache Cocoon and NICE EnginFrame	Materials science, plasma physics and life sciences respectively
EGEE	NICE EnginFrame, P-GRADE, gEclipse	Used for various gateways

Australasia

This is not a complete list. As examples, we mention BeSTGRID in New Zealand and VeRSI in Australia (*http://versi.edu.au*). VeRSI is a joint venture between Multimedia Victoria, the Department of Primary Industries and the universities of Melbourne, Monash and La Trobe.

Many of the VeRSI projects use the Meta Access Management System (*http://www.mams.org.au*) as a collaboration toolkit for their virtual organisation to manage access. GridSphere can be used with this as a portal framework. VeRSI uses TRAC as a support tool.

Table A.8 Portals and science gateways in Australia and New Zealand

Name	Technology	Domain and URL
BeSTGRID	Sakai, Shibboleth, GridSphere, Access Grid and other computational and data grid technologies	Various, see below http://www.bestgrid.org/index.php/BeSTGRID:Community_Portal
VeRSI Life Science	Web 2.0, workflow, portal	Life sciences, see below http://versi.edu.au/activities/lifesciences.html
VBL: VeRSI Virtual Beamline	Web	Remote collaboration for synchrotron experiments including education and training http://versi.edu.au/activities/vbl.html
Monash E-research Centre	Sakai	http://www.monash.edu.au/eresearch/activities/sakai

223

VRE projects hosted on BestGrid currently include the following:

- *New Zealand Social Statistics Network*: developing quantitative social science methods;
- *Primary Care in an Ageing Society (PCASO)*: developing a computer-based model of the primary care system;
- *Network of Excellence for CNC*: developing a community sharing information on technology in computer numerically controlled manufacturing;
- *Macraes TerraSpec*: collaboration to study drill cores from the Macraes gold mine in central Otago;
- *Austronesian Basic Vocabulary and Bantu Language Databases*: sharing information about 580 Austronesian languages spoken throughout the Pacific region plus six Bantu languages.
- *Auckland NZ Network for Earthquake Engineering Simulations (NEES)*: a collaboration that includes partners from USA, UK, Taiwan and China.

Projects listed under VeRSI Life Science currently include the following:

- *Mouse Brain Map*: instrument interfaces, databases, computing, portal development, workflows;
- *Ambulatory Motion*: instrumental interface, databases, portal development, data analysis tools, worksflows, data mining;
- *Neuro-imaging*: databases, computing, portal development, data analysis tools, workflows, large-scale storage, data mining;
- *Meta-bolomics*: instrumental interfaces, databases, portal development, workflows, large-scale storage;
- *Radiotherapy Treatment Planning*: databases, computing, portal development, data analysis tools, large-scale storage, data mining;
- *Genome Dataset Mining*: databases, computing, portal development, large-scale storage, data mining;
- *Uro-oncology Informatics Grid*: database;
- *Laboratory Supervisor Management*: instrument interfaces, databases, computing, portal development, workflows;
- *Eco-informatics*: data architecture, collaborative environment, data visualisation;
- *Bio-informatics Toolbox*: grid computing, collaborative environment;

- *Shared Laboratory Instrumentation*: instrument interfaces, collaboration, workflows.

Workshops and conferences

The eResearch Australasia conference has been held annually since 2007 (*http://www.eresearch.edu.au/*).

Appendix B: E-research tools and services

We list here some information which may be useful for portlet and portal developers. This gives an indication of the range of generic tools and services which are available for use in e-research portals:

- BEA WebLogic has provided a useful online portlet development guide (*http://edocs.bea.com/wlp/docs92/portlets/index.html*).
- In 2003 and 2006, we organised international conferences named 'Portals and Portlets', which were hosted at the National e-Science Centre in Edinburgh. Conference talks are available online for both 2003 (*http://www.nesc.ac.uk/action/esi/contribution.cfm?Title=261*) and 2006 (*http://www.nesc.ac.uk/action/esi/contribution.cfm?Title=686*). A technical report from the 2003 conference is also available (*http://www.grids.ac.uk/TechReports/Portals_2003/portals.pdf*).

Portlet registry

Over the years there have been several discussions about setting up a portlet and tools repository for VRE developers. Despite fairly widespread agreement that this would be a good idea, it has not proven to be straightforward. The main reason is that portlets, while mostly complying with the JSR 168 standard, still need to be tested in all the available frameworks and some support has to be provided. This is best done by the authors of the portlets themselves. Some potentially useful portlet codes are therefore listed below. Note that these are not all open source, but the ones which are may prove to be useful templates for further development.

Adenin Technologies

The Adenin Technologies catalogue (*http://www.adenin.com/Portlets Catalog.asp*) lists: mypages, tag cloud, report viewer, RSS, remote desktop, world clock, notes, Citrix nfuse integration, MS Excel integration, Crystal reports integration, SAP integration, MS Exchange 5.5 integration, news feeds and web services integration, Flash portlet, role member, counter, MS Outlook web access, usage stats, terminal services client, Snitz forum, workflow, image grabber, natterchat, document management, workgroup management, discussion, calendar, application management, Google, conversion tools, dictionary and thesaurus search, calculator, translations, daily information.

AlFresco

The AlFresco (*http://www.alfresco.com*) content management systems have a portlet interface, as mentioned in the context of JBoss below.

BEA WebLogic

BEA WebLogic lists portlets in two locations (*http://dev2dev.bea.com/products/wlportal/psc/index.jsp* and *http://e-docs.bea.com/workshop/docs81/doc/en/core/index.html*). The latter has useful information on portal and portlet development. Some contributions are from business partners such as SAP, Siebel and Comergent. The catalogue lists application areas as follows: collaboration/knowledge management, content management, content syndication, customer relationship management (CRM), document management, e-commerce, enterprise search, human resource management, intranet/extranet, reporting/analytics/BI, search/intelligent interaction, security/single sign-on, supply chain management (SCM/ERP), web/legacy application integration, web services management, wireless integration.

Each category lists a number of applications that run in the BEA WebLogic portal server. For instance, the section on collaboration and knowledge management includes: participate systems discussion forum, discussion forum featured posts, dynamic member profiles, expert events, expert exchange, expert exchange featured questions, knowledge bank and natural language parser, knowledge bank sample questions, knowledge review, management, tracking and analysis, open questions, polls and surveys.

Campus EAI

The Campus EAI consortium maintains a development centre which features a list of contributed portlets (*https://ceai1.campuseai.org*). CEAI uses Oracle technology to underpin its portal and can provide grants to developers. Tools are also listed for uPortal, Microsoft SharePoint, JBoss, BEA and Liferay. CEAI membership is required in order to access the code. The following list contains a number of tools (note that some of these are actually uPortal channels): library service, slide show, courses, external editor integration, customise column, Mirapoint portlet, RSS, comics, grades, invite a friend, announcement for uPortal, PWCL, OEAPlogin, webmail, customise style, calendar, bug report, course management portlet, iTunes music source, password reset, Microsoft Exchange portlet suite, word of the day, this month in campus history, web drag and drop, Amazon search, WebCT Vista 6.4, comments, user acceptance policy portlet, WebCT campus edition integration, gradulator, shoutbox, cruntimeinfo, Yahoo! stock portlet, JNDI portlet, Ajax portlet, clistservassist, custom login portlet, exlibris, cmenuchannel, CNETnews portlet, discussion forum, datel webadvisor secure extension, NOAA current conditions, external app secure, Slashdot portlet, showtime portlet, scientific fiction portlet, WebCT campus edition for uPortal, weather portlet suite, cuser manager, personalise column portlet, moreover news portlet, Yahoo! stock ticker, bookmark portlet, mymemos, feedback portlet, shared bookmarks portlet, NOAA forecast, today in history portlet, HR caught doing something good, JSR 168 internet movie database, early alert system, iframe portlet, announcements, Campus EAI setup, classifieds, file upload example, banner, cmenu, database stats recorder, courses PL-SQL, bookmark manager, PeopleSoft, search portlet, cjavamail, registration portlet, gebrowser os info and run stats, dm tools, notepad portlet, central authentication service, campus view portlet, mashup portlet, smart popcorn news portlet, account info, rotation pages portlet, RSS and blog portlet, channel parameter store, OSTN portlet, universal login on LDAP, JAAS portlet, video portlet, internet movie database portlet, personalise column portlet, marquee portlet, elections, RSS portlet, password change, iframe portlet, flickr portlet, JSR 168 today in history, mylibrary account, dndpreferences, eannounce, webadvisor integration, enews, blog portlet, MSN stockticker portlet, trivia of the day.

Incidentally, this list gives some idea of what tools might be available in a typical university campus portal.

Virtual Research Environments

Cogix ViewsFlash

Cogix mentions a portlet version (*http://www.cogix.com/vf2/Portals168.shtml*). This runs in a number of frameworks and is intended to create surveys, feedback forms, polls, quizzes, tests and assessments.

GEMS

GEMS (*https://gems.dev.java.net/*) provides a free collection of portlets that could be used in any JSR 168 compliant portal platform. Although some are noted as being still under development, GEMS has the following portlets that are or will be, available under Apache licence: e-mail, calendar, address book, weather, sports scores, blog, RSS feed, calculator, image viewer, horoscope, Google search, ads by Google, Google groups, Amazon, UPS tracking, Fed-Ex tracking, hangman game, cards game, cartoon of the day, quote of the day, dictionary, thesaurus, generic datasource search (Wikipedia data, corporate, etc.), acronym search (internal personnel directory, etc.), voting.

GridSphere

As its name implies, GridSphere is widely used for grid gateways. Portlets are classified as: SRB portlets, personal grid library, blue squid (collaboration portlets including forum, blog, chat, list, e-mail, RSS), CMAG: China meteorological application grid, GAMA portlets (grid security via credential management), CSF: community scheduler framework for submitting applications to remote computers. Some screenshots are provided on the website (*http://www.gridsphere.org/gridsphere/gridsphere*). Separate portlets include: login, logout, locale, user manager, group manager, layout manager, profile settings, user layout, tutorial portlets (helloworld, uihelloworld, actionhelloworld, photo portlet, address portlet), extras (web clipping, file commander, banner, charts, poll and photo album), credential retrieval, file browser, job submission portlet, resource browser, resource registry, grid slide (webdav), Sun and IBM samples, Sun JSF sample.

IBM

WebSphere and Lotus portal tools are listed online (*http://www-01.ibm.com/software/brandcatalog/portal/portal/*), and many are partner business oriented. There are many portlets in the catalogue, which is searchable by product, industry, provider and solution area. Entries from an older version were listed under the following headings: asset management, business intelligence, business process management, business-to-business integration, collaboration, commerce, content delivery, content management, corporate performance management, customer relationship management, data management, digital media, enterprise resource planning, financial management, human capital management, human resources, knowledge management, mergers and acquisitions, personal tools, product lifecycle management, search, security, software as services, straight through processing, supply chain management, training, web exploitation.

Examples under the personal tools heading include: calculator application, document viewer, droplets chat, database reporter, e-mail, interactive calendar, UI server and SDK, IBM quicklinks, IBM reminder, integrate people, LDAP search, Stellent authenticated library, authenticated search, basic search, contribution, library, metadata administration, saved search, workflow queue, webradar, world clock, agent finance, Altiolive studio enterprise, Altiolive Websphere, Athoc active portlet, Athoc enterprise alert, Athoc portal toolbar, portal toolbar and desktop alerts, portal toolbar, autonomy agents, breaking news, community, expertise locator, hot news, portlet administration, profile, retrieval, similar people, spectrograph, bookmarks, buddyscript server, Citrix metaframe sp, content management, Convera retrieval ware, corporate news, corporate 411, correlate k-map, desktop grabber, divine federated search, mindalign collaboration, periodicals, print publications, real time news, tracker, easy ask search and navigation, enfavourites, execcommand, FAST smart connector, federated search, Greenax, HR agent, HR quickstart, IBM Lotus extended search, DN2 portlets, logomarc, Moreover technologies CI builder, MQWF worklist, my proactiveportal, newslocker, newspublisher, news viewer, notes2pdf, paybox mobile financial services, portal site map, private expertise portlet, proactive portal server, proactive portal, search sitemap, SharePoint events calendar, statistic chart, super-bookmark, task component, Verity K2 search, ultraseek, integrator, Websphere host on demand, XML news services.

JBoss

The JBoss portlet swap catalogue (*http://labs.jboss.com/portal/portlet swap/portlets_collab.html*) gives screenshots and notes what licences may apply. Contributed portlets are in subcategories: framework, collaboration, miscellaneous and helloworld. A small sample includes: Alfresco CMS, contact, infoview, JBoss wiki, Kosmos (project monitoring suite), Hudson, Pentaho business intelligence, Syncex collaboration suite (MS Exchange and Domino).

Jetspeed

The Apache Jetspeed 2 site (*http://portals.apache.org/jetspeed-2*) currently has: HTML, JSP, RSS, Velocity portlet, generic MVC, web page, XSL, database browser, logfile viewer, web clipping, Java applet. A few contributed portlets for Jetspeed 1.4 include: mail, todo list, web surf, iframe, web browser portlet. There are also portlet bridges from the Apache project for Struts, JSF, Velocity, Perl and PHP.

jPortlet

jPortlet (*http://jportlet.sourceforge.net/road_map.html*) is a Sourceforge project. It currently lists: bookmarks, RSS feed, menu, Google search, discussion forum, contacts, calendar, e-mail client, document manager, login portlet.

Liferay

Liferay has a software catalogue (tools) portlet which links to remote repositories to download and configure other portlets. The website (*http://ww.liferay.com*) states that over 60 tools are available with the portal download. An example of this is from caBIG, the US Cancer Biomedical Informatics Grid project which supports its own community catalogue of over 40 tools (*https://cabig.nci.nih.gov/inventory*). These are in the areas of clinical trials management, bio-specimens, imaging, genome annotation, proteomics, microarrays, pathways, data analysis and statistical tools, data sharing, infrastructure, vocabularies, and translational research. They are based on open source software and are free to use. Training is offered to caBIG consortium members.

Magnolia

The Magnolia content management systems have a portlet interface.

Appendix B

MyOffice24x7

MyOffice for SMEs uses Liferay (*http://www.myoffice24x7.com*). It currently has a suite of electronic records managements system (ERMS) portlets integrated with JBoss JBPM backend, a suite of radio frequency identification (RFID) portlets (requiring ERMS), a suite of payment management portlets, integrated with various banking and third-party gateways via hot deployed plugins.

OGCE2

Version 2 of OGCE NMI portal (*http://www.collab-ogce.org*) uses uPortal and GridSphere. This currently has: proxy manager, GridFTP, GRAM, GPIR, Condor, QBETS, workflow, etc. A Velocity tool allows you to port Jetspeed Velocity portlets into JSR 168 containers. Other portlet independent services are available, for example sharing data. TeraGrid staff are also investigating use of Google gadgets and Javascript applications for similar functionality via iGoogle or a rich desktop application.

Oracle

Portlets available for the Oracle portal from partners can be found by searching the Oracle site (*http://www.oracle.com/technology/products/ias/portal/index.html*). There are said to be hundreds of third-party portlets available, many subject to licensing.

POST

Portlet Open Source Trading, on Sourceforge (*http://portlet-opensrc.sourceforge.net/* and *http://sourceforge.net/projects/portlet-opensrc/*) is a collaboration between Plumtree, Documentum, BEA and Sun. Disappointingly, only Google API, wizard, mail, RSS and upload are currently listed.

Sun

The Java.net repository (*https://portlet-repository.dev.java.net*) is a workspace for open source developers to contribute a variety of JSR 168

233

compliant portlets. The repository includes portlets for enterprise integrations, web technologies, collaboration and much more. This project is part of the overall POST project. Currently listed portlets include the following: Ajax, blog, bookmark, bluminate, Flickr, iframe, JAAS, JNDI, mashup, notepad, mvforum, photoshow, photo viewer, privacy guard, RSS, suggest and search, secure global desktop, shared bookmarks, session counter, inter-portlet communication (JSR 286), showtime, video, weather, XML and XSL translation, workflow.

SyncEx

The SyncEx Portlets To Go suite has portlets available for the following: IBM websphere portal, BEA WebLogic portal, Sun Java system portal, Liferay portal, Oracle iAS portal, Vignette application portal, eXo platform portal, SAP enterprise portal, TIBCO portal builder, Jetspeed portal, uPortal. The catalogue lists the following: employee directory, corporate calendar, forum, blog, calendar portlet, e-mail, team calendar, tasks, contact portlet, poll, minutes of meeting, information sharing and FAQ portlet, mini mail, mini calendar, bookmark, content viewer, RSS, feedback, alert, issue and bug tracking (see *http://www.syncex.com/portlet_catalog/portlet_catalog.htm*).

uPortal

The uPortal site (*http://www.uportal.org/implementors/portlets/workingWithPortlets.html*) lists a few sample portlets which can be used as templates. Pluto test suite sample, RSS, Google, functional tests, WSRP, etc.

Appendix C: Generic portal engines

The tables below list a number of generic portal engines and some related software from commercial vendors and developers in the public domain. The products marked with '(1)' support JSR 168 portlets, (2) support JSR 286 and those marked '(3)' claim to support Ajax.

Commercial

Some of these portals are designed for e-learning or e-business applications.

Table C.1 Generic commercial portal engines

Portal engine	Domain/URL
Adobe ColdFusion (3)	http://www.adobe.com/products/coldfusion
Adenin Enterprise portal (1)	http://www.adenin.com
ASP.NET (3)	http://www.asp.net
ATG Portal (1)	http://www.atg.com
BEA AquaLogic*	http://www.bea.com
BEA/Oracle WebLogic (1)*	http://edocs.bea.com
BI Portal suite	http://www.viador.com
Blackboard Community Portal	http://www.blackboard.com
CA CleverPath Portal	http://www.ca.com
Elipva	http://www.elipva.com
Epicentric	See vignette below
IBM Lotus Domino	http://www.lotus.com
IBM WebSphere Portal (1) (2)	http://www.ibm.com/websphere

Virtual Research Environments

Table C.1 Generic commercial portal engines (*Cont'd*)

Portal engine	Domain/URL
Intrexx Xtreme	http://www.intrexx.com
Jahia (1)	http://www.jahia.org
Merant Collage	http://www.serena.com
Microsoft Exchange 2007	http://www.microsoft.com/exchange
Microsoft SharePoint 2007	http://www.microsoft.com/sharepoint
NICE EnginFrame (1)	http://www.nice-italy.com
Oracle Portal (1)	http://www.oracle.com/portal
SAP Enterprise Portal (1)	http://www.sap.com
Serco Facility VLE	http://www.serco.com
SITS Vision	http://www.tribalgroup.co.uk/sitsvision
Sun ONE Portal Server (1) (2)	http://docs.sun.com/app/docs/coll/S1_Portal Server_30
Sungard Luminis (1)	http://http://www.sungardhe.com/products/luminis-platform
Sybase Enterprise portal	http://www.sybase.com
SyncEx Portal services (1)	http://www.syncex.com
Tibco Portal Builder (1)	http://www.tibco.com/software/portal
Unicon Portal Services	http://www.unicon.net
Vignette Application Portal (2)	http://www.vignette.com
WebCT Vista	http://www.webct.com/products/viewpage?name=products_vista

*This is migrating to the Oracle Technology Network in 2009

Public domain

The following are either open source or free to download and can be used for a variety of purposes.

Table C.2 Generic public domain portal engines

Portal engine	Domain/URL
CHEF	*http://www.chefproject.org*
Enhydra	*http://www.enhydra.org*
ExoPlatform (1) (2)	*http://www.exoplatform.org*
FreshMeat PHP Portal	*http://freshmeat.net/projects/phportal*
Gluecode Portal Foundation Server	Now part of IBM WebSphere Application Service Conity Edition
GridPort	*http://www.gridport.net*
GridSphere (1)	*http://www.gridsphere.org*
HubZero	*http://hubzero.org*
iPoint Portal	*http://www.c2b2.co.uk/iPoint/1.page*
JBoss Portal (2)	*http://www.redhat.com*
JetSpeed-2 (1) (2)	*http://portals.apache.org*
jPortlet (1)	*https://jportlet.dev.java.net*
LifeRay (1) (2)	*http://www.liferay.com*
Lutece Portal (1)	*http://dev.lutece.paris.fr/*
Mambo server	*http://www.mamboserver.com*
MyLibrary	*http://mylibrary.library.nd.edu*
OpenPortal (1)	*https://portal.dev.java.net/*
PHP-Nuke	*http://www.phpnuke.org*
Pluto (1)	*http://portals.apache.org*
PostNuke	*http://www.postnuke.com*
Sakai (1)	*http://www.sakaiproject.org/portal*
StringBeans (1)	*http://www.nabh.com/projects/sbportal*
uPortal(1)	*http://www.uportal.org*
Zope	*http://www.zope.org*

Appendix D: Glossary

A glossary with many relevant entries can be found at: *http://www.grids.ac.uk/ReDRESS/glossary_v2/glossary_v2.html*. For more generic explanations, the reader is referred to Wikipedia (*http://www.wikipedia.org*). Acronyms for specific projects are not listed, only those for established services or standards.

Abbreviations and acronyms

Specific abbreviations and acronyms used in this book are listed below:

AAA: authentication, authorisation and accounting

Access Grid: virtual interaction technology supported by JISC (*http://www.agsc.ja.net*)

ADS: Atlas Data Store, petabyte tape store at the Harwell Campus

AFS: Andrews File System

AHDS: Arts and Humanities Data Service

AHRC: Arts and Humanities Research Council – formerly AHRB (*http://www.ahrc.ac.uk*)

AJAX: asynchronous JavaScript and XML

API: application programming interface

BADC: British Atmospheric Data Centre, one of the NERC funded UK data centres (*http://www.nerc.ac.uk/research/sites/data*)

BBSRC: Bio-technology and Biological Sciences Research Council (*http://www.bbsrc.ac.uk*)

Castor: CERN Advanced Storage Manager (*http://castor.web.cern.ch/castor*)

CCLRC: Council for the Central Laboratory of the Research Councils, now part of STFC

239

CCP: Collaborative Computational Projects (*http://www.ccp.ac.uk*)

CECAM: Centre Européen de Calcul Atomique et Moléculaire (*http://www.cecam.fr*)

CERN: Centre Européen pour la Récherche Nucleaire (*http://www.cern.ch*)

CML: chemical markup language

CNI: Coalition for Networked Information (*http://www.cni.org*)

CNR: Consiglio Nazionale delle Ricerche – the Italian National Research Council (*http://www.cnr.it*)

CROWN: China Research and Development environment Over Wide Area Network – middleware being produced by a number of institutions in China

CSCW: computer supported collaborative working

CURL: Consortium of University Research Librarians (*http://www.curl.ac.uk*)

CWE: collaborative working environment

DCC: Digital Curation Centre (*http://www.dcc.ac.uk*)

DEEWR: Australian Department of Education, Employment and Workplace Relations – formerly DEST (*http://www.deewr.gov.au*)

DEISA: Distributed European Infrastructure for Supercomputing Applications (*http://www.deisa.eu*)

DEST: Australian Department for Education, Science and Training (*http://www.dest.gov.au*) now DEEWR

Diamond: Diamond Light Source – see DLS

DIUS: UK Government Department for Innovation, Universities and Skills (*http://www.dius.gov.uk*)

DLS: Diamond Light Source (*http://www.diamond.ac.uk*)

DOI: digital object identifier, e.g. as provided by CrossRef (*http://www.crossref.org*)

DRM: digital rights management

E-Framework: the E-Framework for Education and Research (*http://www.e-framework.org*)

EDINA: the JISC national academic data centre based at the University of Edinburgh (*http://edina.ac.uk*) – it is not an acronym, but the old poetic name for Edinburgh as used by Robert Burns

EGEE: Enabling Grids for E-science in Europe (*http://www.eu-egee.org*)

ePubs: STFC ePubs open access repository (*http://epubs.cclrc.ac.uk*)

ESRC: Economic and Social Research Council (*http://www.esrc.ac.uk*)

ESRF: European Synchrotron Radiation Facility in Grenoble (*http://www.esrf.eu*)

FTP: file transfer protocol

GDA: Generic Data Acquisition system (*http://www.gda.ac.uk*)

GGF: see OGF

gLite: grid middleware being produced by the EGEE project

GSI: grid security infrastructure

GridPP: UK particle physics data grid for LHC data analysis, funded by STFC (*http://www.gridpp.ac.uk*)

GSSAPI: generic security service application program interface

HCI: human–computer interface

HEI: higher education institution

HPC: high-performance computing

HTML: hyper text markup language

ICT: information and communication technologies

IEEE: Institute of Electrical and Electronic Engineers (*http://www.ieee.org*)

IEMSR: Information Environment Metadata Schema Registry (*http://iemsr.ac.uk*)

IESR: Information Environment Service Registry (*http://iesr.ac.uk*)

IETF: Internet Engineering Task Force, an international standards body (*http://www.ietf.org*)

IGTF: International Grid Trust Federation (*http://www.igtf.net*)

InCHI: international chemical identifier

IPC: inter-process communication

IPR: intellectual property rights

ISO: International Standards Organisation (*http://www.iso.org*)

J2EE: Java platform, enterprise edition

JANET: Joint Academic Network – UK public network for education and research (*http://www.ja.net*)

JCIE: JISC Committee for the Information Environment

JCSR: JISC Committee for the Support of Research

JDBC: Java data base connectivity

JISC: UK Joint Infrastructure Systems Committee (*http://www.jisc.ac.uk*)

JISCmail: JISC mail service (*http://www.jiscmail.ac.uk*)

JSDL: job submission description language OGF specification

JSF: Java Server Faces

JSP: Java Server Pages

LAN: local area network

LDAP: lightweight directory access protocol

LHC: the large hadron collider at CERN

LSID: life sciences identifier

MDS: monitoring and discovery system – a component provided in Globus that provides information about the status of available resources

MIMAS: Manchester Information and Associated Services – JISC and ESRC supported national data centre at the University of Manchester (*http://www.mimas.ac.uk*)

MIME: multi-purpose internet mail extensions

MRC: Medical Research Council (*http://www.mrc.ac.uk*)

MVC: model, view, control programming pattern

NACTeM: National Centre for Text Mining (*http://www.nactem.ac.uk*)

NCeSS: National Centre for e-Social Science (*http://www.ncess.ac.uk*)

NERC: Natural Environment Research Council (*http://www.nerc.ac.uk*)

NeSC: UK National e-Science Centre (*http://www.nesc.ac.uk*)

NGS: National Grid Service (*http://www.ngs.ac.uk*)

OAI: Open Archives Initiative (*http://www.oai.org*)

OAIS: open archival information system

OASIS: Organization for the Advancement of Structured Information Standards (*http://www.oasis-open.org*)

ODBC: open data base connectivity

OGF: Open Grid Forum, formerly known as the Global Grid Forum (GGF) – a body that is attempting to standardise and document the processes and protocols that are, or will be, required to construct grids for research (*http://www.ogf.org*)

OGSA: open grid services architecture – describes an abstract architecture for a service oriented grid environment

OGSA-DAI: open grid services architecture data access and integration

OMII: Open Middleware Infrastructure Initiative (*http://www.omii.ac.uk*)

ONS: UK Office for National Statistics (*http://www.statistics.gov.uk*)

OpenURL: URL link creation standard and resolver

OWL: web ontology language, a Semantic Web technology

P2P: peer-to-peer

PAM: pluggable authentication modules

PDB: Protein Data Bank – a service hosted at the European Biomolecular Institute

PKI: public key infrastructure

PPARC: Particle Physics and Astronomy Research Council, now part of STFC

PSE: problem solving environment

RAT: robust audio tool – an open source audio conferencing and streaming application from University College London

RCUK: UK Research Councils (*http://www.rcuk.ac.uk*)

RDF: resource description framework, a Semantic Web technology

RDN: Resource Discovery Network, now known as Intute (*http://www.intute.ac.uk*)

RFC: request for comment (see *http://www.rfc-editor.org/rfc.html*)

RFID: radio frequency identifier

RPC: remote procedure call

RRM: research reference models, now referred to as SUMs in the e-Framework, (*http://www.grids.ac.uk/Papers/Classes/classes.html*)

SAGA: simple API for grid applications – OGF specification

Sakai: Sakai collaborative learning framework adapted for research purposes (*http://www.saksiproject.org/portal*)

SAML: security assertion markup language

SCUFL: simple conceptual unified flow language

SMTP: simple mail transfer protocol

SOA: service oriented architecture

SOSIG: Social Science Information Gateway – now Intute Social Sciences (*http://www.intute.ac.uk/socialsciences*)

SPP: Subject Portal Project (*http://www.portal.ac.uk/spp*)

SQL: structured query language

SRB: Storage Resource Broker (*http://www.npaci.edu/DICE/SRB*)

SSL: secure socket layer, an internet communication protocol which uses encryption

SSO: single sign-on

STFC: Science and Technology Facilities Council – formed in April 2007 by merging CCLRC and PPARC (*http://www.stfc.ac.uk*)

SUM: service usage models as defined in the e-Framework for Education and Research (*http://www.e-framework.org*)

SURF: Dutch organisation for higher education and research institutions aimed at innovations in ICT (*http://www.surf.nl*)

TLS: transport layer security – formerly known as SSL (see above)

UKDA: UK Data Archive (*http://www.data-archive.ac.uk*)

UKOLN: a centre of excellence in information management based at the University of Bath and funded by the Council for Museums Libraries and Archives and JISC (*http://www.ukoln.ac.uk*)

UNICORE: Uniform Interface to Computing Resources, grid middleware

URL: uniform resource locator

UUID: universally unique identifier

VDT: virtual data toolkit comprising grid middleware

VeRSI: Victorian e-Research Strategic Initiative (*http://versi.edu.au*)

VFS: virtual file system, part of the Apache Commons project (*http://commons.apache.org/vfs*)

VIC: video conference tool from University of California, Berkeley and Lawrence Berkeley National Laboratory

VNC: virtual network computing

VO: virtual organisation

VRC: virtual research community – an alternative term to VO

VRVS: virtual room videoconferencing system developed at CERN

W3C: World Wide Web Consortium (*http://www.w3.org*)

WAN: wide area network

X.509: The standard format for digital certificates used in PKI security frameworks

Web services nomenclature

Some terms which are met in the web services literature are used in this book. They are collected here for reference:

BPEL: business process execution language

BPML: business process modelling language – now referred to as BPMN or business process modelling notation

DOM: document object model – creates the full XML data structure in memory so that element contents can be referenced using XPath – can be very memory-intensive

Endpoint: a URL from which the remote service can be invoked, sometimes referred to as a 'proxy', but not to be confused with an HTTP proxy

Hosting environment: sometimes referred to as a SOAP engine, this is equivalent to a web server (e.g. Apache) but includes XML parsers to do marshalling and demarshalling and despatch to the web service referenced by the proxy endpoint

HTTP: hyper text transfer protocol – protocol based on PUT, GET and POST methods with widely recognised headers and MIME types used for data transfer on the internet

HTTPS: secure HTTP using TLS protocol

Namespace: unique identifier for the set(s) of tags used in XML documents; some namespaces have public definitions allowing for interchange of documents with known semantics, e.g. HTML

SAML: security assertion markup language

SAX: simple access to XML – traverses the document and signals events each time a tag is met so that the user can interpret the attributes and elements; can be time-consuming if the document must be traversed more than once

Serialisation/deserialisation: converts a language-specific data structure into an XML document in a form suitable for transmission over HTTP or vice versa

SGML: standard generalised markup language

SMIL: synchronised multimedia integration language

SOAP: once known as simple object access protocol, it is an XML-based language with predefined tags to encapsulate remote method calls and data in an XML document

SOAP demarshalling/marshalling: converts a SOAP request message body into elements which define the input and output data (messages), required methods and endpoint so that the service may be called (this involves de-serialisation and parsing); similarly, for a reply, the data and status are converted into a SOAP message body

UDDI: universal description, discovery and integration – a platform-independent XML-based registry for publishing information about service provider and their services

WS-I: basic web services interoperability profile from the WS-I Consortium (*http://www.ws-i.org*)

WSDL: web services description language – XML-based language with predefined tags to describe a remote service in terms of its methods and endpoint

WSIL: web services inspection language

Appendix D

WSRF: web services resource framework – a set of specifications dealing with the association of web services with stateful resources on a grid

XAML: extensible application markup language

XML: extensible markup language – ASCII 'language' consisting of tagged elements with names, attributes and contents. Tags and attributes are placed between angular brackets < and >. They are similar to HTML, but XML tags have no predefined meaning (but see *Namespace* above). An XML document is essentially a tree-structured data format with elements nested inside other elements. Elements must be correctly nested and have closing element tags for a document to be 'well formed'.

XML parser: interprets an XML document, separating the tags and content – DOM and SAX-based parsers are available for most programming languages

XPath: an XML language for navigating tree-like information structures, similar to UNIX directory notation

XSD: XML schema definition – defines elements and attributes and their nesting with possible restrictions on content value that are permissible in a given XML document; a document that adheres to a schema is said to be 'valid'

XSLT: XML stylesheet transformation language – using parsers, one XML document can be translated into another with a different layout and different tags; this is one of the most powerful uses of XML, and the basis of many higher-level tools

Bibliography

Abbas, A. (2004) *Grid Computing: A Practical Guide to Technology and Applications* (2nd edn), New Delhi: Laxmi Publications.

Abbott, D. (2006) 'What is digital curation', DCC briefing paper, available at: *http://www.dcc.ac.uk/resource/briefing-papers/what-is-digital-curation/* (accessed 15 June 2009).

Addison, C., Allan, R. J., Brooke, J. M. and van Ark, T. (2008) 'NW-GRID: North West Grid – Final Report', NW-GRID technical report, available at: *http://www.grids.ac.uk/NWGrid/Evaluation-Report-Final.pdf* (accessed 15 June 2009).

Akram, A., Chohan, D., Meredith, D. and Allan, R. (2007) 'CCLRC portal infrastructure to support research facilities', *Concurrency and Computation: Practice and Experience* 19(6): 751–66.

Alameda, J., Christie, M., Fox, G., Futrelle, J., Gannon, D., Hategan, M., Kandaswamy, G., von Laszewski, G., Nacar, M. A., Pierce, M. E., Roberts, E., Severance, C. and Thomas, M. (2007) 'The Open Grid Computing Environments Collaboration: portlets and services for science gateways', *Concurrency and Computation: Practice and Experience* 19(6): 921–42.

Allan, R. J. (2005) 'Service classes', STFC Daresbury Laboratory technical report, available at: *http://www.grids.ac.uk/Papers/Classes/classes.html* (accessed 15 June 2009).

Allan, R. J. and Kewley, J. (2007) 'GROWL: Grid Resources on Workstation Library', available at: *http://www.growl.org.uk/GROWL_FinalReport.pdf* (accessed 15 June 2009).

Allan, R. J. and Severance, C. (2006) 'Discussions about Sakai integration with portals', discussion at 3rd JISC VRE Programme Meeting, Oxford, 16 January.

Allan, R. J. and Yang, X. (2008) 'Using role based access control in the Sakai collaborative framework', STFC Daresbury Laboratory technical report, available at: *http://www.grids.ac.uk/Sakai/sakai_framework_doc.pdf* (accessed 15 June 2009).

Allan, R. J., Wang, X. D. and Hanlon, D. (2003) 'An introduction to web services and related technology for building an e-science grid', UK High End Computing Initiative technical report, available at: *http://www.ukhec.ac.uk/publications/reports/webServices_doc.pdf* (accessed 15 June 2009).

Allan, R. J., Allden, A., Boyd, D., Crouchley, R., Harris, N., Lyon, L., Robiette, A., de Roure, D. and Wilson, S. (2004a) 'Roadmap for a UK virtual research environment', JISC VRE Working Group technical report, available at: *http://www.jisc.ac.uk/uploaded_documents/ VRE%20roadmap%20v4.pdf* (accessed 15 June 2009).

Allan, R. J., Awre, C., Baker, M. and Fish, A. (2004b) 'Portals and portlets 2003', National E-Science Centre technical report, available at: *http://www.nesc.ac.uk/technical_papers/UKeS-2004-06.pdf* (accessed 15 June 2009).

Allan, R. J., Chohan, D., Wang, X. D., McKeown, M., Colgrave, J. and Dovey, M. (2004c) 'UDDI and WS-Inspection for e-Science', STFC Daresbury Laboratory technical report, available at: *http://epubs.cclrc .ac.uk/bitstream/1452/uddi.pdf* (accessed 15 June 2009).

Allan, R. J., Nave, C., Keegan, R., Meredith, D. J., Winn, M. D., Winter, G., Dolomanov, O., Launer, L., Young, P. and Berry, I. (2005) 'Portal design, synchrotron and HPC services in e-HTPX', paper presented at UK e-Science All Hands Conference, Nottingham, 19–22 September, available at: *http://www.allhands.org.uk/2005/proceedings/papers/385.pdf* (accessed 15 June 2009).

Allan, R. J., Crouchley, R. and Ingram, C. (2006a) 'JISC information environment portal activity: comparison of surveys', CSI Consultancy technical report, available at: *http://epubs.cclrc.ac.uk/bitstream/3688/ eRes%20Comparison%20of%20surveys.pdf* (accessed 15 June 2009).

Allan, R. J., Crouchley, R. and Ingram, C. (2006b) 'JISC information environment portal activity: e-research, portals and digital repositories workshop', CSI Consultancy technical report, available at: *http:// epubs.cclrc.ac.uk/bitstream/1143/dr_workshop.pdf* (accessed 15 June 2009).

Allan, R. J., Crouchley, R. and Ingram, C. (2006c) 'JISC information environment portal activity: final report', STFC Daresbury Laboratory technical report, available at: *http://epubs.cclrc.ac.uk/bitstream/3693/ final.pdf* (accessed 15 June 2009).

Allan, R. J., Crouchley, R. and Ingram, C. (2006d) 'JISC information environment portal activity: interim report', STFC Daresbury Laboratory technical report, available at: *http://epubs.cclrc.ac.uk/ bitstream/3692/interim.pdf* (accessed 15 June 2009).

Allan, R. J., Crouchley, R. and Ingram, C. (2006e) 'JISC information environment portal activity: scenarios, use cases and reference models', STFC Daresbury Laboratory technical report, available at: *http://epubs .cclrc.ac.uk/bitstream/3691/use_cases.pdf* (accessed 15 June 2009).

Allan, R. J., Crouchley, R. and Ingram, C. (2006f) 'JISC information environment portal activity: the information environment and e-research portals', STFC Daresbury Laboratory technical report, available at: *http://epubs.cclrc.ac.uk/bitstream/3690/ie_portals.pdf* (accessed 15 June 2009).

Allan, R. J., Crouchley, R. and Ingram, C. (2006g) 'JISC Information environment portal activity: web-based library and information services', STFC Daresbury Laboratory technical report, available at: *http://epubs.cclrc.ac.uk/bitstream/3689/library_services.pdf* (accessed 15 June 2009).

Allan, R. J., Yang, X., Crouchley, R., Fish, A. and Gonzalez, M. (2007) 'Virtual research environments: Sakai VRE Demonstrator', paper presented at the UK e-Science All Hands Conference, Nottingham, 10–13 September, available at: *http://www.allhands.org.uk/2007/ proceedings/papers/814.pdf* (accessed 15 June 2009).

Allan, R. J., Yang, X. and Crouchley, R. (2008) 'ESRC e-infrastructure portal requirements', STFC Daresbury Laboratory technical report, available at: *http://epubs.cclrc.ac.uk/bitstream/3635/e-IP_portal_report.pdf* (accessed 15 June 2009).

Allen, G., Goodale, T., Russell, M., Seidel, E. and Shalf, J. (2003) 'Classifying and enabling grid applications', in F. Berman, G. C. Fox and A. J. G. Hey (2003) *Grid Computing: Making the Global Infrastructure a Reality*, Chichester: J. Wiley and Sons, pp. 601–14.

Anderson, C. (2007) *The Long Tail*, New York: Random House.

Atkins, D. E., Droegemeier, K. K., Feldman, S. I., Garcia-Molina, H., Klien, M. L. and Messerschmitt, D. G. (2003) 'Revolutionizing science and engineering through cyberinfrastructure', National Science Foundation Blue-Ribbon Advisory Panel on Cyberinfrastructure technical report, available at: *http://www.communitytechnology.org/ nsf_ci_report/report.pdf* (accessed 15 June 2009).

Atkinson, M. (2003) 'Rationale for choosing the Open Grid Services Architecture', in F. Berman, G. C. Fox and A. J. G. Hey (2003) *Grid Computing: Making the Global Infrastructure a Reality*, Chichester: J. Wiley and Sons, pp. 199–215.

Atkinson, M., Crowcroft, J., de Roure, D. and Dialani, V. (2002) 'UK role in open grid services architecture', National E-Science Centre technical report, available at: *http://www.nesc.ac.uk/teams/UK_ OGSA_v0.7_12Mar02.pdf* (accessed 15 June 2009).

Baker, M., Ong, H. and Allan, R. (2005) 'Grid services in the UK and beyond', STFC Daresbury Laboratory technical report, available at: *http://epubs.cclrc.ac.uk/bitstream/1041/ogsa_testbed_report.pdf* (accessed 15 June 2009).

Barga, R. S., Andrews, S. and Parastatidis, S. (2007) 'A virtual research environment for bioscience researchers', paper presented at International Conference on Advanced Engineering Computing and Applications in Sciences, Papeete, French Polynesia, 4–9 November, available at: *http://ieeexplore.ieee.org/stamp/stamp.jsp?tp=&arnumber= 4401895&isnumber=4401884* (accessed 15 June 2009).

Beckles, B., Coveney, P., Ryan, P., Abdallah, A., Pickles, S., Brooke, J. and McKeown, M. (2006) 'A user-friendly approach to computational grid security', paper presented at UK e-Science All Hands Conference, Nottingham, 18–21 September, available at: *http://www.allhands.org .uk/2006/proceedings/papers/636.pdf* (accessed 15 June 2009).

Baru C., Moore, R., Rajasekar A. and Wan M. (1998) 'The SDSC Storage Resource Broker', paper presented at CASCON, Toronto, 30 November to 3 December, available at: *http://www.npaci.edu/DICE/ Pubs/srb.pdf* (accessed 15 June 2009).

Berg, A. and Korkuska, M. (2009) *The Official Sakai Handbook: Creating Content, Installing and Using the Open Source Learning Management System*, London: J. Wiley and Sons.

Berman, F., Fox, G. C. and Hey, A. J. G. (2003) *Grid Computing: Making the Global Infrastructure a Reality*, Chichester: J. Wiley and Sons.

Binns, J., DiCarlo, J., Insley, J. A., Leggett, T., Lueninghoener, C., Navarro, J.-P. and Papka, M. E. (2007) 'Enabling community access to TeraGrid visualization resources', *Concurrency and Computation: Practice and Experience* 19(6): 783–94.

Borda, A., Careless, J., Dimitrova, M., Fraser, M., Frey, J. and Hubbard, P. (2006) 'Report of the Working Group on Virtual Research Communities', OSI e-Infrastructure Steering Group technical report, available at: *http://www.nesc.ac.uk/documents/OSI/vrc.pdf* (accessed 15 June 2009).

Borel, E. (1913) 'Mecanique statistique et irreversibilité', *Journal de Physique* 5(3): 189–96.

Borgman, C. L. (2005) 'Building a usable infrastructure for e-science: an information perspective', keynote presentation at UK e-Science All Hands Conference, Nottingham, 19–22 September, available at: *http://www .nesc.ac.uk/talks/ahm2005/keynote1.ppt* (accessed 15 June 2009).

Bibliography

Borgman, C. L., Wallis, J. C. and Enyedy, N. (2006) 'Building digital libraries for scientific data: an exploratory study of data practices in habitat ecology', paper presented at 10th European Conference on Research and Advanced Technology for Digital Libraries, Alicante, 17–22 September, available at: *http://polaris.gseis.ucla.edu/cborgman/pubs/CBJWNE_REV_ECDL.PDF* (accessed 15 June 2009).

Bruin, R. P., White, T. O. H., Walker, A. M., Austen, K. F., Dove, M. T., Tyer, R. P., Couch, P. A., Todorov, I. T. and Blanchard, M. O. (2008) 'Job submission to Grid computing environments', *Concurrency and Computation: Practice and Experience* 20(11): 1329–40.

caGrid Project (2008) 'caGrid Portal v2.1 user's guide', available at: *http://cagrid-portal.nci.nih.gov/web/guest/home* (accessed 15 June 2009).

Calleja, M., Bruin, R., Tucker, M. G., Dove, M. T., Tyer, R. P., Blanshard, L. J., van Dam, K. K., Allan, R. J., Chapman, C., Emmerich, W., Wilson, P. B., Brodholt, J. P., Thandavan, A. and Alexandrov, V. N. (2005) 'Collaborative grid infrastructure for molecular simulations', *Molecular Simulations* 31: 303–13.

Carr, N. (2007) 'The ignorance of crowds', available at: *http://www.strategy-business.com/press/freearticle/07204* (accessed 15 June 2009).

Catlow, C. (1992) 'Research Requirements for High Performance Computing', Scientific Working Group to the SERC Supercomputing Management Committee technical report, Swindon: SERC.

Chin, J. and Coveney, P. V. (2004) 'Towards tractable toolkits for the Grid: a plea for lightweight, usable middleware', National E-Science Centre technical report, available at: *http://www.nesc.ac.uk/technical_papers/UKeS-2004-01.pdf* (accessed 15 June 2009).

Christie, M. and Marru, S. (2007) 'The LEAD portal: a TeraGrid gateway and application service architecture', *Concurrency and Computation: Practice and Experience* 19(6): 767–81.

Cobb, J. W., Geist, A., Kohl, J. A., Miller, S. D., Peterson, P. F., Pike, G. G., Reuter, M. A., Swain, T., Vazhkudai, S. S. and Vijayakumar, N. N. (2007) 'The Neutron Science TeraGrid Gateway: a TeraGrid science gateway to support the spallation neutron source', *Concurrency and Computation: Practice and Experience* 19(6): 809–26.

Collins, H. (2001) *Corporate Portals*, New York: Amacom.

Coveney, P., Saksena, R., Zasada, S., McKeown, M. and Pickles, S. (2007) 'The Application Hosting Environment: lightweight middleware for Grid based computational science', *Computer Physics Communications*, 176: 406–18.

Cox, A. (2004) 'Building collaborative e-research environments', University of Loughborough technical report compiled for JISC.

Crouchley, R. and Allan, R. J. (2008) 'Longitudinal statistical modelling on the Grid', in N. Fielding, R. Lee and G. Blank (eds) *Handbook of Online Research Methods*, London: Sage, pp. 471–90.

Crouchley, R. and Fligelstone, R. (2002) 'The potential for high end computing in the social sciences', Lancaster University technical report, available at: *http://redress.lancs.ac.uk/resources/Crouchley_Rob/ The_Potential_for_High_End_Computing_in_the_Social_Sciences/ HECreport2.pdf* (accessed 15 June 2009).

Crouchley, R., van Ark, T., Pritchard, J., Kewley, J., Allan, R. J., Hayes, M. and Morris, L. (2005) 'Putting social science applications on the Grid', 1st International Conference on e-Social Science, Manchester, 22–24 June, available at: *http://www.epubs.stfc.ac.uk/bitstream/1453/NCeSS.pdf* (accessed 15 June 2009).

Crouchley, R., Allan, R. J., Fraser, M., Baker, M. and van Ark, T. (2007) 'Sakai VRE Portal Demonstrator – Final Report', Lancaster University technical report, available at: *http://www.grids.ac.uk/Sakai/sakai_ final_report.pdf* (accessed 15 June 2009).

Crouchley, R., Berridge, D., Grose, D., Stott, D. and Pritchard, J. (2009) *Multivariate Generalised Linear Mixed Models (sabreR)*, London: Chapman and Hall.

Daw, M., Procter, R., Lin, Y., Hewitt, T., Jie, W., Voss, A., Baird, K., Turner, A., Birkin, M., Miller, K., Dutton, W., Jirotka, M., Schroeder, R., de la Flor, G., Edwards, P., Allan, R. J., Yang, X. and Crouchley, R. (2007) 'Developing an e-infrastructure for social science', 3rd International Conference on e-Social Science, Michigan, 7–9 October, available at: *http://epubs.cclrc.ac.uk/bitstream/1788/e-Infrastructure4 SocSci.pdf* (accessed 15 June 2009).

De Roure, D. and Goble, C. (2007) 'myExperiment, a Web 2.0 virtual research environment', paper presented at International Workshop on VRE and CWE, Edinburgh, 23 May, available at: *http://www.myexperiment .org.http://eprints.ecs.soton.ac.uk/13961* (accessed 15 June 2009).

Dolphin, I., Miller, P. and Sherratt, R. (2002) 'Portals PORTALs everywhere', *Ariadne* 33(12), available at: *http://www.ariadne.ac.uk/ issue33/portals* (accessed 15 June 2009).

Dothen, P. (2004) 'Developing the UK's e-infrastructure for science and innovation', OSI e-Infrastructure Working Group technical report, available at: *http://www.nesc.ac.uk/documents/OSI/report.pdf* (accessed 15 June 2009).

Dove, M. T., Calleja, M., Wakelin, J., Trachenko, K., Ferlat, G., Murray-Rust, P., de Leeuw, N. H., Du, X., Price, G. D., Wilson, P. B., Brodholt, J. P., Alfredsson, M., Marmier, A., Tyer, R. P., Blanshard, L. J., Allan, R. J., van Dam, K. K., Todorov, I. T., Smith, W., Alexandrov, V. N., Lewis, G. J., Thandavan, A. and Hasan, S. M. (2003) 'Environment from the Molecular Level', paper presented at UK e-Science All Hands Conference, Nottingham, 2–4 September, available at: *http://epubs.cclrc .ac.uk/bitstream/381/emin2.pdf* (accessed 15 June 2009).

Environmental Protection Agency (2007) 'Report to Congress on server and data center energy efficiency', US EPA ENERGY STAR Programme. Public Law 109–431.

Erl, T. (2004) *Service-Oriented Architecture*, Upper Saddle River, NJ: Prentice Hall.

Erl, T. (2007) *SOA Principles of Service Design*, Upper Saddle River, NJ: Prentice Hall.

Erwin, D. (2002) 'UNICORE – a Grid Computing Environment', *Concurrency and Computation: Practice and Experience* 14: 1395–410.

Foster, I. and Kesselman, C. (1997) 'Globus: a meta-computing infrastructure toolkit', *International Journal of Supercomputer Applications* 11: 115–28.

Foster, I. and Kesselman, C. (1998) *The Grid: Blueprint for a New Computing Infrastructure*, San Francisco, CA: Morgan Kaufmann.

Foster, I., Kesselman, C. and Tuecke, S. (2001) 'Anatomy of the Grid: enabling scalable virtual organizations', *International Journal of Supercomputer Applications* 15, available at: *http://www.globus.org/ alliance/publications/papers/anatomy.pdf* (accessed 15 June 2009).

Foster, I., Kesselman, C., Nick, J. M. and Tuecke, S. (2003) 'The physiology of the grid', in F. Berman, G. C. Fox and A. J. G. Hey (2003) *Grid Computing: Making the Global Infrastructure a Reality*, Chichester: J. Wiley and Son, pp. 217–50.

Fox, G. and Walker, D. W. (2003) 'E-science gap analysis', National E-Science Centre technical report, available at: *http://www.nesc.ac.uk/ technical_papers/UKeS-2003-01* (accessed 15 June 2009).

Fraser, M. (2005) 'Virtual research environments overview', *Ariadne* 44(7), available at: *http://www.ariadne.ac.uk/issue44/fraser* (accessed 15 June 2009).

Gannon, D. (2009) 'On the TeraGrid, what is a science gateway?', available at: *http://www.teragrid.org/cgi-bin/kb.cgi?portal=1&docid= ascm* (accessed 15 June 2009).

Gleaves, M. T. and Ashtun, A. (2006) 'Summary of user requirements for the Diamond e-infrastructure', STFC Daresbury Laboratory technical report, available at: *http://www.grids.ac.uk/Diamond/SummaryUser RequirementsDiamond8.pdf* (accessed 16 June 2009).

Goldenberg-Hart, D. (2004) 'Libraries and changing research practices: a report of the ARL/CNI Forum on E-Research and Cyberinfrastructure',

Association of Research Libraries Bi-monthly Report 237: 1–5, available at: *http://dlist.sir.arizona.edu/770* (accessed 15 June 2009).

Graham, S., Simeonov, S., Boubez, T., Daniels, G., Nakamura, Y. and Neyama, R. (2004) *Building Web Services with Java: Making Sense of XML, SOAP, WSDL and UDDI* (2nd edn), Indianapolis, IN: SAMS.

Grose, D. (2009) 'High throughput distributed computing using R: the multiR package', *Journal of Statistical Software*, available at: *http://e-science.lancs.ac.uk/multiR/multiR-paper.pdf* (accessed 15 June 2009).

Grose, D., Crouchley, R., van Ark, T., Kewley, J., Allan, R. J., Braimah, A. and Hayes, M. (2006) 'SabreR: Grid-enabling the analysis of multi-process random effect response data in R', paper presented at 2nd International Conference on e-Social Science, Manchester, 26–28 June, available at: *http://www.epubs.stfc.ac.uk/bitstream/1162/NCeSS06.pdf* (accessed 15 June 2009).

Habermas, J. (2006) prize speech [in German], Renner Institute, Austria, March, available at: *http://www.renner-institut.at/download/texte/habermas2006-03-09.pdf* (accessed 15 June 2009).

Hashimi, S. (2003) 'Service-oriented architecture explained', available at: *http://www.ondotnet.com/pub/a/dotnet/2003/08/18/soa_explained.html* (accessed 15 June 2009).

Hayes, M., Crouchley, R., Grose, D., Allan, R. J., Kewley, J. and van Ark, T. (2007) 'GROWL VRE – Final Report', JISC technical report, available at: *http://www.growl.org.uk/GROWL_FinalReport.pdf* (accessed 15 June 2009).

Heery, R. and Anderson, S. (2005) 'Digital repositories review', UKOLN and AHDS technical report, available at: *http://www.jisc.ac.uk/uploaded_documents/digital-repositories-review-2005.pdf* (accessed 15 June 2009).

Hyphen (2007) 'What is eResearch?', available at: *http://www.bestgrid.org/index.php/What_is_eResearch%3F* (accessed 15 June 2009).

Ingram, C. S. (2005) 'JISC Information Environment (IE) inventory with diagrams', CSI Consultancy technical report, available at: *http://www.grids.ac.uk/VRE/IE inventory with images 1.3.pdf* (accessed 15 June 2009).

Jacobs, N. (2006) *Open Access: Key Strategic, Technical and Economic Aspects*, Oxford: Chandos Publishing.

James, H., Ruusalepp, R., Anderson, S. and Pinfield, S. (2003) 'Feasibility and requirements study on preservation of e-prints', JISC technical report, available at: *http://www.jisc.ac.uk/uploaded_documents/e-prints_report_final.pdf* (accessed 15 June 2009).

Jensen, J. (2007) 'SSO use cases', STFC Rutherford Appleton Laboratory technical report, working paper.

JNT (2006) 'Skype and JANET', JNT Association technical report, available at: *http://www.ja.net/documents/development/voip/skype-and-janet.pdf* (accessed 15 June 2009).

Johnson, C., Parker, S., Weinstin, D. and Hefferman, S. (2002) 'Component-based problem solving environments for large-scale scientific computing', *Concurrency and Computation: Practice and Experience* 14: 1337–49.

Jones, C. (2007) *Institutional Repositories: Content and Culture in an Open Access Environment*, Oxford: Chandos Publishing.

Keen, A. (2007) *The Cult of the Amateur*, London: Nicholas Brealey Publishing Ltd.

Klobas, J. (2006) *Wikis: Tools for Information, Work and Collaboration*, Oxford: Chandos Publishing.

Klyne, G. (2005) 'Sakai VRE Demonstrator project user requirements', available at: *http://wiki.oss-watch.ac.uk/SakaiVre/UserRequirements* (accessed 15 June 2009).

Lawson, I. and Butson, R. (2007) 'E-research at Otago', University of Otago technical report, available at: *https://docushare.otago.ac.nz/docushare/dsweb/Get/Document-3584/eResearchatOtagoReport.pdf* (accessed 15 June 2009).

Leadbeater, C. (2008) *We-think: The Power of Mass Creativity*, London: Profile Books Ltd.

Li, M. and Baker, M. (2006) *The Grid: Core Technologies*, London: J. Wiley and Sons.

Litzkow, M., Livney, M. and Mutka, M. (1988) 'Condor – a hunter of idle workstations', paper presented at 8th International Conference on Distributed Computing Systems, San Jose, 13–17 June, available at: *http://www.cs.wisc.edu/condor/doc/icdcs1988.pdf* (accessed 15 June 2009).

Lord, P. and MacDonald, A. (2003) 'JISC e-science curation report', JISC technical report, available at: *http://www.jisc.ac.uk/uploaded_documents/e-ScienceReportFinal.pdf* (accessed 15 June 2009).

Lyon, L. (2003) 'E-Bank UK: Building the links between research data, scholarly communication and learning', *Ariadne* 36(4), available at: *http://www.ariadne.ac.uk/issue36/lyon* (accessed 15 June 2009).

McGarva, G. (2006) 'Curating geo-spatial data', DCC briefing paper, available at: *http://www.dcc.ac.uk/resource/briefing-papers/curating-geospatial-data/* (accessed 15 June 2009).

McLean, N. and Lynch, C. (2004) 'Interoperability between information and learning environments – bridging the gaps', IMS and CNI white paper, available at: *http://www.imsglobal.org/digitalrepositories/CNIandIMS_2004.pdf* (accessed 15 June 2009).

Meredith, D. J., Akram, A. and Allan, R. J. (2006) 'Best practices in web service style, data binding and validation for use in data-centric scientific applications', paper presented at UK e-Science All Hands Conference, Nottingham, 18–21 September, available at: *http://www.allhands.org.uk/2006/proceedings/papers/621.pdf* (accessed 15 June 2009).

Microsoft Corporation (2005) 'Towards 2020 science', available at: *http://research.microsoft.com/en-us/um/cambridge/projects/towards 2020science/downloads/t2020s_reporta4.pdf* (accessed 15 June 2009).

Miller, K. (2007) 'Primary selection of datasets', ESRC e-Infrastructure Project technical report, deliverable D1.1.1, available at: *http://www.grids.ac.uk/NCeSS/e-INF_D1.1.1_V2.doc* (accessed 15 June 2009).

Miller, P. (2003) 'Towards a typology for portals', *Ariadne* 37(7), available at: *http://www.ariadne.ac.uk/issue37/miller* (accessed 15 June 2009).

Neumann, B.C. (1998) 'Security, accounting, and assurance', in I. Foster and C. Kesselman (eds) *The Grid: Blueprint for a New Computing Infrastructure*, San Francisco, CA: Morgan Kaufmann, pp. 395–420.

Novotny, J. (2002) 'The Grid Portal Development Kit', *Concurrency and Computation: Practice and Experience* 14: 1129–44.

Novotny, J., Tuecke, S. and Welch, V. (2001) 'MyProxy: an on-line credential repository for the Grid', paper presented at 10th IEEE Symposium on High Performance Distributed Computing, San Francisco, 7–9 August.

Novotny, J., Russell, M. and Wehrens, O. (2004) 'GridSphere: a portal framework for building collaborations', *Concurrency and Computation: Practice and Experience* 16: 503–13.

OAI (2004) 'Protocol for metadata harvesting', available at: *http://www.openarchives.org/OAI/openarchivesprotocol.html* (accessed 15 June 2009).

OASIS (2003a) 'WSRP: Web Services for Remote Portlets', available at: *http://www.oasis-open.org/committees/download.php/3343/oasis-200304-wsrp-specification-1.0.pdf* (accessed 15 June 2009).

OASIS (2003b) 'WSRF: Web Service Resource Framework', available at: *http://www.oasis-open.org/committees/wsrf* (accessed 15 June 2009).

O'Brien, L. (2005) 'E-Research: an imperative for strengthening institutional partnerships', *Educause Review* 40(6): 65–76.

Okerson, A. S. and O'Donnell, J. J. (1995) 'Open Access: scholarly institutions at the crossroads: a subversive proposal for electronic publishing', ARL technical report, available at: *http://www.arl.org/scomm/subversive/toc.html* (accessed 15 June 2009).

O'Reilly, T. (2005) 'What is Web 2.0?', available at: *http://www.oreillynet.com/pub/a/oreilly/tim/news/2005/09/30/what-is-web-20.html* (accessed 15 June 2009).

Pennock, M. (2006) 'Curating e-mails' DCC briefing paper, available at: *http://www.dcc.ac.uk/resource/briefing-papers/curating-e-mails/* (accessed 15 June 2009).

Periorellis, P. (2007) *Securing Web Services: Practical Usage of Standards and Specifications*, Hershey, PA: Idea Group.

Phifer, G., Valdes, R., Lundy, J., Shegda, K.M., Driver, M., Natis, Y.V. and Gootzit, D. (2005) 'Gartner Hype Cycle for Portal Eco-systems 2005', available at: *http://www.gartner.com/DisplayDocument?doc_cd= 127798&ref=g_fromdoc* (accessed 15 June 2009).

PITAC (2005) 'Computational Science: Ensuring America's Competitiveness', President's Information Technology Advisory Committee technical report, available at: *http://www.nitrd.gov/Pitac/reports/20050609_ computational/computational.pdf* (accessed 15 June 2009).

Powell, A. (2004) 'The JISC information environment and Google', UKOLN technical report, available at: *http://www.ukoln.ac.uk/ distributed-systems/jisc-ie/arch/ie-google* (accessed 15 June 2009).

Powell, A. (2005) 'The JISC resource discovery landscape', UKOLN technical report, available at: *http://www.ukoln.ac.uk/distributed-systems/jisc-ie/arch/resource-discovery-review* (accessed 15 June 2009).

Powell, A. and Lyon, L. (2001) 'The DNER Technical Architecture: scoping the information environment', UKOLN technical report, available at: *http://www.ukoln.ac.uk/distributed-systems/jisc-ie/arch/dner-arch.pdf* (accessed 15 June 2009).

Preston, S. M. (2000) 'Virtual organization as process: integrating cognitive and social structure across time and space', Michigan State University technical report, available at: *http://www.msu.edu/~ prestons/virtual.html* (accessed 15 June 2009).

RCUK (2007) 'RCUK position on issue of improved access to research outputs', available at: *http://www.rcuk.ac.uk/research/outputs/access* (accessed 15 June 2009).

Ruh, B. (2003) 'Succeeding at service oriented architecture', available at: *http://www.zdnet.com.au/builder/architect/work/story/0,2000034884, 20276810,00.htm* (accessed 15 June 2009).

Schuchardt, K., Didier, B. and Black, G. (2002) 'ECCE – a problem solving environment's evolution toward Grid services and a web architecture', *Concurrency and Computation: Practice and Experience* 14: 1221–39.

Sergeant, D. M., Andrews, S. and Farquhar, A. (2006) 'Embedding a VRE in an Institutional Environment EVIE). Workpackage 2: User Requirements Analysis', University of Leeds technical report, available at: *http://www.leeds.ac.uk/evie/workpackages/wp2/evieWP2_User RequirementsAnalysis_v1_0.pdf* (accessed 15 June 2009).

Severance, C., Hardin, J., Golden, G., Crouchley, R., Fish, A., Finholt, T., Kirshner, B., Eng, J. and Allan, R. J. (2007) 'Using the Sakai collaborative toolkit in e-research applications', *Concurrency and Computation: Practice and Experience* 19(12): 1643–52.

Shirky, C. (2008) *Here Comes Everybody*, London: Allen Lane.

Smith, M. J. (2005) 'Use case compendium of derived geo-spatial data', available at: *http://www.edina.ac.uk/projects/grade/usecasecompendium.pdf* (accessed 15 June 2009).

Soddemann, T. (2007) 'Science Gateways to DEISA: User Requirements, Technologies and the Material Sciences and Plasma Physics Gateway', *Concurrency and Computation: Practice and Experience* 19(6): 839–50.

Stanley, T. (2007) 'Developing a VRE in a portal framework', *Ariadne* 51(4), available at: *http://www.ariadne.ac.uk/issue51/stanley/* (accessed 15 June 2009).

Stevens, M. (2003) 'The benefits of a service-oriented architecture', available at: *http://www.developer.com/services/article.php/1041191* (accessed 15 June 2009).

Sun Microsystems (1998a) 'Introduction to public key cryptography', available at: *http://developer.mozilla.org/en/Introduction_to_Public-Key_Cryptography* (accessed 15 June 2009).

Sun Microsystems (1998b) 'Introduction to SSL', available at: *https://developer.mozilla.org/en/Introduction_to_SSL* (accessed 15 June 2009).

Surowiecki, J. (2005) *The Wisdom of Crowds*, New York: Random House.

Surridge, M. (2002) 'A rough guide to grid security', University of Southampton technical report, available at: *http://www.nesc.ac.uk/technical_papers/RoughGuidetoGridSecurityV1_1a.pdf* (accessed 15 June 2009).

Tabor, G. B. (ed.) (2006) *The Emergence of Grid and Service-Oriented IT: An Industry Vision for Business Success*, San Diego, CA: Tabor Communications.

Tapscott, D. and Williams, A. (2007) *Wikinomics*, London: Atlantic Books.

Thain, D., Tannenbaum, T. and Livny, M. (2005) 'Distributed computing in practice: the Condor experience', *Concurrency and Computation: Practice and Experience* 17: 323–56.

Thomas, J. M. H., Tyer, R., Allan, R. J., Rintelman, J. M., Sherwood, P., Dove, M. T., Austen, K. F., Walker, A. M., Bruin, R. P., Petit, L. and Durrant, M. C. (2007a) 'Science carried out as part of the NW-GRID Project using the eMinerals infrastructure', paper presented at UK e-Science All Hands Conference, Nottingham, 10–13 September, available at: *http://www.allhands.org.uk/2007/proceedings/papers/892.pdf* (accessed 15 June 2009).

Thomas, J. M. H., Kewley, J., Allan, R. J., Rintelman, J. M., Sherwood, P., Bailey, C. L., Wander, A., Searle, B. G., Harrison, N. M., Mukhopadyhay, S., Trevin, A., Darling, G. R. and Cooper, A. I. (2007b) 'Experiences with different middleware solutions on the NW-GRID', paper presented at UK e-Science All Hands Conference, Nottingham, 10–13 September, available at: *http://www.allhands.org.uk/2007/proceedings/papers/893.pdf* (accessed 15 June 2009).

Thomas, M., Dahan, M., Mueller, K., Mock, S., Mills, C. and Regno, R. (2002) 'Application portals: practice and experience', *Concurrency and Computation: Practice and Experience* 14: 1427–43.

US Library of Congress (2006) 'Information retrieval (Z39.50) application service definition and protocol specification', available at: *http://www.loc.gov/z3950/agency* (accessed 15 June 2009).

US Navy (2003) 'Kerberos FAQ', available at: *http://www.cmf.nrl.navy.mil/CCS/people/kenh/kerberos-faq.html* (accessed 15 June 2009).

Von Laszewski, G., Gawor, J., Lane, P., Rehn, N. and Russell, M. (2002) 'Features of the Java Commodity Grid Kit', *Concurrency and Computation: Practice and Experience* 14: 1045–55.

Walker, A. M., Bruin, R. P., Dove, M. T., White, T .O. H., Kleese van Dam, K. and Tyer, R. P. (2008) 'Integrating computing, data and collaboration grids: the RMCS tool', *Philosophical Transactions of the Royal Society A* 367: 1047–50.

Wang, X. D., Gleaves, M., Meredith, D., Allan, R. J. and Nave, C. (2006) 'E-science technologies in synchrotron radiation Beamline – remote access and automation', *Macromolecular Research* 14: 140–5.

Wellcome Trust (2007) 'Wellcome Trust position statement in support of open and unrestricted access to published research', available at: *http://www.wellcome.ac.uk/About-us/Policy/Spotlight-issues/Open-access/Policy/index.htm* (accessed 15 June 2009).

Weller, M. (2007) *Virtual Learning Environments: Using, Choosing and Developing your VLE*, Oxford: Routledge.

Willinsky, J. (2005) *Open Access, The Access Principle*, Massachusetts: MIT Press.

Wilson, S., Olivier, B., Jeyes, S., Powell, A. and Franklin, T. (2003) 'A technical framework to support e-learning', JISC technical report, available at: *http://www.jisc.ac.uk/uploaded_documents/Technical%20Framework%20feb04.doc* (accessed 15 June 2009).

Yang, X. and Allan, R. J. (2007a) 'Sakai VRE Demonstrator Project: realising e-research through virtual research environments', *World*

Scientific and Engineering Academy and Society Transactions on Computers 6: 539–45.

Yang, X. and Allan, R. J. (2007b) 'Bringing AJAX to Grid portals', paper presented at International Symposium on Collaborative Technologies and Systems, Orlando, May, available at: *http://epubs.cclrc.ac.uk/bitstream/1419/paper07A.pdf* (accessed 15 June 2009).

Yang, X., Chohan, D., Wang, X. D. and Allan, R. J. (2005) 'A web portal for the National Grid Service', paper presented at UK e-Science All Hands Conference, Nottingham, 19–22 September, *http://www.allhands.org.uk/2005/proceedings/papers/445.pdf* (accessed 15 June 2009).

Yang, X., Wang, X. D. and Allan, R. J. (2006) 'JSR 168 and WSRP 1.0 – how mature are portal standards?', paper presented at WEBIST2006, Setubal, 22–23 April, available at: *http://epubs.cclrc.ac.uk/bitstream/1082/paper06A.pdf* (accessed 15 June 2009).

Yang, X., Akram, A. and Allan, R. J. (2007a) 'Developing portal/portlets using Enterprise Java Beans for grid users', *Concurrency and Computation: Practice and Experience* 19(12): 1633–41.

Yang, X., Wang, X. D. and Allan, R. J. (2007b) 'Development of standards-based grid portals, Part 1: Review of grid portals', available at: *http://epubs.cclrc.ac.uk/bitstream/1418/article07A.pdf* (accessed 15 June 2009).

Yang, X., Wang, X. D. and Allan, R. J. (2007c) 'Development of standards-based grid portals, Part 2: JSR 168 grid portlets', available at: *http://epubs.cclrc.ac.uk/bitstream/1434/article07B.pdf* (accessed 15 June 2009).

Yang, X., Wang, X. D. and Allan, R. J. (2007d) 'Development of standards-based grid portals, Part 3: WSRP and the future of grid portals', available at: *http://epubs.cclrc.ac.uk/bitstream/1454/article07C.pdf* (accessed 15 June 2009).

Yang, X., Allan, R. J. and Finch, J. (2008) 'The NCeSS Portal – a Web 2.0 enabled collaborative virtual research environment for social scientists', paper presented at 4th International Conference on Semantics, Knowledge and Grid, Beijing, 3–5 December, available at: *http://epubs.cclrc.ac.uk/bitstream/2844/paper08A.pdf* (accessed 15 June 2009).

Index

Access Grid, 84–5, 87, 90, 170, 183
AgentX, 35, 149–51
agile programming, 104
Agora, 91–2
AHE: application hosting environment, 139, 145, 147, 151
authentication, 95–8
authorisation, 53, 84, 95, 112

BeSTGrid, 6, 10, 223
BOINC: Berkeley Open Infrastructure Network Computing, 136–7

CASPAR: Cultural, Artistic and Scientific Knowledge for Preservation, Access and Retrieval, 49–51
CCLRC, see STFC: Science and Technology Facilities Council
CCP: Collaborative Computational Project, 34, 40, 44–7, 86, 137, 198
citation index, 26, 103
cloud, 17, 134–5
    campus, 135–6
collaboration, 3, 11, 79–94, 122
    tools, 86–7
computational science, 41, 43, 48–9
    heritage application, 12, 27, 137
Condor, 108, 129, 135, 141–3, 149

CORBA, 16, 111
CSCW: computer supported cooperative work, 85–6, 89, 104–5
CWE: collaborative working environment, 85
cyberinfrastructure, 5, 203

data, 1–2, 4, 21–3, 39–42, 47–55, 74, 103, 138–41
    experimentation, 40, 194, 200
    observation, 40, 178–81
    simulation, 41
DataPortal, 51–3, 202
DCC: Digital Curation Centre, 49, 68, 126
DEEWR, 7, 18, 61
DEST, see DEEWR
digital repository, 68–70, 76, 177
DLS: Diamond Light Source, 37, 53, 61, 71, 193–207

e-HTPX: High Throughput Protein Crystallography, 34, 37, 40, 198–9, 201
e-learning, 14, 100, 125
e-research, 3–9, 73, 100, 124
    management, 130, 169–71, 183, 191
    training, 184, 203

263

eFER: e-Framework for Education and Research, 9, 18–19, 99, 107, 178, 185, 188
EGEE: Enabling Grids for e-Science in Europe, 41, 134, 144, 156
eMinerals: Environment from the Molecular Level, 80–1, 138, 149–50
eReSS: e-Research Interoperability and Standards, 108, 158, 188
ETF: Grid Engineering Task Force, 7
EVIE: Embedding a VRE in an Institutional Environment, 25, 56, 101, 153–4

folksonomy, 72

GEANT, 5
gLite, 144–5
Globus, 3, 118, 134, 140, 143–4, 150
Go-Geo, 32–3
Google, 4, 27, 37, 63–4, 71–2, 76, 134, 154, 158, 184
grey literature, 36, 68, 74
grid, 1, 4, 41, 79–80, 133–9, 145–7, 151, 175
  campus, 16, 135, 149
  client problem, 110, 145
  computational, 16, 146, 167
  data, 1, 41–2
  security, 118–19
GridSphere, 2, 14, 85, 90, 104, 155–6
groupware, 85, 87, 190
GROWL: Grid Resources On Workstation Library, 35, 147, 149–50, 181, 183

HEFCE: Higher Education Funding Council for England, 25

iCAT: Information Catalogue, 51–3, 199, 201
IE: information environment, 8, 28, 35, 74, 102–3, 176
IM: instant messaging, 93
information, 21–2, 51, 55–77, 99–101, 126–7
  personal, 74, 76
ISPyB: Information System for Protein crYstallography Beamlines, 199, 201–2

JANET: UK Joint Academic Network, 5, 121, 196
JISC: Joint Infrastructure Systems Committee, 8, 18, 21, 55–6, 61, 68, 99, 102, 104, 107, 122, 129–30
JISCmail, 36–7, 68, 94–5
JSR 168, 14, 108, 163–4
JSR 286, 108, 163

knowledge, 8, 21, 23

library services, 4, 75
LifeRay, 16

metadata, 22–3, 47–8, 51–3, 108, 113, 194, 200–1
Microsoft, 209
middleware, 84, 105, 108, 114, 118, 127, 133–4, 139–44
multiR, 181
myExperiment, 24, 69, 87, 191, 212
myProxy, 110, 120, 155

N-tier architecture, 110–12, 120, 145, 161
NCeSS: National Centre for e-Social Science, 164, 170, 173, 178, 190
  CQeSS, 182–3

Index

DAMES, 181
e-Infrastructure, 185–90
GENESIS, 191
GeoVue, 191
MoSeS, 184, 191
Policy Grid, 191
ReDReSS, 184
NGS: National Grid Service, 32, 36, 121, 134, 190, 194, 202
portal, 15, 54, 155, 191
NICE Portal, 156
NSF, 10
NVO: National Virtual Observatory, 2
NW-GRID, 134, 149, 164, 170

OAIS: Open Archival Information System, 50
OGCE: the Open Grid Computing Environment, 15, 121, 156, 165
OGF: Open Grid Forum, 122
  JSDL, 151
  SAGA, 151
open access, 6–7, 55, 60–1, 74, 130
OWL: Web Ontology Language, 23

P-GRADE Portal, 156–7
philanthropic computing, 136
PITAC: President's Information Technology Advisory Committee, 41, 48
PKI: public key infrastructure, 95–6, 118
portal, 2, 14–16, 26, 30–1, 85, 87, 152–7
  gateway, 14–16, 107, 154, 180
  grid, 32, 155–7
  institutional, 26, 152–3
  service, 155

quantitative social science, 182–3

R Project, 183
RAE: Research Assessment Exercise, 25, 190
RBAC: role based access control, 54, 165–7
RCUK: UK Research Councils, 7, 21, 37, 43, 60–1, 74, 99, 153
RDF: resource description framework, 23, 150
research lifecycle, 21–2, 24, 28, 49–50, 101–2
RMCS: Remote MyCondor Submit, 147, 149–51

Sabre, 182–3
Sakai, 13, 15, 36, 87, 153, 161–6
  VRE Demonstrator, 14, 24, 91, 164, 167–8
SAML: the Security Assertion Markup Language, 23, 120
scholarly communication, 6, 39
Semantic Web, 23, 47, 150, 209
Shibboleth, 85, 119–20, 127
Skype, 92–3
SOA: service oriented architecture, 3, 16–17, 107, 110, 143
SOAP: Simple Object Access Protocol, 23, 112, 114
social anthropology, 173
SRB: Storage Resource Broker, 54, 141, 147–8, 181, 206
SSL, *see* TLS
SSO: single sign-on, 96–8, 120, 183, 196
STFC: Science and Technology Facilities Council, 46, 51, 53, 61, 75, 94, 193, 201, 203–4
StringBeans, 14, 164
SURF, 18, 61

TeraGrid, 7, 107, 134, 137
　gateway, 15, 107, 203
　user portal, 121, 156
TLS: transport layer security, 96, 119

UNICORE: Uniform Interface to Computing Resources, 133, 137, 139, 142, 147
Univa UD, 137
uPortal, 14, 153, 164
usability, 6, 98, 104–6

VBL: Virtual BeamLine, 202–3
VDT: Virtual Data Toolkit, 143
VeRSI: Victorian e-Research Strategic Initiative, 8, 82, 193, 203
virtual research community, 82
visualisation, 14, 139, 156
VLE: virtual learning environment, 7, 16, 161

VO: virtual organisation, 79, 82, 85, 152, 154, 165, 211
VOMS: virtual organisation membership service, 84–5, 143
VRE: virtual research environment, 5, 7, 9, 11–13, 24, 26, 75, 82–5, 107–11, 122–8, 161

web 2.0, 15, 47, 71–3, 76, 81, 86, 134, 158–9, 165, 190–1, 209
　mashup, 158–9
web applications, 162
web services, 16, 23, 108, 111–15
Wikipedia, 4, 72, 103
WSRF: Web Services Resource Framework, 16, 143–4
WSRP: Web Services for Remote Portlets, 14, 165, 168

XML: eXtensible Markup Language, 23, 112–14